The **Body and Psychology**

The Body and Psychology

edited by

Henderikus J. Stam

SAGE PUBLICATIONS
London • Thousand Oaks • New Delhi

First published 1998

Chapter 10 was previously published in the journal of *Theory &
Psychology*, volume 7, number 4, 1997; all other chapters were
previously published in the journal of *Theory & Psychology*, volume 6,
number 4, 1996.

Thanks to Caterina Pizanias for her photo research and conceptual
thoughts on the cover design.

SAGE Publications Ltd
6 Bonhill Street
London EC2A 4PU

SAGE Publications Inc
2455 Teller Road
Thousand Oaks, California 91320

SAGE Publications India Pvt Ltd
32, M-Block Market
Greater Kailash - I
New Delhi 110 048

British Library Cataloguing in Publication Data

A catalogue record for this book is
available from the British Library

ISBN 0 776119 5533 X
ISBN 0 7619 5534 8 (pbk)

Library of Congress catalog card number 98–060208

Typeset by Photoprint, Torquay, Devon
Printed in Great Britain by The Cromwell Press Ltd, Trowbridge,
Wiltshire

Contents

Notes on contributors   vii

PART I: INTRODUCTION

1   THE BODY'S PSYCHOLOGY AND PSYCHOLOGY'S BODY: 1
    Disciplinary and Extra-disciplinary Examinations
    Henderikus J. Stam

PART II: SOCIAL AND PSYCHOLOGICAL BODIES

2   DISPLAYS AND FRAGMENTS   13
    Embodiment and the Configuration of Social Worlds
    Alan Radley

3   ESTABLISHING EMBODIMENT IN PSYCHOLOGY   30
    Edward E. Sampson

4   MIND AS BODY MOVING IN SPACE   54
    Bringing the Body Back into Self-Psychology
    Harry J. G. Kempen

PART III: SEXED AND GENDERED BODIES

5   'LOVING THE COMPUTER'   71
    Cognition, Embodiment and the Influencing Machine
    Elizabeth A. Wilson

6   FEMINISM, PSYCHOLOGY AND MATTERS OF THE BODY   94
    Betty M. Bayer and Kareen Ror Malone

7   SITUATED KNOWLEDGES OF PERSONAL EMBODIMENT   120
    Transgender Activists' and Psychological Theorists' Perspectives
    on 'Sex' and 'Gender'
    Mary Brown Parlee

8   *HABITUS*: FROM THE INSIDE OUT AND THE
    OUTSIDE IN   141
    Caterina Pizanias

PART IV: SICK AND HEALING BODIES

9   THE BODY AS A SELFING DEVICE   161
    The Case of Anorexia Nervosa
    Cor Baerveldt and Paul Voestermans

10 THE PSYCHOLOGY AND MANAGEMENT OF PAIN   182
    Gate Control as Theory and Symbol
    Robert Kugelmann

11 FROM DYSAPPEARANCE TO HYPERAPPEARANCE:
    Sliding Boundaries of Illness and Bodies   205
    Arthur W. Frank

Index   *233*

Notes on contributors

COR BAERVELDT is a Junior Researcher in the Department of Cultural Psychology, University of Nijmegen. He obtained his master's degree with a thesis on the cultural constitution of expressive bodily skills, especially in relation to eating disorders. He is currently working on a dissertation on New Age practices. His main fields of interest are the epistemological foundations of the human sciences, human embodiment and the cultural constitution of self.

BETTY M. BAYER is an Assistant Professor at Hobart and William Smith Colleges. She has published articles pertaining to theory and history in social psychology, critiques of sociobiology, and research into women's self-help books on the body. She is co-editor, with John Shotter, of *Reconstructing the Psychological Subject: Bodies, Practices and Technologies* (forthcoming). She is currently working on a cultural history of gender constructions and human–machine investigative practices in small group research.

ARTHUR W. FRANK is Professor of Sociology at the University of Calgary, Calgary, Alberta, Canada. He is the author of *At the Will of the Body: Reflections on Illness* (1991) and *The Wounded Storyteller: Body, Illness, and Ethics* (1995). He is also editor of the Case Stories series in the journal *Making the Rounds in Health, Faith and Ethics* (Chicago, The Park Ridge Center). His work concerns the power of telling one's own story as a way of living through suffering.

HARRY J.G. KEMPEN lectures in general and comparative cultural psychology at the Psychological Laboratory of the University of Nijmegen. Primarily assigned to cross-cultural personality research, he has gradually moved into cultural psychological theory development. His long-term interest is in classical and contemporary interdisciplinary theories within the social sciences. He is co-author, with Hubert Hermans, of *The Dialogical Self: Meaning as Movement* (Academic Press, 1993), a study viewing the self as composed of multiple I-positions in dialogue with each other and the collective voices of society.

ROBERT KUGELMANN is an associate professor of psychology and author of two books: *The Windows of Soul* (1983) and *Stress: The Nature and History of Engineered Grief* (1992). Current research includes an empirical phenomenological and social constructionist approach to chronic pain, and a study of the implications of the work of Emmanuel Lévinas for the nature of psychology.

KAREEN ROR MALONE is an Associate Professor of Psychology at West Georgia College. She has researched and published in areas related to the fields of feminism, social construction, humanistic psychology and psycho-analysis. Her main interests are Lacanian psychoanalysis, its understanding of the structures of subjectivity, and its possible (non-reductive) relevance to issues in social psychology, especially questions of body and desire.

MARY BROWN PARLEE is Visiting Professor in the School of Humanities and Social Science at the Massachusetts Institute of Technology, where she teaches courses in the Women's Studies Program. Her research interests include women's health, premenstrual syndrome and (drawing on feminist, historical and science studies approaches) the social construction of women's health 'issues'. She is author most recently of chapters in *The Good Body: Asceticism in Contemporary Culture* (Yale University Press, 1994), *Premenstrual Dysphorias: Myths and Realities* (American Psychiatric Press, 1994), *Psychology of Women: A Handbook of Issues and Theories* (Greenwood, 1993) and of forthcoming essays in *The Women's Studies Encyclopedia* (Harvester Wheatsheaf) and (with Stephanie J. Bird) the *Encyclopedia of Neuroscience* (Elsevier Science).

CATERINA PIZANIAS is an itinerant academic who received her PhD in 1992 in the sociology of knowledge from the University of Alberta. She is interested in expressive culture—in both its everyday and 'learned' manifes-tations. Her research documents and attempts to understand the traffic of cultural 'texts' and 'values' within the academy and other social worlds.

ALAN RADLEY is Reader in Health and Social Relations in the Department of Social Sciences at Loughborough University, UK. His research interests include, specifically, the problems of coping with heart disease and, more generally, issues concerning the social context of health and illness. He also researches in the field of charitable giving. His book publications include *Prospects of Heart Surgery: Psychological Adjustment to Coronary Bypass Grafting* (Springer, 1988); *In Social Relationships: An Introduction to the Social Psychology of Membership and Intimacy* (Open University Press, 1991); *The Body and Social Psychology* (Springer, 1991); and *Making Sense of Illness: The Social Psychology of Health and Disease* (Sage, 1994); and *Worlds of Illness: Biographical and Cultural Perspectives on Health and Disease* (Routledge, 1993) and co-author with M. Billig, S. Condor, D. Edwards, M. Gane and D. Middleton of *Ideological Dilemmas: A Social Psychology of Everyday Thinking* (Sage, 1988). He is the editor of the journal *Health*.

EDWARD E. SAMPSON is a Professor of Psychology at California State University, Northridge. For the last 25 years, he has sought to develop a critique of his field, social psychology, by taking seriously the social aspect of the field's name. He has been especially concerned with the political implications of social psychological work and has written widely in this regard, including *Justice and the Critique of Pure Psychology*, Plenum, 1993; *Celebrating the Other*, Harvester Wheatsheaf/Westview, 1993 and the forthcoming *Dealing with Differences: The Social Psychology of Prejudice.*

HENDERIKUS J. STAM is Professor of Psychology at the University of Calgary. His research interests are in the historical and theoretical foundations of psychology. He is the editor of the journal *Theory & Psychology* and co-editor with L. Radkte of *Power/Gender: Social Relations in Theory and Practice* (1994).

PAUL VOESTERMANS is Associate Professor of Cultural Psychology at the University of Nijmegen. His research has focused on theories of culture and their application to the cultural patterning of behaviour. His main area of interest is the cultural and embodied forms of feeling. He has published several articles in Dutch and English dealing with this theme of emotion and feeling, embodiment and culture.

ELIZABETH A. WILSON is a research fellow in the Department of Women's Studies at the University of Sydney, NSW. She is the author of *Neural Geographies: Feminism and the Microstructure of Cognition*. (Routledge, 1998).

1

The Body's Psychology and Psychology's Body
Disciplinary and Extra-disciplinary Examinations

Henderikus J. Stam

This volume is an invitation to reconstrue psychology as a discipline of bodies. It is an invitation to conceptualize cognition and behavior, perception and development, attitudes and traits as the mere surface or transient manifestations of the body; as the inscriptions, productions, reproductions and other features of the body and embodiment that are commonly taken for the content of the psychologically real subject/object, packaged into disciplinary and sub-disciplinary units to be consumed by students and clients of psychology. The history of this discipline is an object lesson in what can be done when all of the many manifestations of the human body are figured along functional, mechanical, systemic or technological lines.

Psychology's Body

> It is necessary to begin with a definition.
> Behavior is only part of the total activity of an organism,
> and some formal delimitation is called for.
> (B F. Skinner, 1938, p. 6)

Of the two great metaphors that have organized research in the discipline of psychology in the twentieth-century, that of *organism* dominated the period in the first half of this century. Organisms are just organized bodies, "consisting of mutually connected and dependent parts constituted to share a common life" (*OED*). That very organization, however, leaves them capable of description in terms of stimulus and response, reflex and energy. As Danziger (1997) has noted, the adoption of an organismic language had its

roots in nineteenth-century physiology and allowed the language of physiology to move smoothly into the psychological domain. The net effect of this
move however was to make the *body*, not the mind, the central concern of
the nascent discipline. For had Skinner written, in 1938, a work called *The
behavior of organized bodies: An experimental analysis* it would have
required little change in conception. At the same time this body was not the
same as the body conceptualized by the physiologists. Indeed it became a
quasi-physiological entity, interchangeably human and animal, neither the
body of any particular species nor a generalized mammalian body. Instead
this body was abstract, precisely so that the attributes of stimulus and
response, reflex and habit, drive and behavior could form a universal
psychological language.

This body was also a mechanized body, but not mechanical. For psychologists in the early twentieth-century, it was a requirement that subjectivity be
made precise, that it be measurable. Thus, as the behaviorists worried about
the external problems of the body, researchers in sensation and perception
concerned themselves with the need to quantify and hence eliminate the
uncertainty associated with sensing and movement. Once quantified precisely, subjectivity was indeed eliminated, reduced to manageable measure-
ments. Subjectivity was replaced by the quantifiable body that was, at the
same time, a machine (Deleul, 1992; Stam, Lubek & Radtke, 1998). It came
to incorporate the mechanical ethos of the twentieth-century in an organic
form that was both organic *and* mechanical, or rather represented the
mechanization of the organic.

What the fascination with normative, data-driven, statistical knowledge
hid was the need to find the secrets of the body while regulating subjectivity.
Thus G. Stanley Hall's Child Study Movement formed a foundation for
determining the rate and progress of childrens' mental and physical growth.
Alfred Kinsey made the sexualized body normal, if only by counting the
variety of sexual acts and their frequency of occurrence. Mental tests
quantified the very contents of mind, if not intelligence. What such movements gradually produced was a belief that the mind, for all its complexity,
could be understood as a range of quantifiable events, a limited scale of
possibilities. The body, on the other hand, came to occupy the place of the
vehicle of this quantified mind. It too had its capacities and limitations, but
these could be known normatively, even in the case of the preverbal infant -
as Arnold Gesell showed. Bodies were no longer the source of consciousness and feeling so much as the casement for its expression. Indeed, the
body was given in a pre-fabricated fashion. Consciousness and feeling
however were the province of a science that sought out the range of its
possibilities in its quantifications.

The body so delimited was not necessary to the further development of
the discipline despite its organicist metaphor. If anything, psychology never
took the problem of the organism seriously, misconstruing it as a species of

mechanism instead of a version that saw organic structure as fundamentally different from mechanical structure (see McDonough, 1997). Had psychology developed a notion of emergent organic structures seriously it might have avoided a sterile behaviorism altogether.

By mid-century however the abstract organism and its body failed to satisfy the burgeoning profession and the abandonment of the organic metaphor was inevitable. This was not so much the outcome of a dissatisfaction with the metaphor but instead followed from the requirement that psychology address the concerns of a modern society, first one at war and subsequently one in rapid post-war development simultaneously preoccupied with a new, Cold War to consume the energies of science and technology. It was to be the new technological sciences and the engineering fields that would provide psychology with its second great metaphor in the twentieth-century, that of *system*.

From Organism to System

> . . . the input/output behavior of the hypothesized primitive operations of the
> cognitive architecture must not itself depend on goals and beliefs . . .
> it must be what I refer to as cognitively impenetrable.
> (Zenon Pylyshyn, 1989, p. 81.)

The metaphor of system was closely allied to what passes through systems, namely information. In the developments of industrialized nations, information and its movement had already become a preoccupation of the corporate world. With the development of corporate structures, information had to flow both vertically and horizontally. It was the appearance of cybernetics and complex machines capable of self-regulation that supported the extension of the metaphor of system, originally a biological term, to all manner of machine, as well as to corporate structures themselves. Systems carried information in visible ways in technology (e.g., radar detectors, heart monitors). The corporate problem of information flow was manifest in mechanism, and it required no more than a small step to incarnate itself in the psychology of human information processing. Suddenly we were all carriers of information.

Notwithstanding the dubious nature of the term, what kind of body was to carry this *information*? It was to be a model, predicted Kenneth Craik in 1943, that included any "physical or chemical system which has a similar relation-structure to that of the processes it imitates" (p. 51). This relation-structure should mirror the processes it parallels, argued Craik long before the advent of the digital computer. Although the language of people as "intermittent correction servomechanisms" no longer informs, it does reference the beginning of a move to the adoption of a language of system, an organization of units that is open and capable of forming part of larger systems. Cybernetics, the science of control, has so come to dominate thinking about bodies that the mechanical organism no longer requires a biological reference point except in those cases where explicit acknowledgment needs to be made to the limits of feedback devices.

The body in cognitive science has evolved into the sexless hull of the robomind, the complex machinery of information systems brought to its highest level of abstraction in the human facsimile. Despite this, it controls a body that, outside the rarefied sphere of cognitive science, is the object of bitter conflicts over gender, race, reproductive rights, health care, genetic modification and mapping, and is the crucible of new and more deadly epidemic diseases. Yet within the cognitive sciences it rarely rates more than secondary notice, having already been relegated to the mechanical realm or the problem of architecture. Even when cognitive scientists address the problem of the body, they can do no more than point to the fact that it is missing altogether from the transcendental fixtures of cognition that tie meaning to the relations between words and the world. When the body does secure a place in cognition, the presented alternative is often no more than an escape to mysticism (Varela, Thompson & Rosch, 1991). Whether concerned with the symbolic architectures of computational mechanisms or the so-called "brain-style" computation of connectionist systems, the body remains almost entirely the subject of the special sciences of biology and neurology.

While psychology continues its Cartesian dream, the body is finding a new place in the lexicon elsewhere in the academy, where it had previously been limited to an object of scientific investigation. Now it is a vehicle for social theory, a mainstay of cultural studies, a permanent fixture in gender studies and queer theory, and a host of other locations previously enamored only of the linguistic and representational problems of modernity. Gradually, more traditional disciplines have risen to the challenge of studies that claim a space for a political, gendered, social and racial body by encouraging and sometimes appropriating body topics that insist that bodies are more than mere vehicles. In its first moment, then, body talk crosses disciplinary lines; it is not interdisciplinary so much as it its *trans*disciplinary. Bodies resist boundary maintenance.

Yet disciplines exert a strong pull. Psychology's functionalized, physiological body remains the backdrop of the discipline. To approach the body as the object of disciplinary practices, as the inscribed carrier of social life, as the phenomenological origin of psychological life itself, requires that we bracket, if not undermine, that original conception of the body as a collection of sophisticated drips and squirts. More than this, body talk undermines the notion of disciplinary boundaries altogether. At the same time, disciplines move quickly to withstand the challenger as the body becomes another topic domesticated for slow and careful excision and consumption within the confines of the investigative and rhetorical practices which define the field.

The Body's Psychology

> *What is at stake in the struggle for control of the body, in short,*
> *is control of the social relations of personal production.*
>
> (T. Turner, 1994)

As body topics challenge psychology to rethink and reconceptualize its subject matter, psychology is in turn capable of challenging certain contested notions in the literature on embodiment. To claim this is to understand the capacities for the new language of bodies to deceive. The body emerges as a topic at the same moment as the politics of identity have come to dominate the human sciences. As *personal* identity is created in the context of a mass market of individualistic consumption, *collective* identities are being re-claimed around categories of gender, race and religion. Thus topics from sexuality and health to fashion and sport are the domain of a new embodied politics of choice and identity because bodies have become the "material infrastructure ... of the production of personhood and social identity" (Turner, 1994, p. 28). Yet, as Turner implies in the opening quote to this section, the body also remains the site of oppression and inequality. To limit our exploration of the body in contemporary culture to the expression of personal identities or to manifest forms of oppression is, as Turner has it, to see all of these in strictly individualistic terms and to negate their possible social nature.

We are in danger here of construing the body as a new Cartesian entity, taking the place of the discarded dualism of mind with equally opaque categories that would psychologize the body into a language of discourse, desire, style, performativity and the like while jettisoning its sociality and materiality. The language of bodies can take on a highly individualized and ethereal character, being at one remove from both the social and the psychological. In this language bodies are no longer seen as constituted in social relations or, rather, the sensuous existence of the body cannot be seen as the primary prerequisite of all that emerges from persons. Whereas psychology splits and compartmentalizes the body into functions that deny the embodied nature of psychological life and experience, so can an individualistic language of 'bodies in discourse' deny the crucial manner in which the body is already and always social in its expressions and im-pressions. This is no attempt to hearken back to a universal physical body but a way of questioning the limits of a rarefied discourse of bodies that continues under new conceptions the abstract project of an asocial and ahistorical mind. It is precisely here that we must ask what a psychology can offer the body if we agree both to replace a cognitivized but bloodless subject and revitalize a more or less passive body filled with "crypto-subjective desires and proclivities" (Turner, 1994, p. 30). It is just at this juncture that the historical, classed, gendered, racial body intersects with disciplinarity. For in refusing to be misled by the project of glorified systems theories or seduced by a desiring body, psychology can insist that the subjectivity reclaimed for the body be historically specific and not just the application of a set of theories appropriated from the new scholasticism of high theory.

How then might psychology, on the one hand, be reformulated from the vantage of the lived body, from the body that is both the source and experience of subjectivity and is also the object seen, stylized, and acted upon from without? How, in other words, can psychology understand the body as both subject and object, as "the very intertwining of self and Other" (Leder, 1990, p. 6)? How can the question of the body, on the other hand, be made psychologically real so that it is neither merely the phenomenology of perception nor the source of abstract desire? These questions are far from traditional disciplinary problems. Indeed, they already presume a reformulated conception of the 'psychological' beyond the narrow boundaries of the North-Atlantic anglo-conception of the discipline.

The papers in this collection, all of which come from recent issues of *Theory & Psychology*, provide a remarkable range of answers to these problems. All agree that psychology has not taken the body seriously in most of its current manifestations. The degree to which the authors take this to be telling in psychology's relationship with the body is widely divergent. They range from a wholesale rejection of psychology's traditional project to a reconceptualization of certain contents in some or other specialty topics. Other papers are entirely unconcerned, if not downright hostile, to disciplinary intentions. Whatever the case, each paper was included in this collection for its unique contribution to an understanding of the psychological dimensions of embodiment, and the body's expressions and dependencies in social life, gendering, and illness. Even this is insufficient as an introductory pointer however if only because "the body" is already a misnomer, a product of the social-scientific penchant for reification and abstraction. Elsewhere Radley (1995) argues that it is "the nature of the body-subject to be elusory" (p. 5). By this he means that the body is not just elus*ive* in its avoidance of social control but that it is elus*ory* because it retains a capacity to configure experience. To talk of *the* body in this context is to try to reconstruct boundaries and disciplinary discourses. But the alternative, that is, that there are only bodies that are now ill, now at play, now desirous, and so on, is equally unsatisfactory for its incapacity to specify just what it is that the body brings to understanding and experience. The authors try to work through this dilemma by locating the body in dialetical relations with self, culture, gender, race, history and more.

Social and Psychological Bodies

One of the crucial problems in the body literature is how it is that the mundane claim of the body's inherent capacities to be at once social and individual are theorized. This remains a problem for those who want not just to invite a reductionist take on the body as social artifact but want, with Leder (1990) and others to appreciate the simultaneous presence of the body as a first-person actor who lives through it from within while being, always, a third-person object of an external gaze. If we acknowledge the ever meaningful constitution of the body in its multiple manifestations as the accomplishment of culture, then an entirely new psychology ought to follow. In the first section, three papers address this question from divergent starting points. Each author argues that a psychology based on the traditional Cartesian subject is incapable of addressing the problems of embodiment. Moreover, none of these three authors is convinced that social construction-ism can provide further insights into this problem. Instead, each struggles to return to more primitive categories to comprehend and do justice to the embodied, as well as social, world of subjectivity.

In the first paper, Alan Radley provides an insightful analysis based on Simmel's work on displays. In particular he notes that Simmel was careful to distinguish between displays that are in the order of alignments and stylizations, that are no more than our deployment of the body for a particular social purpose, and the manner in which individuals can "take up and . . . transform features of the mundane world in order to portray a 'way of being.'" This distinction is of more than passing value to Radley who notes that this is also the root of understanding that in engaging the world through a material body, the body makes itself understood. It is not only that this is an action of the body on the world or an "incorporation" of the world into the body but it consists of nothing less than the "con-figuring" of possible social worlds. Radley urges an important shift here from conceiving the body as merely expressing itself, as it does in emotions, to an under-standing of displays as indications of how we constitute and are constituted not just through our bodies but with them.

Edward Sampson adopts a different strategy in his paper. Arguing that neither cognitivism nor social constructionist metatheories have taken the question of *embodiment* seriously, he distinguishes the latter from a notion of the *object-body*. This body is an aspect of the ocularcentric bias of the western tradition and is shared by both the scientific and social con-structionist traditions. Although phenomenology does take embodiment seriously, Sampson argues that this tradition excludes history, culture and community. Instead he urges a conception of embodiment that includes discourses among its phenomena. In his historical reading of the changes taking place in the western tradition, Sampson notes that three movements have contributed to our changing conceptions of embodiment. These are feminism, the appropriation of Buddhist practices, and the pentecostal religious revival. All of these, in some measure, ensure a continued focus on and acceptance of embodiment as a vehicle of knowledge and practice. Sampson calls for a politics of embodiment that transcends even those writings in the social sciences that explicitly call for an epistemology based on the body. He hints at what might be a project for a future psychology that concerns itself with the bodily pedagogy of the oppressed.

Like Sampson, Harry Kempen too wants to return the body to psychology and avoid the turn to social constructionism and its implications of a culturally relativistic human nature. Instead, he argues that the human body "becomes filled with a self, a self that is embodied: a *corps-sujet.*" Vico's corporeal imagination is the foundation of this newly conceived self and Kempen elaborates this into a notion of the self as a biological necessity that has five tasks. These tasks, that are carried out by a subjectifying body, are variables insofar as they can be carried out in different ways. Thus the subjectifying body is faced with a wide range of possible ways in which it can orient itself to the world in its boundary, its evaluations of the world, its activities and so on. It is at this juncture that culture intervenes and reduces the wide array of possible selves we might be by providing powerful constraints on the body. Or, in other words, culture is both the starting point and landing place of self-construction.

Sexed and Gendered Bodies

If the topic of the body has made any inroads in the academy then it is surely in the domain of the sexed and gendered body. Prodded in large measure by feminism, queer theory, psychoanalysis and the contributions from social and historical studies of human sexuality, most of the human sciences have been altered by the radical singularity and embeddedness of the subjective world in an always sexed and gendered body. The four papers that make this problem explicit in this collection each tackle an important set of questions and, in turn, raise serious and hitherto unaddressed problems for psychology.

Elizabeth Wilson interrogates both the Turing test and cognitive psychology on their stance towards the body and in particular for their indebtedness to a masculine morphology. Wilson argues that Turing enacts cognition in a fashion that makes the computer isomorphic with man, not woman. Cognition in this incarnation is nothing less than a masculine desire to shed the body. In cognitive psychology the binary logic is replaced with an "active, reconstructive, cultural, embodied, affective, non-conscious, non-unitary and over-determined" process, that is, an interpretive process, the very existence of which is denied by the creators of information-processing models. As such, these models will always be limited by the repressed necessity of interpretation as the arbiter of what is "processed" in cognition. Following Irigaray, Wilson shows us the male imaginary at work in cognitive psychology and asks us to press the case not for a neutral cognitive science but for an intervention that makes explicit the masculine orientation behind disembodied cognition.

Pursuing a similar line of questioning, Betty Bayer and Kareen Malone relate questions of the body in psychology to a more general crisis in late 20th-century thought in which the body represents woman, the concrete, the Other, all in opposition to the phallogocentrism of dominant epistemologies. The body, in a stubborn refusal of universalization, has become a prominent figure in feminist theorizing, questioning long-held dualist traditions, the sexualization of science and a denaturalized body. Bayer and Malone argue that psychology too has, in its discourse and practices, brought about a displacement that has opposed woman to the body while failing to notice women's resistance to "master discourses." Although the place of the body in feminism and contemporary scholarship remains contested, Bayer and Malone find that there is no easy feminist way out. It is neither a home to return to nor the site of a final freedom. For these authors the "body can cleave to representations" yet "representation and body collaborate in undermining one another."

Mary Brown Parlee invites alternative readings of the traditional binary sex/gender categories by listening to those whose embodiment falls outside such distinctions. She is critical of academic constructions of sex and gender, noting how these typically privilege the former over the latter. In their stead she demonstrates how transgender activists undermine scientific and medical discourses of what counts as 'natural' categories. Claiming a name is an activity that constitutes identities and relationships and Parlee rightly notes that psychology does not have a tradition of discussing the ethics of representational strategies. The very range of terms used by both activists and medical communities raises not only ethical questions about the accountability of professionals but points to the limits of our knowledge. For those whose lives do not fit neatly into "the grid" of binary sex/gender categories, official ways of knowing, speaking and acting are deeply flawed and incapacitates our understanding, our ways of coming to know, those whose lives are gendered in ways that academic/medical traditions do not comprehend. It is here that different embodied experiences call for a change in academic practices.

In a related vein, Caterina Pizanias unearths the story of Susan Stewart's exhibit *Lovers and Warriors* after it had failed to leave its "mark in the art world." In the story of the show's creation and short life, Pizanias examines the boundaries of disciplinarity in the academy as well as the world of art. Incorporating Bourdieu's concept of *habitus* into her work, she attempts to uncover the representational politics in art and the social sciences. Her journey through the art world becomes a case study in its own right of the "*habitus* in action," the "*habitus* that includes those aspects of identity and praxis which are only partially surveyed in the standard social sciences' theoretical frames." Susan Stewart's intervention of including in her photographic exhibit the narratives of her collaborators becomes the occasion for her exclusion from the world of professional art. By presenting subject spaces for lesbian women she transgresses the rules of the gallery's *sanctum sanctorum*. Pizanias presents the case as one way of coming to comprehend the *habitus* as fluid and unfinished, and to note that "to speak of the body outside disciplinary bounds" is fraught with dangers.

Sick and Healing Bodies

It is in illness and pain that the body undergoes a change that makes it incapable of being taken for granted. As Leder (1990) notes, our temporal horizon shrinks, and the body may appear both alien and threatening while demanding continued ministrations. At the same time, it is Radley's (1991) contention that a chronic illness is not just something to which one adapts but rather the very adjustments made come to constitute the illness with which one must cope. The illness is "refigured through one's efforts to maintain daily life" (p. 149). There is no singular path for doing so, narratives of illness express varied and difficult ways of living with illness and of re-figuring one's bodily life to bear one's illness. We have argued elsewhere that persons with a chronic illness such as cancer who explicitly integrate their illness into biographical narratives live different lives from those who "leave their bodies to medicine," and who remain disinterested observers of what transpires biomedically (Stam & Mathieson, 1995). Illness remains a problematic for a psychology of the body precisely because modern "biopsychosocial" accounts are incapable of dealing with the body. In effect, such accounts reduce to functional, dualist conceptions that either privilege biology or abstract properties (such as "coping") that have no meaning to the suffering body.

The papers that follow deal with the question of pain and illness but hold to very different conceptual agendas. Cor Baerveldt and Paul Voestermans walk through the problem of the body in anorexia nervosa as a way to a critique of psychology's body and to validate the embodied experience of women who are anorectic. They note that accounts of anorexia have either ignored the body by focusing on a host of non-specific psychological variables or have argued for a "mannequin body," one that is dressed up in culture but has no flesh. Turning to social constructionist accounts, they find that these have far too limited a take on the body as a vehicle for communicative acts and miss the body as cultural practice. To include bodily conduct which is meaningful as well as socially regulated within communication they suggest the broadening of the latter term to 'co-regulation.' This notion recognizes not only the fact that presentations can lack an explicit structure and hence can do more than merely "communicate" but also that bodily skills are slowly acquired through the refinement of a bodily sensitivity that can be expressive. Anorexia nervosa can now be recast without denying the anorectic's competence to "claim and sustain an identity." Baerveldt and Voestermans introduce the notion of the body as a 'selfing' device, a concept that has close affinities to Bourdieu's notion of *habitus*. On this account, anorectics objectify their bodies to the extent that they are no longer meaningfully engaged in the social world and their bodies become objects to be controlled. Thus, rather than focus on the meaning associated with the eating habits of anorectics, Baerveldt and Voestermans argue that the focus should be on the competence of anorectics to deploy their bodies in the social world and the manner in which this competence becomes restricted. This paper, then, travels across a wide conceptual and empirical domain to argue for a renewed conception of the lived body.

Robert Kugelmann provides a thorough critique of the psychology of pain in general, and the gate control theory of pain specifically, motivated by an attempt to understand the way in which medicine has come to "treat" all of a patient's existence under the new biopsychosocial models. Pain is emblematic of the changing landscape of bio-medicine and psychology has played an important supporting role. Kugelmann tells the history of this development noting how the theory and treatment of pain began to change dramatically after 1950, albeit not in tandem. It was not until the emergence of the gate-control theory in 1965 that a model of pain encapsulated both the divergent theoretical strands in the pain literature as well as changing clinical conceptions of pain management. According to Kugelmann, pain could now be seen as a process rather than a strictly sensory matter. One implication drawn from this and other developments was that pain was now an "experience" that allowed for a much wider variety of treatment and intervention, including the scientific expropriation of cultural healing techniques. Kugelmann argues that this constitutes an extension of the limits of bio-medicine into all aspects of a patient's life, an account of the gate control theory that provides a corrective to the rather more optimistic versions found elsewhere in the body literature (e.g., Scarry, 1985).

Anyone who has attempted to chart the process of the problems of embodiment and illness in the contemporary literature will know how vastly it has reached into many disciplines and subject areas of the academy. In an encyclopedic and insightful account, Arthur Frank reviews ten major book-length studies of the body, focusing particularly on the "narrative construction of the lived body." Frank organizes his review around a set of propositions that bring into focus the very important works on the body now reshaping social scientists' understanding of illness. This understanding is not so much above the body, observed as it were from outside, but a recognition that we come to know ourselves and the world through our bodies and we had better not allow this insight to be suppressed in the name of medical treatments if we want to retain that self through an illness or if we want to reclaim ourselves on the other end of illness.

These papers are neither an introduction to theorizing the body nor do they provide any closure on the topic. They invite further elaboration, contradiction and dialogue. If they can be said to have a common theme it is, as Frank notes, the ethics of body talk. Each author invites us to consider certain questions and possibilities of psychological and social life that the body opens for valuation. They request a suspension of belief in scientized psychological categories for the empirical problems bodies pose. By empirical I mean it in its older and etymological sense of *experience* or *skill*, the experience and skill of embodied life.

References

Craik, K. J. W. (1943). *The nature of explanation*. Cambridge: Cambridge University Press.

Danziger, K. (1997). *Naming the mind: How psychology found its language*. London: Sage.

Deleule, D. (1992). The living machine: Psychology as organology. In J. Crary & S. Kwinter (Eds.), *Incorporations. Zone*, Vol. 6 (pp. 203-233). New York: Zone.

Leder, D. (1990). *The absent body*. Chicago: University of Chicago Press.

McDonough, R. (1997). The concept of organism and the concept of mind. *Theory & Psychology*, 7, 579-604.

Pylyshyn, Z. W. (1989). Computing in cognitive science. In M. I. Posner (Ed.), *Foundations of cognitive science* (pp. 51-91). Cambridge, Mass.: MIT Press.

Radley, A. (1991). *The body and social psychology*. New York: Springer-Verlag.

Radley, A. (1995). The elusory body and social constructionist theory. *Body & Society*, 1(2), 3-23.

Scarry, E. (1985). *The body in pain*. New York: Oxford University Press.

Skinner, B. F. (1938). *The behavior of organisms: An experimental analysis*. New York: Appleton-Century-Crofts.

Stam, H. J., Lubek, I., & Radtke, H. L. (1998). Repopulating social psychology texts: Disembodied "subjects" and embodied subjectivity. In B. Bayer & J. Shotter (Eds.), *Reconstructing the subject* (pp. 153–186). London: Sage.

Stam, H. J. & Mathieson, C. M. (1995). Psychological perspectives on the body. In I. Lubek, R. van Hezewijk, G. Pheterson, & C. Tolman (Eds.), *Trends and issues in theoretical psychology* (pp. 119-125). New York: Springer.

Turner, T. (1994). Bodies and anti-bodies: flesh and fetish in contemporary social theory. In T. J. Csordas (Ed.), *Embodiment and experience* (pp. 27-47). Cambridge: Cambridge University Press.

Varela, F. J., Thompson, E., & Rosch, E. (1991). *The embodied mind: Cognitive science and human experience*. Cambridge, Mass.: MIT Press.

Part II
SOCIAL AND PSYCHOLOGICAL BODIES

2

Displays and Fragments
Embodiment and the Configuration of Social Worlds

Alan Radley

ABSTRACT. This paper draws a distinction between the concepts of embodiment and the body. It focuses upon embodiment as a central condition of social life, through which individuals are able to symbolize their world. The physically bounded body is often seen as a matter relating either to individual experiences of corporeality, or to social evaluations and constraints concerning its scope of action. Embodiment, however, is fundamental to how people collectively and individually 'take a stand' towards each other, and in so doing define or propose the worlds in which they meet. The paper explores this idea through an examination of display in social life, drawing upon the work of Goffman and of Geertz on expression, Simmel on style and Goodman on exemplification. It argues that display enables us to reconfigure possible 'ways of life'. This involves us, as embodied beings, in entering into and transforming the present moment. This refiguring of everyday experience is achieved by virtue of our appearing as exemplars of the social worlds portrayed (i.e. those that we embody), such as the spheres of play, ecstasy or danger.

In this paper I try to show that *embodiment*, rather than the body, is central to psychological life and to social relationships. This is because it is the medium for individuals to display things that matter to each other, and how they matter. If being a medium of display is key to the body's role in social life, and if display is more than a matter of establishing, endorsing or challenging our social identities, then what is it that we are able to do because we are embodied beings? The broad answer is—to engage the world so as to fashion semblances and configure social worlds: in short, to symbolize. It is the capacity to do such things as mime, flirt, play at, invite moods or close off possible futures. The question then becomes: how can our physical appearance, manner and what at first sight are merely mundane actions make this possible?

Before addressing this issue, it is worth dealing with the objection that the body is not essential to all such occurrences. People are able to use words expressively, and can convey moods through written texts and by means of the plastic arts. Metaphor is everywhere: why, one might ask, focus upon the body? The argument implied by this objection is misleading, because it attempts to reinsert the division between the (physical) body and discourse, insisting that the former be considered only as a field or material resource, while the latter be accorded signifying powers. Once this happens, the question of embodiment is side-stepped in favour of making the body into just one object (or medium) amongst others.

One way of answering the question posed in the opening paragraph is to reanalyse some proposals about the nature of expression in social life. While the idea of the body being expressive—or having some expressive function—is by no means new, the claim that this capacity is fundamental to people's conceptions of their situation, and thereby to an understanding of the body in psychology, does make a novel challenge for the discipline. Much of the writing about the body in recent years has been stimulated by the aim of determining what is special about our corporeal existence. The fact that we are fleshy beings is clearly important: we feel pain and are ill, we have desires, we are conscious of our practical dependence upon the material world, we shape cultural norms to contain or to proscribe bodily functions and capacities. All these things redirect our attention towards the body as a focal entity in psychological life. They tend to make it distinct in our analyses, suggesting that social scientists have managed to catch under the spotlight of their inquiries something particular, bounded and coherent. Under certain circumstances this might be true, but to adhere to this position alone renders the puzzle of embodiment in general into one concerning 'the body' in particular, as if questions about the former could be satisfactorily answered in terms of the latter. They could if embodiment was only about 'the body' considered as individual being: they cannot, because embodiment is also about social worlds, not just those which are material and extant, but also those which are ephemeral and possible.

This argument underlines the fact that human beings would not be what they are if they did not have bodies (Wertz, 1987). More to the point, socio-psychological life would not be what it is if it were not embodied through and through. This means, for example, that we are individuals who do not just happen to find ourselves in male or female bodies. Instead, our existence as sexual beings is involved in all aspects of our lives. This does not mean that sexuality is a blind factor in all of life's equations, but that the ground from which an individual acts is a gendered ground, and that its features can be sought in the largest or in the smallest actions. Again, this is not meant to imply that sexuality is a natural characteristic: the marking and cultivation of physical difference is cultural and symbolic (Laqueur, 1990). The remaking or undoing of that difference in action is, however, an endorsement of the fact that we are differentiated in our being, not just in our social identities.

Because embodiment has both a material and a sentient aspect to it, we do more than know a ready-made physical reality through our separate bodies: we transform it through the actions that we make together. In the case of something like flirtation, what is conveyed is not simply an emotion but an invitation, a call to the other to participate. The material aspect of the body then takes on a greater significance, because the physical world is now defined in relation to social projects, cultural mores, shared and contested meanings. What we are capable of showing through our embodied actions, therefore, are matters concerning our social condition. While this includes face-to-face relationships between individuals, such as those involving flirtation or play, it also extends to all kinds of groupings and crowds in which matters of collective feeling are nurtured and conveyed by virtue of the physical presence of those concerned. For example, the technological innovations of the funfair make new bodily sensations possible, but they do not of themselves make the atmosphere of enjoyment. For this to happen something else must occur, something involving the way that people lose and recover balance (and dignity) in each other's eyes.

This reference to the mutual visibility of bodily conduct is the stuff of display; how this relates to questions of the body is the core issue for the remainder of this paper. However, an analysis based upon display cannot be one of 'the body in total'. There are important reasons why this should be the case. First, of course, an argument based upon display is limited to the body's appearance in movement, and has no concern for the individual's sensing of or reflection upon his or her physical condition. But there is a more important reason. The idea that there might be an explanation of the body assumes that there is a single entity to be explained. I have already said that the specific question of the body is not to be confused with the broader issue of embodiment. It is not the (physical) body that concerns us here so much as what is made possible because we are embodied—in brief, what can be shown forth about ourselves and our situation.

Display: Embodiment as Expressive Form

The concept of display is useful because it highlights the fact that embodiment not only provides the ground of being, but places us in relation to each other in our mutual visibility. For phenomenologists, the individual body 'conceals itself as it projects itself across the physical world', so that understanding it is a matter of revealing its role in the tacit basis of individual action (Leder, 1990). However, in social life individuals do not merely stand somewhere: they also see where each of them stands, and how they stand, to put this point metaphorically as well as literally. As this paper argues, this goes well beyond the notion of communicating impressions about 'ourselves' as particular kinds of persons, having characteristics that we impute one to the other. The idea of impression management assumes the body to be either a kind of prop or else an elaborate signalling system for communicating ideas emanating from, and presumed to be about, the individual sender. Such a notion abandons entirely any critical reanalysis of embodiment as a serious issue for psychology. To recapture it one must look again at what it means to be embodied in the social world, and indeed what it means to be social in an embodied world.

It is a truism that individuals can express themselves with their bodies. However, what this is usually taken to mean is that they can convey something about their feelings or present orientation in a way that another person can understand. Expression is, then, a kind of communication of ideas about something or someone, that happens to employ the special channels available because people have bodies. This is why the word 'expression' is made redundant by the term 'non-verbal communication'. This view also assumes the body to exist, as it were, in some sort of ether with respect to the material world. It is no more than an interesting device expanding the possible ways for individuals to communicate with one another.

In this section I argue that displays are expressive forms, and that they do much more than communicate ideas about selves in abstraction. In order to show why this is so, it is necessary to re-examine how the concept of expression has been used in relation to display. Two points are made, both having implications for an analysis of embodiment in social life. The first is that displays involving expression are not reducible to the function of denoting or categorizing; the second point is that expression involves an engagement with aspects of the material world and, indeed, a transformation of them. Because we are dealing here with what is shown, it is necessary that we make use of examples to illustrate the points being made.

In one of his earliest publications, Goffman (1951) made a distinction which is potentially useful to an understanding of what is significant about embodiment for social life. Writing about symbols of class status, he said that these carry both categorial and expressive significance. The former is concerned with matters of denoting or claiming identity; the latter expresses the style of life or point of view of the person concerned. Goffman backed up his distinction using the example of duelling in earlier times, which, although a marker of gentlemanly status, was largely redundant in this regard because duelling was not extended to the lower classes. As an expression of a way of life, however, it portrayed the conception of a man who would not spurn danger in the defence of his self-respect, of a style that permeated all of this person's actions.

The idea that, in some important way, expression is different to categoriz-ation remained implicit in Goffman's writings about the ritual order, where, for example, he used the distinction between information being 'given' and 'given off' to establish what are constructed, though effectively categorial selves. In his later work, Goffman (1976) was to re-emphasize the im-portance of displays for the alignments that individuals make in order to establish their social identities. In that sense, expressive work is in the service of establishing claims to category membership, and so appears to be embraced as a phenomenon by the practice of maintaining identity or the giving of accounts. In spite of being accorded what might be seen as a secondary role, the concept of expression continually resurfaces in his treatment of interpersonal encounters, particularly in discussions of the limitation of (institutional) membership and of (bodily) accident, as being sufficient to explain the emergence of the actor's situated self. His essay on 'role distance' (Goffman, 1961) is a masterly attempt to elucidate 'the problem of expression'. In fact, what he provides is a thorough description of the way that a working self may be claimed through the full or partial disowning of the virtual role imputed by the position held. The result of this analysis, however, is that the problem of expression becomes resolved into the question of how people play at, rather than merely play, roles they are seen to occupy.

A re-examination of one example that Goffman gives shows the relevance of this analysis for our discussion of embodiment. The analysis makes use of an illustration of young people on a merry-go-round, who make fun of their situation (i.e. distance themselves from it) by such activities as standing on the saddle, or holding on to the post with one hand while leaning back as far as possible. This is clearly different from the situation of the child who embraces the role of merry-go-round rider, for whom the physical sensations of riding the horse are integral with his or her experience of the ride as constituting the reality of the situation.

The difference between the two kinds of rider lies, in one regard, in the obvious deployments of posture, and in the apparent risk and recovery of loss of muscular control conveyed by those who treat the ride as 'a game'. The expressive features of role distance, in this as in other cases Goffman describes, are to do with the adoption and refusal of selves, and the fabrication of appearances in relation to the presence of an audience of one kind or another. And yet, the stylistics of this fabrication are made possible only through changes in bodily comportment. This comportment—as a key feature of the display—involves a variation of, or departure from, the use of the body in the conventional setting. In the course of his discussion of role distance, these changes become assimilated to the concepts that Goffman develops. As features of display, the detailed descriptions of physical life become merely the means for analysing the establishment of social iden-tities; expression is seen to be in the service of categorization. In spite of this, examples like that of the merry-go-round can be used to explore further the claim that the involvement of the body in expressive displays is more than a secondary affair.

A different illustration, though one having interesting similarities to the merry-go-round example, was provided by Willis (1975) in his description of a motor-bike gang in central England. The gang members made a point of discarding, or wearing loosely, the usual protective items of clothing associated with conventional riding, as well as removing baffles to increase the noise of the bike's exhaust. By doing this, they opened out the inherent characteristics of the motor-cycle, heightening the physical sensations of speed and the presence of excitement and danger. Compared with the conventional rider, whose clothes and helmet tend to make him or her impersonal and anonymous, the motor-bike boys became more visible to others. This had two different but associated effects. On the one hand, it distinguished the gang from conventional riders in the eyes of themselves and others; and on the other, it allowed them to experience, collectively, the reverberations of the machines and the danger of the ride.

In both of these examples, the concept of display (with its associated idea of expressiveness) points, as it were, in two directions. In one direction, the fabrication of a shared, pleasurable way of life when riding (bikes or wooden horses) transcends the immediate situation. This transcendence is the evocation of a 'social world' which, though it might be fleeting and ephemeral, is significant to the extent that it refigures the experience of the actors and the perceptions of the audience. The other direction concerns the engagement of individuals in the physical world, in which the possibility of danger and excitement is encountered by virtue of entering further, faster or more fleetingly into its particulars. While the merry-go-round riders depend upon the rigidity of the horse in order to deploy their movements, the motor-bike boys created their experience through the repositioning and recontextualizing of cultural commodities (the parts of the bike, the conventional clothes worn by bikers). Both cases show, however, that displays do not just take place in particular settings: they transform them in ways made possible because we do not float in some sociopsychological vacuum, but inhabit the world as both symbolic and material beings (Merleau-Ponty, 1962).

This double aspect of display involving the body—transcendence on the one hand, immediacy on the other—has been noted particularly in the world of artistic endeavour (Langer, 1957) and more generally by anthropologists studying ritual (Bateson, 1987; Turner, 1974). One fine example is given by Geertz (1972) in his description of the Balinese cockfight. This involves a series of staged matches between fighting cocks, over which spectators will urge their chosen protagonist against the background of bets having been placed. In Bali, Geertz points out, cocks (like motor-bikes in the western world) are things with which the men identify themselves, not least because of the association of these birds with metaphysical powers. The cockfight is not (for the players) essentially about establishing status—its function is not primarily categorial. It is, like any social display, essentially expressive, in that it renders ordinary life comprehensible by presenting it in terms of acts and objects that are reordered or transformed. As Geertz (1972) describes it:

> The cockfight is a means of expression; its function is neither to assuage social passions nor to heighten them ... but, in a medium of feathers, blood, crowds, and money, to display them. (p. 23)

Displays, then, depend upon transformations of the world, upon the reordering of cultural artifacts, and the deployment of the corporeal body in its material settings. In order that these things could occur, it is necessary to conceive of our ability to dwell in the particulars of the material world, to take them into ourselves and to transform them. In the earlier example of the motor-bike gang, the resistance of the wind, the speed of the bike over the ground, the weight of the machine, the noise of the exhaust, were such particulars for the bikers. These things are sensual, of the moment and concrete: and yet they are fundamental to the creation of an aura that, in colouring other aspects of the riders' daily round, expressed a style of life that transcended the immediacy of the moment, of the riding as an instance of motor control.

This suggests that displays are important because they can be more than a portrayal, the demonstration of a claim or the avowal of a belief (Shotter, 1981). This 'more than' involves precisely those features through which individuals fabricate a 'world in itself', a fragment of life that is self-contained in being distinguished from the mundane, and yet can reconfigure those who are caught up in it, either as actors or as witnesses. This raises two points that are important to note about displays, as we have discussed them so far. First, even if they do not require an audience to occur, the presence of an audience would often seem to be assumed in the form of their execution. The everyday meaning of display connotes a 'showing off', an exhibiting to others. This would seem less so in the case of the Balinese cockfight, though this is perhaps because the protagonists in the drama are birds, allowing the human actors to participate at a distance, so to speak. However, in the case of riders (of bikes or wooden horses), the presence of an audience is implicit in their riding displays, one whose reactions (perhaps of amazement, of outrage) are responses that fuel the course of the action.

To see the full implication of this we need to note one further feature of expressive display; as part of the sense of a particular world, it can create the idea of being bounded by its own time. As Geertz (1972) says, the dramatic shape of the cockfight creates a world unto itself; it is an expressive form which, in order to articulate significant features of Balinese life, 'lives in its own present—the one it itself creates' (p. 24).

Putting together the two features of visibility and sense of time, it can be argued that an important feature of displays is a drawing of others' attention, a delineation of a time–space in which something significant is to occur. Arguably, the duellist, those involved in watching the cockfight, and the bike-rider all exemplify this important condition (as does the dancer). At first sight, it might seem that this is nothing more than saying that they draw attention to themselves: however, this is not just the case, if we mean by this 'pointing to themselves'. In evoking another bounded world, the actors conjure powers and meanings that they dispose of, which yet appear to derive from a location other than their 'ordinary' selves. (This is the sense, when watching a dramatic scene, that the actors are invigorated by passions or can draw upon powers that have their source beyond the immediate setting or their physical capacities.)

What the actors draw attention to is to an impending (or ongoing) rearrangement of objects and symbols within a field involving the body. An attempt to convey this idea has been set out previously in terms of the concepts of meta-communication (Bateson, 1987) and framing (Goffman, 1975). However, these concepts do not emphasize sufficiently the crucial point that the ground of the display indicates itself; it is self-referential. It is embodied beings who, by virtue (*not* by means) of their physical presence, can portray transmutations of the 'here and now' which delineate the immediate as a fragment of some different, or new, totality of meaning. This underlines the point made by Merleau-Ponty (1962) that the immediate moment is transcended, or achieves significance, not in spite of our physical form, but because of it.

Fragments of Society, Total Worlds

At this point it is necessary to say more about the issue of transcendence as it relates to the question of individuals and society. In particular, there remains the problem of what it is that is 'expressed', although, from what has been said already, this must be more than information about selves and identities. Displays, as we have seen, are enactments with the body that symbolize certain ways of being, that make certain social worlds appear. These worlds may be small, as in the time two people spend together where the movements of the body are minimized but allude to intimacy. (Displays do not have to be grand or loud—or even public.) On the other hand, these worlds may be large, as when they encompass many people involved in social ritual (e.g. carnival), or who form the audience watching a play. In each case, however, the key point is that the term 'world' is appropriate because a totality of meaning is conjured. It is not that displays produce a section from an alternative lifestyle, or a piece of it. The invitation that lies at the core of true flirtation is to an entry into a different way of being in relation to each other, not to the hastening of a brute act of sexual congress. While displays are, in their immediacy, necessarily fragments of life when viewed from a distance, they signify in the ways described here only because they partake of a different totality. Embodiment involves both immanence and transcendence together.

One can approach this issue, as previously, through the work of Goffman (1976), who provided a critique of the notion that expression is natural, in the sense that the body is a vehicle for making signs that can be read as marks of the individual's enduring (essential) nature. Dealing with the question of gender, he argued that men and women use their faces and bodies to engage in a form of 'social portraiture'. In doing this, they both provide and read depictions of masculinity and femininity, and show a greater or lesser willingness to adhere to the accepted schedule for presenting these portraits. In doing these things, they are not merely affirming the ritual order, but in fabricating the form and degree of variation about this schedule, their displays also constitute the social hierarchy. In his words, these expressions are both 'the shadow and the substance' of social life.

One of the problems that this account is intended to solve relates directly to the source of the codes used in these behavioural styles, and indirectly, therefore, to the role of the body. For Goffman, it is not enough to say that codes are in society, because there still remains the issue of how the ingredients are formulated in action—effectively the styling of displays. Having dispatched the natural expression thesis, his argument turned once more to the willingness or the need for people to justify or legitimate their alignment with such social schedules. While there is no requirement that people must endorse these schedules (they can counterbalance or contradict them), this argument once more reduces expression to a matter of consonance or dissonance between what is shown and what might be expected.

The question remains, however, as to the significance of embodiment for the fabrication of displays, in relation both to their styling and to the colouring of episodes that 'live in their own present'. These two aspects are not reducible to one another, although they appear to be related. There is a sense in which bodily style is expressive, but yet falls short of the transformation of experience that can be produced, for example, in religious ritual or artistic endeavour. A useful distinction can be drawn here between stylization as a reflection of general form and the uniqueness implicit in the fabricated moment, the social world that is conjured, for example, in the Balinese cockfight.

We owe this distinction to Simmel (1991), who argued that stylization always represents the general character of things, its purpose being (in the case of cultural artifacts) to reveal the universal form to which it adheres (i.e. is aligned). So, for example, all manufactured objects—jewellery, furniture, drinking glasses—have their meaning in the generality of the various styles that inform them. In contrast, the ideal of the unique work of art—the painting—is 'closed within itself', and refuses to participate in the everyday world of practicalities. While it is possible to discuss a painting in terms of the styles of the period, or those typical of the works of other painters, its uniqueness lies in its particular way of figuring its subject. The relevance of this distinction for an analysis of embodiment is in the argument that Simmel makes for the place of these two expressive forms in everyday life. On the one hand, the work of art draws us in to a contemplation of life, which it reflects uniquely. On the other, the stylized object (or, rather, objects reflecting various styles) provides the means whereby individuals can locate themselves in the general social sphere. With regard to the latter, which Simmel regarded as a key issue for individuals in modern society, he said that there is a vital need for the individual to create a distance from 'the exaggerated subjectivism of the times', a need which is met by the arrangement of objects marked by typicality. The consequences of these arrangements for psychological life are considerable, in that 'we are saved from absolute responsibility, from balancing on the narrowness of mere individuality' (Simmel, 1991, p. 68).

Having made note of this distinction, it is important to emphasize that the opposition drawn between these terms is an ideal one; it is not an empirical observation. In the world of art and of artifacts, original pictures are sometimes reproduced to be used as living room decorations, while everyday objects are reassembled together and displayed in galleries as art objects. This exchange of materials does not invalidate the argument that, in each case, different social forms are operating. Similarly, it is not suggested here that the body is used discretely, at one time in displays and at another in alignments. As has been shown, expressive behaviour can be employed in the service of establishing one's identity. As far as display is concerned, it relies upon categories (or rather the breaching or transforming of them) to achieve its effect.

When related to the question of embodiment, Simmel's analysis of style makes it possible to argue that alignments with schedules (displays of consonance) and their variation are but one way in which the body is deployed in social life. In these terms, the 'stylized body' is one that portrays the individual not just as a member of a particular group (e.g. women), but as owning (or lacking) certain general qualities that are universal to the group form. In this respect, for example, any particular woman 'will find that the way has been cleared to fall back on the situation of her entire sex to account to herself for why she should refrain from vying with men in matters mechanical, political and so forth' (Goffman, 1976, p. 76). Or consider the family who arrange themselves for a photograph on holiday; they are literally pictured, as well as figuratively portrayed as people having the kind of happy holiday experience thought to be culturally appropriate for people in their situation.

Other examples of alignments can be found in the world of consumer culture, where the transformation and exchange of objects that can be worn, carried or ridden provide the wherewithal not only to display cultural codes, but also to comment on them. For example, the worlds of alternative groupings or subcultures are articulated, in part, through the intentional repositioning and recontextualizing of commodities that bear either directly (e.g. body piercing) or indirectly (clothing) upon the corporeal body (Hebdige, 1979).

How, then, does Simmel's discussion of the other ideal form, the work of art, bear upon the question of embodiment? In this case, what is at work is the opposite of stylization, in that a sense of uniqueness of action or episode is experienced, at least by participants if not by onlookers. As part of this, there is a boundary or frame between it and its surroundings, so that it does not intervene in the mundane world, or 'cannot serve as a necessary extra' (Simmel, 1991, p. 68). The Balinese cockfight is of this form, as are all kinds of lesser rituals in everyday life (e.g. flirtation), in which individuals transcend alignments to configure a time out of the mundane. The role of the body here is more than the conveyance of subtleties of communication, or the making of covert signals. There is a catching up of the threads of the moment to create the possibility of another way of living, or at least of apprehending the world in another hue. The feelings and ideas that are part of this apprehension are configured not only in speech, but by means of actions and facial expressions of 'fleshy' individuals. What is expressed by such episodes are symbols, to be sure, but not always those that can easily be articulated in words. (Note, however, that this does not necessarily make them any the more significant, nor words less so.) The sense of the uniqueness of such an episode is that which allows it to remain a fragment in experience, but at the same time to symbolize something either more general or more important. It alludes to a wider sphere, imaginary or otherwise, which totality of meaning 'lends significance and coherence to the specifics of what was said or done' (Simmel, in Frisby, 1985, p. 50).

We need to tackle this proposal head on in the next section of the paper. For the moment, what matters is that we have made a potentially useful distinction concerning embodied action in social display. On the one hand, there is the use of the body as that through which we may endorse, refuse or distort the forms or schedules defining social groups. This is the stuff of alignments and of stylization by means of which social identities are portrayed. On the other hand, embodiment involves a capacity to take up and to transform features of the mundane world in order to portray a 'way of being', an outlook, a style of life that shows itself in what it is. Like the painted picture in a frame, it has self-referential qualities that allude to something not easily specified. This is the totality of which we spoke earlier, which cannot be isolated in a particular movement or word because it transcends these when taken as a fragment of the mundane (e.g. the physical body). At the same time, it does not exist beyond the particulars of the act because it is only through the specific engagements of embodied people together that such symbolic realms are made to appear.

Rather than trying to conceal or to reify the elusory features of expressive action within some essentialist body, I am arguing instead that these merit the kind of distinction that Simmel made between the stylized and the artistic object. With regard to the latter form of display, the lasting significance of the look, the touch or the posture does not lie in their ability to specify exactly the essence of a class or category (the lover, the duellist). Instead, it resides in the ability to express, in its fragmentary appearance, a totality which it in some way exemplifies.

The Problem of Expression: The Body as Exemplar

If embodiment is a condition for expression, and if displays are the medium by which expression is achieved, then people's actions signify something not only beyond the mundane present, but also about it. In some sense, the totality of which we have spoken must be seen to animate or to be reflected in the particulars that convey its presence. To illustrate, the flirt must not just convey a world of flirtation but somehow exemplify it. This is not the same thing as saying that the flirt must appear flirtatious, which is to reduce the problem to a matter of categories located in the constructions (discourse) of the individuals concerned, and thus to one of social identity. The key point is that expressive displays produce a world of virtual powers on which the actors appear to draw, and which their actions embody. That is, as well as making a certain world appear, the actors are themselves reconfigured in the light of the possibilities that flow from them. What is expressed is not what is intrinsic to individuals, but the virtual forms which displays make possible.

In this section I argue that embodiment is, to follow Merleau-Ponty (1968), the 'exemplar sensible' that makes it possible for us to incorporate things in the fragment of the present, and yet to transcend them in the anticipation and configuring of alternative pasts and futures. Within Merleau-Ponty's scheme, this concept is aimed at showing how individuals know the (physical) world in which they live. For the purposes of this paper, the concept of exemplification is important when trying to answer questions about what it is that individuals express in the course of embodied display.

Expression is symbolization, but of a particular kind. Having already distinguished it from categorization (attribution) we now need to ask what is special about it. The distinction between expression and denotation has been reaffirmed and extended by Goodman (1978) in his analysis of symbolization in art. Whereas to depict is to denote or to specify, to express is to display or to exemplify. So much we have seen already. However, Goodman goes further by underlining the special role of exemplification in display. Using the illustration of a tailor's swatch, he argues that it exemplifies attributes of colour and texture relating to the bolt of cloth, but not its size or shape. Even in the case of literal properties such as these, there remains the question of which ones are to be made salient. What is important about exemplification is that a sample exemplifies—is a sample of—only some of its properties, which are salient in relation to the practical possibilities surrounding it.

Exemplification as symbolization is a form of reference in which the picture (or the person) stands as a sample of that to which it (s/he) refers. It is, says Goodman, a matter of being and doing, of both having properties and referring to them. These might be properties that are literally possessed (e.g. the colour of the swatch), or they might be attributes that are figuratively possessed, as in the sadness conveyed by a painting. In the latter case, what is shown forth as sadness is a property that is metaphorically exemplified: it is not intrinsic to the picture, as are the colours of the paint, but instead can be said to be borrowed. As with all metaphor, the properties something expresses are those it possesses, but which did not originally belong to it. They are not the features by which the work is literally classified (e.g. a grey picture), but are metaphorical imports, so that 'pictures express sounds or feelings rather than colours' (Goodman, 1968, p. 86).

We can use these ideas to pursue the question of how embodiment is key to expression in social life. Two features of the argument can be taken as being useful, at least initially. First, people can express only what they metaphorically (but not literally) possess. Second, individuals exemplify only those attributes that are pertinent to the symbolization intended. This means that displays of pain, fear or anger are not expressions as I am using the word here; they are the (literal) symptoms of different states of being.

A useful illustration of what this means is provided by the case of the motor-bike gang mentioned above. One of the gang-members was a dwarf, with whom more prominent members would engage in mock fights. These fights had all the ceremonial features of ritual, in which the practical (literal) consequences of fighting were removed by the fact that the regular members would feign injury or pretend to be overpowered by the dwarf. This play-fighting involved these protagonists in modulated or exaggerated actions, though in the dwarf's case both his pugilistic efforts and his response to this treatment involved a ready embracing of his role as a fighter. As an ongoing event enjoyed by other gang-members, this was no contest to determine (or reinforce) social status in the group, but a display in which salient features of their world (toughness, a 'rough masculine bonhomie') were more power-fully articulated. The meaning of the display, its symbolization, was carried over in the resulting behaviour of the dwarf, who at other times took on a swaggering comportment, to the delight of his fellows. In effect, Willis

(1975) says, in the affection shown to him by other members, the dwarf came to symbolize the culture and ideology of the group.

This example shows the way in which the dwarf's literal attributes (of smallness, and relative weakness) were precisely those that, through the modulation of action, enabled him to exemplify characteristics of fighting ability that he metaphorically (but not literally) possessed. More than this, he became the symbol, in his bodily comportment, of attributes of the culture of the group. His literal smallness was the vehicle through which the metaphorical toughness of the group could be displayed. Like the example of the Balinese cockfight, this expressive form worked because 'properties conventionally ascribed to certain things are unconventionally ascribed to others, which are then seen to possess them' (Geertz, 1972, p. 26). And like the cockfight, the figurative element is more significant (socially, psychologically) than the literal. Identified as a style of the group, it can (loosely) be compared to a work of art in the way that it refracts life through its medium of appearance. And like art, it does not merely mirror the world, but articulates, in a complex of feeling and action, an approach to the world in general. This approach is lived out by us, as embodied beings, in the course of its dramatic instantiation: it is not merely reflected upon or discussed after the fact. It is for this reason that Simmel saw the style of modern art as that which 'not only possesses truth, it *is* truth' (quoted in Frisby, 1985, p. 47).

Certain key elements are present in this example of the expressive behaviour of the motor-bike gang. It involves 'the body', to be sure, but it is not merely the physical body that is at issue here. What the members said in the course of the mock fight, and what they said about it afterwards, were important to the establishment and selection of attributes that contributed to the group's sense of its own culture. In fact, the fight involved several bodies that engaged one another in a world of symbols. This world was created with(in) a display that made use of both the body's material form and 'its' symbolic capacities. The dwarf's (bodily) limitations and the gang members' exaggerated, yet modulated, actions were a non-discursive fragment which alluded to the totality of meaning (the gang's style of life) in which these matters cohered. This example shows, once again, that what appears in embodied display does so not in spite of the physicality of being, but by virtue of it.

We can conclude from this that the literal or mundane is transcended by our engagement with the world as embodied beings. In Merleau-Ponty's (1962) terms, the body does this because, in being 'sensible', it can take up the world and transform it, so that the meaning swallows up the signs. Then, for example, the physical limitations of the dwarf embody toughness, or the cloud of blood and feathers demonstrate imaginatively the state of Balinese society. This reaffirms the point that embodiment is a condition of both the social and the physical worlds, and because of that the body should never be considered some 'thing' that lies, as it were, between mind and nature, self and other.

Implications

This paper has argued that embodiment is vital to expression, and claimed that expression is as extensive in social life as is categorization. One interesting feature of embodiment is that its involvement in transcending the moment, while yet deepening that fragment of experience, means that it remains a background feature. The condition of phenomenal absence of the body is well documented within analyses that consider the experience of action as a displacing away from the corporeal self (Leder, 1990). However, many of these analyses make use of examples of individuals acting alone within or upon the physical world. The tendency, then, is to consider the body as the ground for knowing that world or for making changes within it, so that questions tend to revolve around the conditions under which the body appears in different balances of absence/presence to consciousness. A major condition for appearance is in times of difficulty (as when the body's capacities are tested) or when it is not functioning as usual (e.g. in times of illness, or pain). Leder (1990) uses the term 'dysappearance' to cover these situations, in which the person's body becomes figured in relation to his or her 'self'.

However, neither the analysis of the body as ground (in relation to individual action) nor the analysis of it when figured (e.g. in pain) addresses the questions that have been raised in this paper. These analyses contribute to a psychology which is unquestionably oriented towards the individual, and which is often directed at how bodies engage the material world, in relation to which 'they' become revealed. The emphasis upon expression in this paper shifts the investigation away from how 'the body' incorporates 'the world' towards embodiment as involved in the con-figuring of possible *social worlds*. These have been considered as symbolic realms in which people dwell by virtue of their ability to indicate *with* their bodies, rather than just through them. Expressive action is not the same as instrumental behaviour, such as occurs when one is unaware of one's arm movements in the course of feeling for the light switch. Nor, in display, are the body's workings to be understood in terms of cybernetic functions such as channels or circuits of information (Bateson, 1987).

There are particular features of embodiment attaching to expressive behaviour which remain to be explored in detail. The point of this paper is that these are not special conditions, but general features of social life. The reason that they have so far been given little consideration is two-fold. First, expressive action has at its centre an elusory aspect which disappears whenever the body or its functions are treated focally (Radley, 1995). Second, displays are often confused with 'expressions' of the body (i.e. emotions), which are taken to be characteristic of groups such as crowds, women and the sick. Traditionally, these have had a secondary claim upon the attention of a discipline born astride the Cartesian divide. For psychology the body is still an unknown quantity, in spite of (or, rather, because of) the fact that its assumptions concerning embodiment underpin all its fields of inquiry (Radley, 1991).

There is, then, a distinction to be made between studying the body in all its separate appearances, technologies and contexts, and the question of embodiment as a condition of human existence. Separating out the body as 'a thing in itself' seems only to make it one more topic for psychological and social theory. Then we have studies of the 'anorexic body', the 'sick body', the 'athletic body' or the 'disciplined body', which, though informative, do not add up to any distinct field of inquiry. It may be that studies of particular instances of how people deal focally with bodies will reveal more general features of significance for psychological theory, but this is not guaranteed. Knowing how the body is controlled, or is talked about, or is used as a means of communication will not necessarily expand psychologists' knowledge of what being embodied makes possible (beyond the instances studied). It does not demonstrate or examine where a study of embodiment might lead.

Conclusion

In spite of the fact that the body is everywhere in our doings, the examples mentioned in this paper show that it is possible, as Simmel insisted, to delineate its workings in any fragment of social life, which always partake of embodiment as a totality. Related to the claims of this paper, this appreciation of embodiment might seem to have limited implications for psychological theory as a whole. However, the argument put forward here underlines the claim that embodiment is the crucial phenomenon (concerning the body) that psychologists must acknowledge. It also reaffirms what sociological analyses of the body have recently rediscovered: that phenomenological descriptions of life-situations are a necessary part of any attempt to make progress in this field (Crossley, 1995). And finally, by showing the key role of embodiment in the formation of symbolic worlds, it puts in question the idea that we can discover much of importance about the body by holding on to the notion that the primary reality of human experience is 'having a conversation'.

References

Bateson, G. (1987). *Steps to an ecology of mind*. Northvale, NJ: Jason Aronson.

Crossley, N. (1995). Merleau-Ponty, the elusive body and carnal sociology. *Body & Society*, *1*(1), 43–63.

Frisby, D. (1985). *Fragments of modernity: Theories of modernity in the work of Simmel, Kracauer and Benjamain*. Cambridge: Polity.

Geertz, C. (1972). Deep play: Notes on the Balinese cockfight. *Daedalus*, *101*, 1–37.

Goffman, E. (1951). Symbols of class status. *British Journal of Sociology*, *2*, 294–304.

Goffman, E. (1961). *Encounters: Two studies in the sociology of interaction*. Harmondsworth: Penguin.

Goffman, E. (1975). *Frame analysis: An essay on the organization of experience*. Harmondsworth: Penguin.

Goffman, E. (1976). Gender advertisements. *Studies in the Anthropology of Visual Communication*, *3* (Whole No. 2).

Goodman, N. (1968). *Language of art: An approach to a theory of symbols*. Indianapolis, IN: Bobbs-Merrill.

Goodman, N. (1978). *Ways of worldmaking*. Indianapolis, IN: Hackett.

Hebdige, D. (1979). *Subculture: The meaning of style*. London: Methuen.

Langer. S.K. (1957). *Philosophy in a new key: A study in the symbolism of reason, rite and art*. Oxford: Oxford University Press.

Laqueur, T. (1990). *Making sex: Body and gender from the Greeks to Freud*. Cambridge, MA: Harvard University Press.

Leder, D. (1990). *The absent body*. Chicago, IL: University of Chicago Press.

Merleau-Ponty, M. (1962). *Phenomenology of perception* (C. Smith, Trans.). London: Routledge & Kegan Paul.

Merleau-Ponty, M. (1968). *The visible and the invisible* (C. Lefort, Ed.; A. Lingis, Trans.). Evanston, IL: Northwestern University Press.

Radley, A. (1991). *The body and social psychology*. New York: Springer.

Radley, A. (1995). The elusory body and social constructionist theory. *Body & Society*, *1*(2), 3–23.

Shotter, J. (1981). Telling and reporting: Prospective and retrospective uses of self-ascriptions. In C. Antaki (Ed.), *The psychology of ordinary explanations of behaviour*. London: Academic Press.

Simmel, G. (1991). The problem of style. *Theory, Culture & Society*, *8*, 63–71.

Turner, V. (1974). *Dramas, fields, metaphors: Symbolic action in human society*. Ithaca, NY: Cornell University Press.

Wertz, F. (1987). Cognitive psychology and the understanding of perception. *Journal of Phenomenological Psychology*, *18*, 103–142.

Willis, P.E. (1975). The expressive style of a motor-bike culture. In J. Benthall & T. Polhemus (Eds.), *The body as a medium of expression*. London: Allen Lane.

3

Establishing Embodiment in Psychology

Edward E. Sampson

ABSTRACT. The dominant discourse within the western tradition and within the psychology it has spawned can be described as exclusionary: history, culture and community are generally not considered as central to understanding what are presumed to be universal psychological processes. Although the challenger and possible successor to the dominant tradition's discourses, social constructionism, is inclusive of history, culture and community, it shares with the dominant tradition an exclusion of embodiment. Other than the object-body (i.e. the body that a third person observer can know), which remains of interest both to the dominant tradition and to social constructionism's examination of how discourse constructs this object-body, neither the dominant nor the successor discourse deals with the inherently embodied character of all social practices, including discursive practices themselves. All exclusions, including the exclusion of embodiment, have serious political ramifications. Establishing an embodied discourse in psychological inquiry, including the inquiry governed by constructionism, will advance both our understanding and, more significantly, those disciplinary applications designed to contribute to human betterment.

A characteristic of the western tradition that continues in force today is the generally exclusionary quality of its dominant discourses on human nature and human knowledge. In its pursuit of what are presumed to be basic elements found in all persons, this tradition and the psychology it has spawned do not consider history, culture and community to be central to its inquiry. Rather, these are considered troublesome particularities to be excluded so that they no longer interfere with the steadfast pursuit of something fundamental and universal about human nature.

For most cognitivist approaches, created in tandem with computer technology, for example, interest centers on a mind that is a kind of abstract calculating device dwelling inside the head of the individual and conducting its operations on symbolic representations of the world outside. The embeddedness of persons and minds in history, culture and community is excluded from the typical cognitivist approach so that the mind's intrinsic structure and processes for representing the world can be discovered (e.g. see Sampson, 1993, pp. 59–65, for one account of this argument).

In the last several years, a challenger and potential successor to this dominant tradition and its psychology has emerged. I refer here to the more inclusive discourses of social constructionism. Social constructionism challenges the exclusionary quality of the dominant tradition by insisting that the very concepts that the dominant tradition has assumed to be the foundational elements of human nature are constructed in and through processes that are inherently historical, cultural and communal (e.g. see Edwards, 1991; Gergen, 1985, 1995; Sampson, 1983, 1993; Shotter, 1990, 1991, 1993, for a sampling of these arguments).

There is one major discourse, however, whose exclusion is shared by the dominant and successor traditions: both exclude the inherently embodied character of human endeavor. Within the dominant tradition, at least in its current formulations, the body has become yet one further interference with its pursuit of basic mental processes. And, while social constructionism is noteworthy for its discourse *about* the body, it too has not included embodiment as central.

At this point, many readers might reasonably argue that my remarks about the absence of embodiment from both the dominant and successor discourses, or from the larger culture of which they are a part, is either an exaggeration or simply inaccurate. Some would suggest, for example, that the body has hardly been excluded from a focal interest within the broader western culture. Endless time and money are spent in nurturing, clothing, decorating, disciplining and, in general, caring for the body (e.g. see Foucault, 1986, for some historical background on this point). Others would insist that many working within the dominant tradition have been profoundly interested in the body, as for instance in the brain, as a source of the basic processes of human nature that they hope eventually to discover (e.g. see Fausto-Sterling, 1992, for both a summary and a critique of many of these ideas). Furthermore, adherents of social constructionism would argue that they have spent a considerable amount of time in probing the manner by which the body has been constructed in history and society: hardly a neglectful treatment of the body (e.g. Butler, 1990, 1993).

Although I readily accede to those who make these claims on behalf of the dominant and successor discourses, I nevertheless insist that both the larger culture and this disciplinary interest, for the most part, have been concerned not with embodiment but rather with what I refer to as the *object-body*: the body that is known as a third-person observer knows any object in the world. Little interest has been shown in embodied social practices, including, especially for the constructionist challenger, embodied discourse.

In my view, therefore, interest in the object-body is not an exception to but rather a further manifestation of the dominant tradition's eschewal of embodiment. Likewise, while social constructionism has challenged most of the dominant tradition's exclusionary tendencies, it has joined with that tradition in focusing its attention on the object-body while excluding the inherently embodied character of human endeavor.

Ocularcentrism and the Object-Body

It is apparent from my preceding remarks that I distinguish between the *object-body*, which has been of some interest to both the dominant and successor traditions, and *embodiment*, which has generally been ignored by both. I shortly examine what I mean by embodiment. But first, it is necessary to develop further the idea of the object-body.

It should come as no surprise that the object-body, that is, the body that a third-person observer encounters much as any other object of knowledge, would have become of general interest to the western scientific community. In great measure this focus on the object-body can be understood to be an aspect of what has come to be known as the *ocularcentric bias* (i.e. vision-dominated) of the western tradition in which vision and visual metaphors dominate our understanding.

Both Jay's (1993) and Levin's (1985, 1993) rather thorough analyses suggest that the privileging of vision and of visual metaphors has been so central to our language and our practices (including our scientific practices) since at least the Greek era that it operates as a kind of *seen but unnoticed* background (as even my own words attest) to all that we think. Others have similarly commented on the West's privileging of vision and its parallel denigration of the other senses, a conclusion that emerges from both historical (e.g. see Lowe, 1982; Romanyshyn, 1992, 1993; Synnott, 1993) and cross-cultural analyses (e.g. see Bremmer & Rodenburg, 1991; Featherstone, Hepworth, & Turner, 1991; Howes, 1991).

Both Jay (1993) and Levin (1985, 1993) among others (e.g. Synnott, 1993) argue that some of the most notable philosophers whose works serve as the foundation of the western paradigm, Plato and Aristotle, for example, extolled the nobility of vision, while the keynoter of modernism, Descartes, employed a visual metaphor as central to his ideas. For example, Jay (1993) describes Descartes as 'a quintessentially visual philosopher' (p. 69) who, while sharing Plato's distrust of the senses, including the illusions of sight, nevertheless built his entire framework upon the inner or mind's eye, whose clear and distinct vision would establish a secure basis for human knowledge and truth itself. The very term Enlightenment describes both the era within which scientific understanding began its hegemonic rise and the use of a visual metaphor to inform the scientific task. In each of these cases, foundational to the western understanding, a visual metaphor that stressed a disembodied, *angelic eye* (e.g. see Jay, 1993, p. 81) became central.

This ocularcentric understanding is nowhere more evident today than in our scientific conceptions. Not only do we demand observation of phenomena in order to understand their workings, but we also insist that these observations be carried out as a spectator, a third-person observer who remains at a distance from what is being observed, so as not to affect or be affected by what is seen (i.e. the angelic eye). It is no wonder then that whenever the body has emerged within this ocularcentric tradition, it has been the object-body: to be seen, observed and manipulated from the outside.

I will shortly argue that social constructionism shares the dominant tradition's ocularcentrism and so, when concerned with the body, likewise focuses on the object-body. But before unfolding that point and introducing a genuinely embodied alternative, I must pause to examine one important challenger within the western tradition to ocularcentrim's otherwise hegemonic object-body: phenomenology's turn to the felt-body. As we will see, however, while returning the body to centrality, the phenomenological challenger carries its own problems.

The Phenomenological Body

There has been a challenger within the western tradition to the ocularcentric metaphor: the phenomenologically experienced body, sometimes also referred to as the tactile–kinesthetic body (e.g. see Sheets-Johnstone, 1990, 1992) and said to be known from the 'inside'. Various authors have drawn a distinction between ocularcentrism's object-body and the phenomenological-body. According to Levin (1985), for example, in seeking to 'resurrect the human body in its truth' (p. 35), Nietszche distinguished between 'the body we experience' and the 'body of scientific observation'. Merleau-Ponty (see Jay, 1993; Zaner, 1971) makes a similar distinction in his analysis of the lived body as the flesh of the world and the physical body we usually treat merely as an object. Heidegger (see Dreyfus, 1991; Jay, 1993; Levin, 1985) formulated a parallel distinction, as did others too numerous to name.

Although these phenomenological challengers to the hegemony of the object-body in western discourse encourage a return to the body, they carry along with this return those exclusionary elements of the western tradition (especially its individualism and foundationalism) that warrant a more critical treatment (e.g. see Gergen, 1995, for a useful summary of some of the incoherences of individualism and foundationalism; also see Sampson, 1977, 1988, 1993). A few examples at this point will help both flesh out the nature of the phenomenological challenger and simultaneously reveal some of the exclusionary qualities that I find troublesome.

Romanyshyn (1992) refers to the object-body as the *corpse* that is the subject of medical scrutiny in contrast to the body which we live. The corpse may be dissected, its neuronal pathways charted, its organs, bones and muscles described. But, says Romanyshyn, the muscles that we describe by means of our medical charts are not the same muscles we know through living:

> One knows one's muscles in and through the heavy boxes of books which one moves . . . in and through the embrace one gives to one's friend, in and through the ball that one throws to one's child. These muscles . . . unlike those of the corpse, are not neutral or detached from one's living situation. (pp. 167–168)

The distinction between the object- and phenomenological-bodies as well as the depth to which the ocularcentric bias has infiltrated into the heart of our thinking is also clearly illustrated by contrasting an argument recently presented by Eleanor Gibson (1994) with the position advocated by Maxine Sheets-Johnstone (1990), both of whom are ostensibly discussing the concept of agency, but appear to be referring to different bodies. Citing research on infants, Gibson argues that the 'control of an observable event by one's own action is the essence of agency. . . . The detection of oneself as a potential agent and controller of observable external consequences foreshadows and leads to knowledge of causal relations and a concept of oneself as agent' (p. 72). It is clear that, for Gibson, the body that helps shape the person's sense of agency is the object-body whose actions are seen and whose consequences are observed. Gibson cites the study reported by Kalnins and Bruner (1973) to illustrate her point and mine. The authors of this study noted how the infant discovers her own agency by *observing* that her sucking movements bring about desired consequences, such as keeping a picture in rather than out of focus.

Gibson's formulation of the development of agency is to be contrasted with Sheets-Johnstone's (1990) account, in which she uses the teeth and chewing to illustrate how people develop their felt sense of agency. Sheets-Johnstone begins by noting that rather than viewing the body as a thing within visual space, 'it is first and foremost the center of a tactile–kinesthetic world that, unlike the visual world, rubs up directly against things' (p. 216). Teeth and their action in chewing are experienced as tools we use both to transform things in our world, and in being so used, to provide us with a tactile–kinesthetic sense of our corporeal powers, or, as Sheets-Johnstone puts it, 'a global domain of *I can's*' (p. 28).

In other words, in the act of chewing, we transform things in our world and gain a felt sense of our powers as a transformative agent. This sense of agency is not an awareness derived from *seeing* our effects on the world, but rather is derived by *tactilely* and *kinesthetically* feeling our power. Sheets-Johnstone uses this as but one of several examples of how our body is the ground of our concepts, thereby linking conceptual knowledge with bodily knowledge.

Phenomenology's exclusions. The contrast between Gibson and Sheets-Johnstone illustrates the ocularcentric bias of the western tradition that has led us to privilege the observed body. In this regard, then, the phenomeno-logical turn to corporeality provides a challenge to the dominant tradition's otherwise hegemonic ocularcentric discourse. On the other hand, a problem with the phenomenological challenger, clearly evident in Sheets-Johnstone's approach, is its uncritical taking of the body as a ground. This effectively excludes history, culture and community by installing something essential and foundational *within the individual* as the ground for all human endeavor.

In short, the phenomenological challenger has brought along with it too much that remains troublesome about the dominant tradition: especially its individualism and foundationalism. The exclusions of history, culture and community that characterize the dominant discourse are reproduced even while the body is added.

Summary

As the preceding review suggests, all approaches, including the dominant discourse, the social constructionist challenger, as well as phenomenology's challenge to the ocularcentric emphasis on the object-body, present us with various lingering issues that my turn to embodiment seeks to address. The dominant discourse not only excludes history, culture and community, but the body, other than the object-body. Phenomenology challenges this focus on the object-body by emphasizing the felt-body, but does so by reproducing the same exclusions of history, culture and community as the dominant tradition. Does social constructionism do any better?

Social constructionism includes history, culture and community, yet for the most part shares with the dominant tradition an exclusion of the body, other than the same ocularcentric object-body. It engages in discourses *about* this body and how it is constructed in history, culture and community, but does not engage in embodied discourses. What is needed, I argue, is a genuinely inclusive discourse that not only addresses the inherently histori-cal, cultural and communal character of human endeavor, but its inherently embodied character as well.

Discourses about the Object-Body vs Embodied Discourses

Let me first establish the plausibility of my claim that social constructionism addresses itself to discourses *about* the object-body but not to embodied discourses by calling upon the recent writings on the body developed by Judith Butler (1990, 1993), one of the prime advocates of a feminist–constructionist conception of the body. Butler argues that the dominant discourse (which she refers to as objectivist) assumes a world of neutral objects and natural meanings, including the biological body, on which culture writes its particular message of sex and gender. In this account, one with which Butler disagrees, sex differences are assumed to be real in that each culture and epoch writes its particular message upon the pregiven natural distinction between the male and the female body and so establishes its own particular accent on an object that has an independent existence in the world.

The constructionist position that Butler favors argues that there is no independently real body, hence no sexed male or female outside culture. Culture does not write on an already existing sexed object, she argues, but rather creates the sexed objects which then appear to be naturally occurring, out there 'in the world'. Butler comments, for example, that the choice of the genitals to mark male and female is a cultural choice, not a feature of nature. Approvingly citing Foucault, Butler (1990) tells us that 'the body is not sexed in any significant sense prior to its determination within a discourse through which it becomes invested with an "idea" of natural or essential sex' (p. 92).

Butler's arguments have been advanced by those theorists of sex difference for whom it is vital to recognize how deeply power differentials are embedded within our cultural tradition (e.g. Connell, 1987; Kitzinger, 1987; Lacquer, 1990; Riley, 1988; Synnott, 1993). According to these proponents of the constructionist approach to the body, power differentials are built into the founding cultural definitions of male and female; thus in order to transform the current hierarchy, those very definitions must be challenged. It is clear, they argue, that if a *precultural* body exists, it may serve as an invitation to house the power differentials with which we have become so familiar: for example, men are *by nature* dominant and aggressive and so are meant to lead. And so, by challenging the naturalness of bodies, Butler and the others hope to challenge those theories of difference that have been grounded in nature rather than in culture.

Objectivism, constructionism and ocularcentrism. On its face, there would seem to be no more severe separation than that which distinguishes the objectivist from the constructionist accounts of the body. Yet, as I unfold my arguments, I believe that we will come to see that both the objectivist and the constructionist positions, as different as they appear to be, are in fact both married to the ocularcentric bias of the western tradition.

Both objectivism and constructionism share an interest in the external world in which we dwell. They differ primarily in their understanding of how that world comes into being. For objectivism, the world pre-exists individuals, culture and history, and the task of the mind is to recover the main features of that world by means of clear mental representations. For constructionism, by contrast, the world does not exist independently of individuals, culture and history, but rather is constituted on the basis of socially generated discourses. Whereas objectivism is concerned with the nature of the fit between representation and reality, constructionism is concerned with how what is taken to be real is socially constructed and appears to be independent of the very human endeavor that makes it possible. Both objectivism and constructionism dwell within an ocular-centric tradition that leads them away from the embodied view that I believe we must establish. Once again, let me call upon Butler's analysis to illustrate this point for constructionism.

As we have already seen, Butler (1993) questions the objectivist view in which any social construction 'happens to a ready-made object, a pregiven thing' (p. 11). The basis for Butler's rejection hinges on her argument that 'to "refer" naïvely or directly to such an extra-discursive object will always require the prior delimitation of the extra-discursive. And insofar as the extra-discursive is delimited, it is formed by the very discourse from which it seeks to free itself' (p. 11). In other words, there must be an initial discursive act that sets forth the boundaries of whatever will become an object in the first place.

In short, according to Butler, in order to have an object on which a culture can write its own message, there must first be a discursive (i.e. cultural/historical) act that discriminates what is to be taken as an object. This inevitably provides a constructionist basis for all theories that would otherwise appear to deal directly with the world of so-called 'natural' objects, including the body.

Although Butler's (and other parallel) arguments are persuasive as far as they have gone, what they exclude is the embodied nature of discourse itself. That is, her emphasis is on how discourse (e.g. the word, talk and conversation) comprises the initial act by which objects are delineated in the first place. What she fails to recognize, however, is that those discourses are themselves not pure in the sense of being carried by disembodied words; rather, embodiment pervades all human endeavor, all human practices, including discursive practices. While it is indeed reasonable to join with Butler and others in insisting that words construct the body, it is also reasonable to insist that those words are themselves embodied.

In this regard, then, Butler reveals the general problem of all con-structionist accounts. In emphasizing language, in engaging in what van der Merwe and Voestermans (1995) refer to as *constructomania* and *narrotomania*, constructionist approaches exclude embodiment, even as some (e.g. Butler) include the constructed object-body. Unlike van der Merwe and Voestermans's call for redressing this exclusion by turning to phenomenology's body, for the reasons I have already indicated, I must reject this approach and call, rather, for a turn (not a return, since it was not present in the first place) to embodiment.

Embodied Discourses

While it is clear that we can and routinely do hold conversations about the object-body and about the phenomenologically experienced body, neither the dominant nor successor (i.e. constructionist) discourses recognize that these discourses *about* the body are in and of themselves embodied. Embodied discourses refer to the inherently embodied nature of all human endeavor, including talk, conversation and discourse itself.

Rather than dividing the world into mind and body, as favored by the dominant discourse, or to talk that is about the body, as favored by the constructionist challenger, or to talk about personal bodily feelings, which the phenomenologists discuss, when I refer to embodied discourse, I am referring to the intrinsically embodied character of human endeavor: to the idea that we are socialized into both a linguistic and a bodily community of practices such that what we say and the embodied quality of how we say it are simultaneously engendered and inextricably intertwined.

I include here things as seemingly mundane as how our mouths, lips, lungs, vocal cords and breath patterns are socialized to form the sounds that are the words we speak. I also include the bodily movements of our head, ears and eyes while listening to another speak or our bodily tensions as we lean forward to speak our own piece. Although he does not develop the details about its embodied quality, Shotter's (1995) rhetorical–responsive model of conversations lends itself to this embodied view. Surely, we are socialized into postures of listening and hearing that are in various ways part of the responsive process that occurs in any conversation. This embodied responsivity, then, is also included in my notion of embodied discourse.

I also include, however, those more complex bodily practices we are so carefully socialized to employ: for example, how we stand and move, how we comport ourselves through the various circumstances of our social lives. Bourdieu (1990) offers a useful illustration of this latter point in his description of how: 'The opposition between male and female is realized in posture, in the gestures and movements of the body' (p. 70). He also refers to the articulatory style of a social class, noting, for example, how a group's very life style becomes embodied (see Bourdieu & Wacquant, 1992, p. 149).

Gleason's (1990) examination of a 2nd-century (CE) text on physiognomy adds further to this idea of embodied social practices, including embodied discourse. Specific directives are provided in that work to help males especially learn how properly to carry their body in walking and sitting:

> The orderly man . . . reveals his self-restraint . . . through his deportment: deep-voiced and slow-stepping, his eyes, neither fixed nor rapidly blinking . . . with a leonine walk . . . [whose] feet and hands move in harmony with all the rest of his person, who moves forward with shoulders calm and carefully controlled, with his neck but slightly inclined. (p. 393)

The similarities with Bourdieu's (1990) more recent account of the male and female bodily practices among the Kabyle are striking. Gleason (1990) continues her own account by commenting on how such bodily comportment was part of every young man's socialization, with nurses going so far as to 'socialize' the body by 'Squeezing and stretching, even hanging the body upside down . . . to mold the infant body into shape' (p. 402).

The key concept, *habitus*, introduced by Bourdieu (1977, 1990; Bourdieu & Wacquant, 1992) and borrowed from Mauss's (1950) earlier treatise on embodiment, clearly carries the meaning of embodied practices and embodied discourse that I am discussing. Habitus is defined as

> . . . a set of historical relations 'deposited' within individual bodies in the form of mental and corporeal schemata of perception, appreciation, and action. (Wacquant, in Bourdieu & Wacquant, 1992, p. 16)

Taylor's (1993) discussion of Bourdieu's concept of habitus expands and illustrates its force as an embodied discourse. He comments, for example:

> Our body is not just the executant of the goals we frame or just the locus of the causal factors which shape our representations. Our understanding itself is embodied. That is, our bodily know-how and the way we act and move can encode components of our understanding of self and world. (p. 50)

Taylor illustrates this view of what I have termed embodied discourse by noting how 'The deference I owe you is carried in the distance I stand from you, in the way I hold myself in your presence' (p. 50). He continues by noting how 'the way I swagger . . . the way I carry myself and project in public space: whether I am "macho" or timid or eager to please or calm and unflappable' (pp. 50–51) are likewise an embodied discourse.

There is little doubt in reading Wacquant's (in Bourdieu & Wacquant, 1992) account, for example, that Bourdieu fully intended habitus to join what we routinely separate: body and discourse. The point of embodied social practices, including embodied discursive practices, is that language itself is embodied, even as the body is en-languaged.

Both the dominant discourse and the social constructionist challenger and would-be successor fail to deal with embodiment. The former deals only with the object-body, the latter only with conversations about the body. We are not only inherently historical, cultural and communal beings, but inherently embodied beings as well. To establish embodiment in psychological discourse, then, is to recognize these embodied qualities of all social practices, including discursive practices.

Let me repeat for emphasis. My point is that the idea of embodied social practices, of which embodied discourse is a major form, does not introduce us to two separate ways of knowing or being. We are socialized into a joint language and embodied community. Therefore, I am not suggesting that we are in the world through language or through the body separately, but because language is in-itself embodied even as the body is en-worded, we are in the world in a unified manner.

Then and Now: Locating the Body in the Western Tradition

There are some significant social and historical bases for the western tradition's exclusion of the body in both its dominant and challenger discourses. And there are some equally good social and historical bases for suggesting that the larger cultural climate is ripe for the body's having a renaissance today. Although it is not my intention to probe all of those reasons, nor to develop a full-blown socio-historical analysis, it will prove useful at this point to examine briefly some of the past (the then) and some of these current trends (the now).

Then

One reasonable conclusion from a careful historical survey is that the body in general, including even the object-body, has generally been neglected, disparaged or both within the larger western tradition. It is true that the medical and biological sciences have made significant inroads in examining the object-body and providing us with a plethora of information to guide our everyday lives. And it is equally true that care of the body has again become a dominant theme in society today even as it was earlier (e.g. see Foucault, 1978, 1985, 1986). Yet I find myself in close agreement with Levin (1985), who, in commenting on the underlying hostility towards the body that has marked the western tradition, notes that whenever we do give the body our attention it 'invariably tends to be caught between forms of negative reinforcement (ascetic disciplining and punishment) and forms of drilling, of repetitive, uniform, mechanistic training' (p. 229).

In his thoughtful historical review, Synnott (1993) clearly establishes that there has been no singular, monolithic understanding of the body within the western tradition: 'Each age seems to have a love–hate relationship with the body' (p. 11). In ancient Greece, for example, opinion ranged from viewing the body as a place of pleasure to regarding it as a tomb for the otherwise helpless soul. But even then, and in Rome as well, we are told that pure pleasure for its own sake was more to be tamed and regulated as a sign of one's upstanding character than to be released to unsocial excess (e.g. see Brown, 1988; Foucault, 1978, 1985, 1986). Early Christian views carried their own ambivalent message. For some early Christians, the body was a temple, for others, it was a dangerous enemy to be watched and tamed (Brown, 1988). Boyarin (1993) argues that while early 'rabbinic Judaism invested significance in the body which ... [Christianity] invested in the soul' (p. 5), in time, Judeo-Christian discourses merged around a body-negative message (also see Brown, 1988, for a similar analysis).

On the other hand, Bynum's (1995) thoughtful analysis of the fate of the body in early Christianity notes how significant the body remained for this tradition at least for several centuries of the common era. She notes, for example, how the separation of a permanent soul from an impermanent body, as well as the idea that the body and flesh were evil, were disputed and even rejected by early Christianity. Early theology argued that the soul was incomplete without the accompanying body; thereby, it was crucial to attend carefully to the body on death in order to ensure that its decay would be redeemed through its eventual resurrection into body-and-soul together. Bynum's discussion of the Eucharist also reminds us of the continuing importance of the body (of Christ) in current religious rituals, hardly an entirely body-negating tradition.

And yet, in spite of both Boyarin's and Bynum's reminders of the more body-positive views in certain segments of the western tradition's Judeo-Christian past, the overwhelming evidence suggests to me that if there is one dominant message that has been carried for many centuries in the western tradition's relationship to the body, it centers on the ideas of danger and control. The bases for these concerns center on three related themes: (1) The body represents our continuing tie to the world of animals and so diminishes that which is distinctly human. (2) The body seems to be something that is always at the edge of our control and so threatens to take us places that we and others prefer we not go. (3) Once later Christianity separated soul from body, the soul took precedence as something that served mortality in a way that the decaying body was incapable of achieving, thus elevating the soul to higher standing than the body. I think it fair to conclude that other than a few notable (and early) exceptions (e.g. see Bynum, 1995), the western tradition has been more body-negative than body-positive, especially viewing the body as a source of potential danger rather than as a source of knowledge or wisdom. No wonder, then, that those scholarly traditions that developed within this context, including both the dominant and challenger discourses we have been considering, either ignored or disparaged the body. There was little if any support within the larger tradition for doing otherwise.

Now

There are three interrelated yet distinct changes now taking place in the western tradition, however, that lead me to suggest not only that the body is returning to a pride of place within this tradition, but also that the current renaissance of interest in the body and in embodiment is part and parcel of an emerging cultural narrative. As interesting and valuable as it might be to provide an in-depth examination of each of these three, such an exploration would be more appropriate to a book-length treatment than a paper of this sort. Let me, however, briefly and in a somewhat truncated form provide at least an introduction to the relevance of each of these for the renaissance in embodiment.

Feminism's reminder of embodiment. There is no simple, uniform feminist view of the body. Differences between the constructionist account offered by persons such as Butler and the contrasting emphasis of writers such as Irigaray (1974, 1977), for example, for whom female bodily specificity remains central, continue to abound in feminist discourse. In spite of these different emphases and understandings, what all of these discussions share is the recognition that feminism requires a return to embodiment. The efforts to exclude the body from philosophy and psychology have been an exclusion only of the female body; the male body has always been secretely housed in these phallocentric discourses, serving as the unstated, normative standard by which the female is inferior because she lacks what the male possesses. In short, feminist discourse has required that the body be taken seriously lest the failure to do so delete women from any standing in philosophical and psychological treatments. A further discussion and analysis of this issue appears in numerous publications (e.g. Eisenstein, 1988; Sampson, 1993; Scott, 1988; Young, 1990). For my present purposes, what is of primary relevance is to note how feminism has demanded that we begin to look closely at embodiment, thus transforming the otherwise body-ignoring qualities of the dominant western tradition.

The western appropriation of eastern-Buddhist thought and practices. Although it somewhat simplifies the complexities contained within each view, it is not unreasonable to suggest that the western and the eastern traditions of knowledge have adopted somewhat oppositional routes to achieve much the same desired goal: enlightenment (e.g. see Nagatomo, 1992; Varela, Thompson, & Rosch, 1991, for a useful summary). Whereas, as we have seen, we in the West have tended to see the body as interfering with the mind's pursuit of genuine knowledge and understanding, the East reverses this view. The body and bodily practices, including 'just sitting' and 'meditation', for example, hold the key to achieve the enlightenment that the mind alone cannot achieve in great measure because one cannot think one's way out of the snares in which thinking itself is entrapped. In short, a bodily practice is required in order to achieve an experience that a purely mental practice, critical reflection for example, cannot reveal, in great measure because critical reflection reproduces the very traps of thinking that it hopes to overcome.

This eastern tradition does not argue that the mental operations of our everyday consciousness are incorrect; rather it sees these operations as offering us only a *provisional* ordering of experience. Bodily practices (e.g. 'just sitting') are thereby required in order to reach beyond this provisional level of understanding. For example, the dualism that continues to animate the western understanding, its separation of subject and object, is said to be a provisional dualism, temporary and useful, but by no means the entire story of humankind. No matter how much we attempt to *think* our way beyond this dualism, we will forever return to it because thinking alone cannot achieve what only a bodily practice can provide.

Once again, it would take me too far afield and into a territory that I am not sufficiently well versed to cover to expand these ideas further. Suffice it to note that this turn to the Buddhist East is not a small intrusion into the West, nor, I believe, a mere passing fancy. There are growing numbers of highly educated and well-informed westerners for whom this turn to eastern religion and its bodily practices holds the key that they find missing in more traditional western forms of belief. At minimum, this eastern turn reflects a concern with embodiment that joins with the other cultural currents to provide a climate that is increasingly receptive to a corporeal turn.

Pentecostal religious revival. A well-known Harvard theologian, Harvey Cox (1995), has argued that the largest religious revival now taking place in the Christian world involves pentecostal churches, 'growing at the rate of 20 million new members a year and . . . worldwide membership . . . some 410 million' (p. xv). Given its humble and recent beginnings, 1906 'in a wooden bungalow . . . in Los Angeles' (p. 45), the growth of this revival is nothing short of astounding.

Central to my present concerns in charting a rather broadly based cultural shift are the actual forms of worship that characterize pentecostalism. These are fully embodied. Here is Cox's own summary description which I freely paraphrase: (1) This most rapidly expanding religion of our times 'works' because it speaks the language of the heart, including speaking in tongues and praying in the Spirit. In these ways, it challenges 'the flattened language of commercial blather of consumer society' (p. 120). (2) In its forms of worship, pentecostalism embraces 'ecstatic praise, visions, healing, dreams, and joyous bodily movement' (p. 120), tapping 'into a raging underground sea of raw religious feeling and turbulent emotion' (p. 120).

Given both its large numbers and rapid rise, far outdistancing its 'competitors' or compelling those more staid competitors to adopt some of its more embodied practices, this movement suggests a larger cultural trend away from mere talk and to the recognition of the embodied nature of human religious endeavor and the key role that embodiment plays in shaping a shared community of worship.

Summary

My intention in undertaking this brief historical interlude was not to offer an in-depth analysis of the fate of the body in the western tradition's past nor its current resurrection in newly emerging facets of that tradition. Rather, my purposes are best served if I have been able to make two points. First, embodiment's past, in which the body was ambivalently received and then hidden away in the dark recesses of the dominant culture's closet, provides a broader cultural framework for understanding why both the dominant and successor discourses failed to include the body (other than the object-body).

Second, however, there are significant transformations now occurring within the larger western cultural tradition that suggest a climate more receptive to a central focus on embodiment. I am not suggesting, however, that my conception of embodiment is being carried by these newly emerging cultural movements. I am suggesting, rather, that the changing cultural climate makes such a move more likely to find a receptive hearing than in even the fairly recent past. If, as Sedgwick (1990) tells us, the closet has become the modern metaphor for many significant movements today, then I think it fair to conclude this brief historical commentary by suggesting that the body is now coming out of the closet.

Psychology's Body

While it is true that embodiment has remained secreted away from the main-stream western tradition, including its psychology, it is also true, as I have noted, that the object-body has continued to receive a modicum of interest even within psychology. There are two traditions of psychological concern with the object-body: an early concern with a few contemporary offshoots with the connection between the body and the emotions; and a more recent concern with the connections between the body and knowledge.

Although neither of these is strictly speaking the turn to embodied discourse that I have described, both trends suggest that in spite of the generally disembodied quality of the psychology nurtured within the western tradition, several pockets of interest remain. Furthermore, the latter interest in the relationship between the body and knowledge suggests a direction towards the focus on embodiment, even though, as we will see, that direction was aborted because of continuing allegiances to the dominant tradition's exclusionary tendencies.

Body and Emotion

While the idea is old, some suggest going back in time to Homer and forward through Darwin (1872/1965) and James (1932) to several more contemporary theorists (e.g. Laird, 1974, 1984), it remains simple to state yet complex both to demonstrate and to fathom in terms of the mechanisms involved. I am referring to the idea that bodily events such as posture and facial musculature shape persons' emotional experiences (see Bremmer &

Rodenburg, 1991; Duclos et al., 1989; Izard, 1990; Riskind, 1984, for a sampling).

In its modern guise, Laird's (1974, 1984; also Duclos et al., 1989; Stepper & Strack, 1993; Strack, Martin, & Stepper, 1988) program of research gives us one important illustration. Laird placed his subjects' faces in physical arrangements that paralleled various emotional states and examined the effects that these had on their emotional experience. For example, through instructions, the subjects' faces were arranged to form a smile; the cartoons they rated when in this pose were experienced as funnier than those when their face had been arranged in a frown. Strack et al. (1988) used a more subtle technique to arrange persons' facial muscles by having them hold a pen in their mouths in a manner that either facilitated or inhibited those muscles associated with smiling. Their results indicated a more intense humorous response to cartoons under the facilitating than the inhibiting conditions. Other investigators, however, have found either no relationship or sufficient methodological fault with many studies in this tradition to warrant caution (e.g. Matsumoto, 1987; Tourangeaux & Ellsworth, 1979).

The work reported by Zajonc, Murphy and Inglehart (1989) provides yet another avenue for exploring the connections between the body and emotional experience. Unlike Laird's substantially cognitivist rationale for the connection between the face and emotional experience based on self-perception theory—I see myself smiling so what I am looking at must be funny—Zajonc et al. rejected any such cognitivist interpretation in favor of a vascular theory. It is their contention, with some intriguing supportive data, that the flow of blood to the brain is modified by various facial movements and that flows that increase cerebral temperatures produce unpleasant feelings states, while movements that decrease blood flow produce more pleasant feelings.

The Body and Knowledge

Given the non-corporeal roots of the western epistemological tradition, to argue that the corporeal serves as a foundational template for human knowledge seems to fly in the face of much of this tradition. After all, Descartes founded the certainty of human knowledge on the *Cogito*, a disembodied thinking being, and saw the body as interfering with the purity and clarity that secure truth demanded. The possibility of grounding thinking and knowledge in the body has tended to escape all but a few within the western tradition.

In this section, I briefly examine two approaches in which the body is not a mere backdrop for more important events taking place elsewhere, not something forgotten in the rush to document the powers of the mind, nor debased and treated as a danger to be governed by the ruling mind. Rather, in these two views, the body becomes the very ground of human knowledge. While several key philosophers have contributed to this focus, including Nietzsche (see Jay, 1993; Levin, 1993), Vico (see Verene, 1981) and Merleau-Ponty (see Jay, 1993), the two strands that I examine here are based on Lakoff and Johnson's (e.g. Johnson, 1987; Lakoff, 1987; Lakoff & Johnson, 1980) *experientialism* or *experiential realism* and Sheets-Johnstone's (1990, 1992) evolutionary approach to understanding the role of the body in human knowledge. I hold off on my critical concerns until both have been presented.

Lakoff and Johnson's experientialism. Mark Johnson's (1987) book title, *The Body in the Mind*, captures the agenda of both his own and Lakoff's experiential realism: 'putting the body back into the mind' (Johnson, 1987, p. xxxvi) by understanding the bodily bases of mental operations and the bodily constraints on human thinking and reasoning. For too long, say both Johnson and Lakoff, the body has been ignored when considering mental events, as though the embodied nature of the organism that thinks plays no role in the nature of what is or what can be thought. By restoring the body to the mind, experiential realism intends to provide an improved understanding of human experience.

In contrast to the Cartesian and current cognitivist approaches, for which the frail particularities of the human body offer a troubling interference with the certainties which only pure thinking is capable of providing, both Johnson and Lakoff insist that the body's preconceptual meaning structure provides the very possibility for human thinking itself. In other words, rather than viewing the body as interfering with thinking, Lakoff and Johnson argue that we are constrained to think in certain ways by virtue of the nature of the embodied organism who does the thinking.

The central idea is amply illustrated throughout both Lakoff's and Johnson's writings on metaphor, but for my present purposes can be usefully illustrated by their analysis of the 'container metaphor'. The argument is that our body is a container, with a boundary separating what is inside and what is outside; our everyday transactions in and with our world involve taking things in and sending things out. These interactions form a preconceptual level of understanding of things that are contained, that have boundaries and that have an inside and an outside. Johnson (1987) argues that this feature of the body 'enters into our understanding of reasoning' (p. 39), providing us with the later emerging understanding of an either/or form of logic (i.e. the law of the excluded middle) as well as the logical principle of transitivity and our understanding of set membership: that is, 'If a marble is in a small bag, which is placed within a second, larger bag, then we know the *obvious* conclusion: the marble is in the larger bag' (p. 39). Lakoff (1987) has reached the same position, concluding that: 'Reason is embodied in the sense that the very structure on which reason is based emerges from our bodily experiences' (p. 368).

Lakoff argues that the body's preconceptual meaning structure can be analyzed into two related components: (1) basic level structures that derive from the capacities for bodily movement and our ability to form images from such movements; (2) kinesthetic image-schematic structures that, like the container example noted above, involve recurring bodily events that form the templates that ground more advanced conceptual understandings. According to this view, 'in order for us to have meaningful connected experiences that we can comprehend and reason about, there must be pattern and order to our actions, perceptions, and conceptions' (Lakoff, 1987, p. 29); the grounding for this meaningfulness, what makes it possible in other words, are the recurring patterns of our bodily physical movements in and with our world.

There can be no doubt that Lakoff and Johnson's experientialism argues that without the body there could be no thinking as we know it. Rather than bodily processes interfering with thinking, they are what makes thinking possible in the first place; they offer the grounding for the later meaningfulness that we experience. To summarize and perhaps somewhat oversimplify, according to experiential realism, we can understand and think as we do because our more abstract understandings are grounded on preconceptual embodied structures.

Sheets-Johnstone's evolutionary view. The title of Sheets-Johnstone's (1990) major book, *The Roots of Thinking*, reveals the similarity between her approach and Johnson's and Lakoff's experientialism, while offering an even broader view of the key role that the living body plays in the formation of meaning:

> Concepts were either generated or awakened by the living body in the course of everyday actions such as chewing, urinating, striding, standing, breathing, and so on. . . . The broad thesis of this book is thus that there is an indissoluble bond between hominid thinking and hominid evolution, a bond cemented by the living body. (p. 4)

Sheets-Johnstone leaves little doubt: our major abstract concepts, including our ideas of death, numbers, agency, and so on, derive from 'an original bodily logos' (p. 6). As her book title suggests, the roots of human thinking lie in the hominid body.

It will not serve my purposes to review the rich material she presents in support of this thesis. We have already seen the direction of her thinking in the earlier illustration of the body's role in the experience of agency. For my purposes, it is her overriding point that is critical to reiterate: 'meanings are generated by an animal's bodily comportment, movement and orientation' (p. 122); thus 'semanticity is a built-in of bodily life' (p. 123).

Critical Commentary

I have previously suggested that while Lakoff, Johnson and Sheets-Johnstone all return the body to its pride of place in our theoretical discourses about human knowledge, in one form or another, the price of this inclusion comes much too high. Specifically, the manner by which the body is included sustains the dominant tradition's trio of exclusions: that is, history, culture and community are excluded even as the body has been added.

In short, by sticking fairly closely both to the individualism that remains dominant in the western tradition and to its never-ending search for transcendent foundations, Lakoff, Johnson and Sheets-Johnstone locate knowledge within the individual and locate the transcendent foundations for such knowledge in an invariant body. That knowledge is historical, cultural and communal—the embodied view I have proposed—is not central to these otherwise body-affirming discourses.

Thus, while the body is included, history, culture and community, for the most part, are not. By contrast, my conception of embodied discourse is neither individualistic nor foundational. It advocates a clearly social and historical perspective by insisting that we are socialized into a joint linguistic and embodied community. It seeks a ground for human understanding neither in words nor in bodies, but rather in the notion that words are embodied even as the body is worded.

The Politics of Embodiment

> Thus the submission of workers, women, minorities, and graduate students is most often not a deliberate or conscious concession to the brute force of managers, men, whites and professors. . . . It is lodged deep inside the socialized body. In truth it expresses the 'somatization of social relations of domination'. (Wacquant, in Bourdieu & Wacquant, 1992, p. 24) . . . an imprisonment effected via the body. (Bourdieu, in Bourdieu & Wacquant, 1992, p. 172)

For those such as myself who have a long-standing interest in the political dimension of psychological work, the topic of ideology and its role in psychology has loomed large (e.g. Sampson, 1977, 1983, 1993). In its usual usage, ideology refers to thoughts, ideas and beliefs: in other words, to matters that emphasize a relatively disembodied understanding. In my earlier works, for example, I addressed the ideological individualism of much work in psychology (e.g. Sampson, 1977). Both myself and others have likewise written about the ideology contained in psychology's conceptions of mental health as involving descriptions of the adult male, of human relationships as involving heterosexual relationships, and so forth (e.g. see Broverman, Vogel, Broverman, Clarkson, & Rosenkrantz, 1972; Sampson, 1993; Tavris, 1992, for a small sampling). In each case, the ideology is discursively established and maintained through language and conversation. The notion of embodied social practices and embodied discourses would lead us to be concerned with the role of the embodied aspects of domination, a concern that has generally not been central.

At this point, it should be apparent that my view of embodied social practices, including discourse, and Bourdieu's similar concerns as expressed, for example, in the passage quoted at the beginning of this section, strongly recommend that we reconsider our understanding of what domination and oppression mean: how they are carried and how they are sustained. If persons' thoughts are embodied, we need to examine the embodiment of domination and not rest content with the disembodied words alone.

So that my position is clear, I am not denying the importance of discourse in ideological practice. Rather, I am suggesting that insofar as discourse is embodied, we need to consider the bodily dimension of politics, a *body politics*. We spend too much of our energy focusing on language and ideology and so miss the embodied character of language and hence of the position of the body in ideological practices. As Bourdieu suggests, the actual body is molded to carry within its very tissues and muscles the story of ideology. Given the depth to which embodied ideological practices have penetrated and remain deeply secreted within us, I am talking about a very difficult area for transformation, one that cannot be changed by thought alone but only by embodied action.

In short, if part of what we learn in growing up within a given society are its relations of domination and our places within that scheme, and if those relations of domination are embodied—that is, learned in how we walk, talk, move in space, etc.—then part and parcel of any emancipatory techniques must be addressed to the body that also needs to learn a new way of comportment. The pedagogy of the oppressed (e.g. Friere, 1970) must be addressed to the deeply embodied quality of oppression.

The body that is worn down by hard labor that Engels (1845/1987) described, for example, or the body weakened by extreme hunger that Scheper-Hughes (1992) examined, are ideologically shaped bodies. The muscles carry the message of social class. Body movements and gestures tell one's life story: the beaten-down body of the oppressed day laborer; the pain-wracked and tortured body of the profoundly undernourished.

I am referring to bodies that know hunger regardless of what or how one has come to talk about it. I am talking about bodies whose muscles have been shaped, hardened and weakened often into debilitating distortion by hard physical labor and minimal nutrition. We need not hold lofty discussions here about oppression; these bodies know oppression; they *are* oppression defined more clearly than perhaps we have been willing to recognize.

Too often, we search for politics, and, in this case, the ideology of oppression and domination, in the words that are uttered and in the disembodied discursive practices that exist within a culture. In this, then, we miss the embodied nature of oppression and domination and thus the necessarily embodied route to eventual emancipation. We cannot discuss our way out of oppression when that oppression is embodied, carved into the muscles and retained in the body's knowledge of its place in the world. Body politics, then, directs us to a rather different kind of psychological practice, at least among those for whom human transformation towards well-being is a valued ideal.

We who wish to transform the human condition in beneficial ways, who hope not simply to undo those 'mind-forg'd manacles' of which Blake (1946/1968) has written, but, in seeing the mind as embodied, to undo the manacles of embodiment as well, have an enormous task before us. For, if social relations of domination are indeed somaticized, as Bourdieu suggests and as my idea of embodiment also recommends, we will need to be certain that our transformative practices are themselves as embodied as are the oppressions we hope to undo. But then, this is the topic of another paper.

References

Blake, W. (1968). London. In A. Kazin (Ed.), *The portable Blake*. New York: Penguin. (Original work published 1946.)

Bourdieu, P. (1977). *Outline of a theory of practice*. Cambridge: Cambridge University Press.

Bourdieu, P. (1990). *The logic of practice*. Stanford, CA: Stanford University Press.

Bourdieu, P., & Wacquant, L.J.D. (1992). *An introduction to reflexive sociology*. Chicago, IL: University of Chicago Press.

Boyarin, D. (1993). *Carnal Israel: Reading sex in Talmudic culture*. Berkeley: University of California Press.

Bremmer, J., & Rodenburg, H. (Eds.). (1991). *A cultural history of gesture*. Ithaca, NY: Cornell University Press.

Broverman, I.K., Vogel, S.R., Broverman, D.M., Clarkson, F.E., & Rosenkrantz, P.S. (1972). Sex role stereotypes: A current appraisal. *Journal of Social Issues, 28*, 59–78.

Brown, P. (1988). *The body and society: Men, women and sexual renunciation in early Christianity*. New York: Columbia University Press.

Butler, J. (1990). *Gender trouble: Feminism and the subversion of identity*. New York: Routledge.

Butler, J. (1993). *Bodies that matter: On the discursive limits of 'sex'*. New York: Routledge.

Bynum, C.W. (1995). *The resurrection of the body in western Christianity, 200–1336*. New York: Columbia University Press.

Connell, R.W. (1987). *Gender and power: Society, the person and sexual politics*. Stanford, CA: Stanford University Press.

Cox, H. (1995). *Fire from heaven: The rise of pentecostal spirituality and the reshaping of religion in the twenty-first century*. Reading, MA: Addison-Wesley.

Darwin, C.R. (1965). *The expression of emotions in man and animals*. Chicago, IL: University of Chicago Press. (Original work published 1872.)

Dreyfus, H.L. (1991). *Being-in-the-world: A commentary on Heidegger's Being and time, Division I*. Cambridge, MA: MIT Press.

Duclos, S.E., Laird, J.D., Schneider, E., Sexter, M., Stern, L., & Van Lighten, O. (1989). Emotion-specific effects of facial expressions and postures on emotional experiences. *Journal of Personality and Social Psychology*, *57*, 100–108.

Edwards, D. (1991). Categories are for talking: On the cognitive and discursive bases of categorization. *Theory & Psychology*, *1*, 515–542.

Eisenstein, Z.R. (1988). *The female body and the law*. Berkeley: University of California Press.

Engels, F. (1987). *The condition of the working class in England*. Harmondsworth: Penguin. (Original work published 1845.)

Fausto-Sterling, A. (1992). *Myths of gender: Biological theories about women and men*. New York: Basic Books.

Featherstone, M., Hepworth, M., & Turner, B.S. (Eds.). (1991). *The body: Social process and cultural theory*. London: Sage.

Foucault, M. (1978). *The history of sexuality: Vol. I. An introduction*. New York: Vintage.

Foucault, M. (1985). *The uses of pleasure*. New York: Vintage.

Foucault, M. (1986). *The care of the self*. New York: Pantheon.

Friere, P. (1970). *Pedagogy of the oppressed*. New York: Continuum.

Gergen, K.J. (1985). The social constructionist movement in modern psychology. *American Psychologist*, *40*, 266–275.

Gergen, K.J. (1995). *Realities and relationships: Soundings in social construction*. Cambridge, MA: Harvard University Press.

Gibson, E.J. (1994). Has psychology a future? *Psychological Science*, *2*, 69–76.

Gleason, M.W. (1990). The semiotics of gender: Physiognomy and self-fashioning in the second century C.E. In D.M. Halperin, J.J. Winkler, & F.I. Zeitlin (Eds.), *Before sexuality: The construction of erotic experience in the ancient Greek world* (pp. 389–415). Princeton, NJ: Princeton University Press.

Howes, D. (Ed.). (1991). *The varieties of sensory experience: A sourcebook in the anthropology of the senses*. Toronto: University of Toronto Press.

Irigaray, L. (1974). *Speculum of the other woman*. Ithaca, NY: Cornell University Press.

Irigaray, L. (1977). *This sex which is not one*. Ithaca, NY: Cornell University Press.

Izard, C.E. (1990). Facial expressions and the regulation of emotions. *Journal of Personality and Social Psychology*, *58*, 487–498.

James, W.T. (1932). A study of the expression of bodily posture. *Journal of General Psychology*, *7*, 405–437.

Jay, M. (1993). *Downcast eyes: The denigration of vision in twentieth century French thought*. Berkeley: University of California Press.

Johnson, M. (1987). *The body in the mind: The bodily basis of meaning, imagination, and reason*. Chicago, IL: University of Chicago Press.

Kalnins, I.V., & Bruner, J.S. (1973). The coordination of visual observation and instrumental behavior in early infancy. *Perception*, *2*, 307–314.

Kitzinger, C. (1987). *The social construction of lesbianism*. London: Sage.

Laird, J.D. (1974). Self-attribution of emotion: The effects of expressive behavior on the quality of emotional experience. *Journal of Personality and Social Psychology*, *29*, 475–486.

Laird, J.D. (1984). Facial response and emotion. *Journal of Personality and Social Psychology*, *47*, 909–917.

Lakoff, G. (1987). *Women, fire, and dangerous things: What categories reveal about the mind*. Chicago, IL: University of Chicago Press.

Lakoff, G., & Johnson, M. (1980). *Metaphors we live by*. Chicago, IL: University of Chicago Press.

Laqueur, T. (1990). *Making sex: Body and gender from the Greeks to Freud*. Cambridge, MA: Harvard University Press.

Levin, D.M. (1985). *The body's recollection of being: Phenomenological psychology and the deconstruction of nihilism*. London: Routledge & Kegan Paul.

Levin, D.M. (Ed.). (1993). *Modernity and the hegemony of vision*. Berkeley: University of California Press.

Lowe, D.M. (1982). *History of bourgeois perception*. Chicago, IL: University of Chicago Press.

Matsumoto, D. (1987). The role of facial response in the experience of emotion: More methodological problems and a meta-analysis. *Journal of Personality and Social Psychology*, *52*, 769–774.

Mauss, M. (1950). The notion of body techniques. In *Sociology and psychology: Essays* (pp. 97–119). London: Routledge & Kegan Paul.

Merwe, W.L., van der, & Voestermans, P.P. (1995). Wittgenstein's legacy and the challenge to psychology. *Theory & Psychology*, *5*, 27–48.

Nagatomo, S. (1992). *Attunement through the body*. Albany: State University of New York Press.

Riley, D. (1988). *'Am I that name?': Feminism and the category of 'women' in history*. Minneapolis: University of Minnesota Press.

Riskind, J.H. (1984). They stoop to conquer: Guiding and self-regulatory functions of physical posture after success and failure. *Journal of Personality and Social Psychology*, *47*, 479–493.

Romanyshyn, R.D. (1992). The human body as historical matter and cultural symptom. In M. Sheets-Johnstone (Ed.), *Giving the body its due* (pp. 159–179). Albany: State University of New York Press.

Romanyshyn, R.D. (1993). The despotic eye and its shadow: Media image in the age of literacy. In D.M. Levin (Ed.), *Modernity and the hegemony of vision* (pp. 339–360). Berkeley: University of California Press.

Sampson, E.E. (1977). Psychology and the American ideal. *Journal of Personality and Social Psychology*, *35*, 767–782.

Sampson, E.E. (1983). *Justice and the critique of pure psychology*. New York: Plenum.

Sampson, E.E. (1988). The debate on individualism: Indigenous psychologies of the individual and their role in personal and societal functioning. *American Psychologist*, *43*, 15–22.

Sampson, E.E. (1993). *Celebrating the other: A dialogic account of human nature*. Hemel Hempstead: Harvester Wheatsheaf.

Scheper-Hughes, N. (1992). *Death without weeping: The violence of everyday life in Brazil*. Berkeley: University of California Press.

Scott, J.W. (1988). *Gender and the politics of history*. New York: Columbia University Press.

Sedgwick, E.K. (1990). *Epistemology of the closet*. Berkeley: University of California Press.

Sheets-Johnstone, M. (1990). *The roots of thinking*. Philadelphia, PA: Temple University Press.

Sheet-Johnstone, M. (Ed.). (1992). *Giving the body its due*. Albany: State University of New York Press.

Shotter, J. (1990). *Knowing of the third kind*. Utrecht: University of Utrecht.

Shotter, J. (1991). Rhetoric and the social construction of cognitivism. *Theory & Psychology, 1*, 495–513.

Shotter, J. (1993). *Conversational realities: Constructing life through language*. London: Sage.

Shotter, J. (1995). In conversation: Joint action, shared intentionality and ethics. *Theory & Psychology, 5*, 49–73.

Stepper, S., & Strack, F. (1993). Proprioceptive determinants of emotional and nonemotional feelings. *Journal of Personality and Social Psychology, 64*, 211–220.

Strack, F., Martin, L.L., & Stepper, S. (1988). Inhibiting and facilitating conditions of the human smile: A nonobtrusive test of the facial feedback hypothesis. *Journal of Personality and Social Psychology, 54*, 768–777.

Synnott, A. (1993). *The body social: Symbolism, self and society*. London: Routledge.

Tavris, C. (1992). *The mismeasure of woman*. New York: Touchstone.

Taylor, C. (1993). To follow a rule . . . In C. Calhoun, E. Lipuma, & M. Postone (Eds.), *Bourdieu: Critical perspectives* (pp. 45–60). Chicago, IL: University of Chicago Press.

Tourangeau, R., & Ellsworth, P. (1979). The role of facial response in the experience of emotion. *Journal of Personality and Social Psychology, 37*, 1519–1531.

Varela, F.J., Thompson, E., & Rosch, E. (1991). *The embodied mind: Cognitive science and human experience*. Cambridge, MA: MIT Press.

Verene, D.P. (1981). *Vico's science of imagination*. Ithaca, NY: Cornell University Press.

Young, I.M. (1990). *Justice and the politics of difference*. Princeton, NJ: Princeton University Press.

Zajonc, R.B., Murphy, S.T., & Inglehart, M. (1989). Feeling and facial efference: Implications of the vascular theory of emotions. *Psychological Review, 96*, 395–416.

Zaner, R.M. (1971). *The problem of embodiment: Some contributions to a phenomenology of the body*. The Hague: Martinus Nijhoff.

4

Mind as Body Moving in Space

Bringing the Body Back into Self-Psychology

Harry J.G. Kempen

ABSTRACT. Critics of psychology's view on personality and self as western and ethnocentric and those with a growing interest in what is called the cultural self both tend to advocate social constructionism as the better paradigm. In social constructionism, however, the production of cultures and concomitant selves seems to start from an empty human biology. For a corrective to this Cartesian 'thinking above the body', I return to Vico's 'wholly corporeal imagination' as the starting-point of social constructions. If the human body is universal and if a selfing process is an evolutionary exigency, we may expect to find self-universals or tasks to be undertaken by anybody in any culture. Some five self-universals, each with its multiple options, are sketched. These universal self-variables can be regarded as a common genotypical matrix from which culturally specific, phenotypical selves are derived. A parallel is sought in the hypothesis of linguistic core notions. If the body is the source of universal self-features and if cultures put restrictions on the feature combinations, we can ask ourselves—countering cultural relativism—whether cultures and selves could be judged from what they do to human bodies.

Cultural Variability and Monocultural Psychology

Growing evidence for the cross-cultural variability of personality conceptions and ideas about the self nowadays converges with a criticism of the monocultural view on personality and self as held in western psychology. Baumeister (1987), for example, analysed historical data and literary sources in order to demonstrate the historicity of the western self. Shweder and Bourne (1982) collected data in search of an answer to the question: 'Do the concept of the person and ideas about the self vary cross-culturally?' Their answer was in the affirmative. Volumes like those of White and Kirkpatrick (1985) and of Marsella, DeVos and Hsu (1985) are entirely devoted to the newly identified phenomenon called the cultural self. For the concomitant criticism of psychology's monocultural, and therefore ethnocentric, view on personality and self, I refer to the more or less continuing discussion in the

American Psychologist. (See there, e.g., Cushman, 1990, 1991; Guisinger & Blatt, 1994; Hermans, Kempen, & Van Loon, 1992; Howard, 1991; Markus & Nurius, 1986; Perloff, 1987; Sampson, 1985, 1988, 1989, 1993; Spence, 1985; Weisz, Rothbaum, & Blackburn, 1984.)

Psychology's growing recognition of the role of culture in the formation and functioning of personality and subjectivity should be welcomed. Wundt's (1897, pp. 8–12) plea for a cultural psychology that would operate side by side with an experimental psychology is nearly a century old. But the realization that culture produces variability should not cause us to shut our eyes to universals in human behaviour.

Recently, Cushman asserted in the *American Psychologist* (1990, p. 599) that there is 'no universal, transhistorical self, only local selves; no universal theory about the selves, only local theories'. Contrary to Cushman's view, I want to defend the thesis that there are self-universals. I consider a self, or 'selfing process', necessary for the biological system called *homo erectus*. Human biology is 'in the large about the same the world over' (Kluckhohn & Morgan, 1951, p. 120) and has not changed, as far as we know, for the last 35,000 years, the era of cultural differentiation (cf. Harris, 1993). If 'selfing' is biologically necessary, and if human biology is universal, we should begin to look for universals in the self.

Before presenting arguments in support of this thesis, a preliminary question should be dealt with: Why should we look for self-universals? Is there not already a tremendously rich discipline called personality psychology? There is. But there seems to be something wrong with the conception of personality in contemporary psychology. The anthropologist Geertz (1974/1984), for example, states that 'the Western conception of the person ... is, however incorrigible it may seem to us, a rather peculiar idea within the context of the world's cultures' (p. 126). The West—according to Geertz—understands personality as an idiocentric and distinctive whole, whereas in non-western cultures the person is conceived of as a less isolated, other-related, sociocentric system. Perhaps psychologists are a bit hesitant to accept such a thesis from an interpretative anthropologist like Clifford Geertz. Therefore, let me quote a statement, in the same vein, from Spence's Presidential Address of 1985 to the American Psychological Association. According to Spence, western individualism leads to 'a sense of self with a sharp boundary that stops at one's skin and clearly demarks self from nonself'. This local self-conception can be set against the Japanese self-sense, which is 'more permeable and more diffuse at its boundaries' (p. 1288).

Local self-conceptions are interrelated with local institutions. A characteristic self-sense is, according to Spence, the product and, at the same time, the producer of local political, economic and social institutions. The institution called psychology is apparently not sufficiently guarded against this kind of embeddedness. Spence maintains that for Americans individualism, and its positive aspects, are 'so taken for granted that it is difficult to conceive of any alternative kind of self-conception' (p. 1287). And the producers of psychology are indeed not immune to this problem: the values related to individualism—such as independence, self-reliance, an emphasis on mastery, competition and the loss of a sense for larger purposes—find, according to Spence, 'full expression within contemporary American psychology' (p. 1288). Therefore, Spence suggests, psychology's pretension that it is capable of discovering universal empirical relationships is only 'probably valid in the case of many relatively basic phenomena' (p. 1285). And, Spence continues, 'it seems indisputable that many of our empirical findings and theoretical concepts must inevitably be bound to particular cultures and times, except perhaps on some highly abstract level that few psychological theories have been able to reach' (p. 1285).

On the European side of the Atlantic, the role of culture is likewise recognized not only in everyday behaviour and experiencing, but also in theorizing and researching. Harré (1986), for example, speaks about 'a sudden realization that much of what passed for psychology in the era of simplistic empiricism may be no more than a projection of local custom and practices, even local political philosophies' (p. vii).

It appears that psychology has become aware of its indigenousness; its ethnocentric, monocultural biases. Robbed of the illusion that they were producing universally valid insights, some psychologists are now redefining their discipline's object. That object should now be: the locally and historically specific practices of individuals and groups. The concept 'practices' here is to be understood in a wide sense. It refers to beliefs, emotions, feelings and overt practices. All these covert and overt routines are seen as human-made constructions 'in the face of chaos' (Berger & Luckmann, 1966, p. 21). These constructions are viewed as, inevitably, locally and historically specific, because 'there is no human nature in the sense of a biologically fixed substratum determining the variability of sociocultural formations' (p. 67).

This construction process proceeds more or less as follows: human beings, who, when compared to animals, are instinctually underdeveloped, are obliged to create a proper environment. This creation, or culture, must be appropriated by anyone who wants his or her behaviour to be judged as proper. By doing so, the participants are in their turn consolidating their culture. In the words of Andrew Lock (1981): 'Selves are constituted within culture and culture is maintained by the community of selves' (p. 19). As a consequence we find on our globe such human-made environments as the North American, the Japanese, the Hindu, the medieval and the Renaissance cultures and, accordingly, we can meet with North American, Japanese, Hindu, medieval or Renaissance self-conceptions.

Social Constructionism Enters; Exit the Human Body

This new look in psychology is called 'constructionism' or 'social constructionism' (Gergen, 1985). In the opinion of Ginsburg (1985, p. 873), the
approach is 'now only a minority view in the field'. But Harré (1988, p. 50)
asserts that constructionism has 'become dominant in contemporary
Europe'. The constructionist movement is, in part, a reaction to a psychology
which neglected and continues to neglect the nowadays well-documented
influence of culture on behaviour. However, I think it is an overreaction.

Compared to animals, humans are indeed instinctually underdeveloped.
They must make culture in order to survive. And this culture works itself
deeply into human beliefs, emotion formation, motor behaviour and self-
conceptions. But the production of culture does not start from nowhere, as is
suggested by contemporary constructionism. The basic outline or blueprint
of constructionism is illustrated in Figure 1.

The starting-point of this dialectical human/culture cycle is human biology, but in constructionism human biology is generally considered as an
empty vessel. Berger and Luckmann, for example, whose *The Social
Construction of Reality* (1966) is a landmark in constructionist thinking,
declare plainly that there 'is no human nature in the sense of a biologically
fixed substratum' (p. 67). In their view, human nature is characterized by
world-openness and instinctual plasticity. Geertz (1973) also is sensitive to
the suggestion that 'there is no such thing as human nature independent of
culture' (p. 49). In the same vein, Heelas (1981), in his plea for the study of
indigenous psychologies, states that 'our nature is quite literally assumed'
(p. 16). This same suggestion of a gap between human nature and culture
can be found in Bruner's (1990) recent plea for a cultural psychology. 'It is',
according to Bruner, 'the character of man's biological inheritance . . . that it

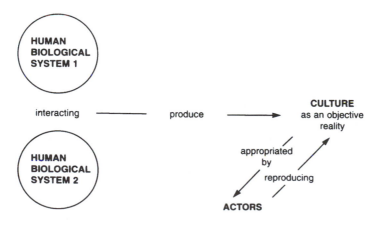

FIGURE 1. Basic outline of social constructionism

does not direct or shape human action and experience, does not serve as the universal cause' (p. 34). And Cushman (1991, p. 206) considers the search for 'the foundational laws of a transhistorical human nature' as itself an artifact of a particular indigenous psychology.

Focusing on the variability of cultures and on the concomitant variability of behaviour, and meanwhile disclaiming any content to human nature, entails at least two problems for psychology. The first one is this: How can a psychology studying practices which are regarded principally as local and historical arrive at scientific, that is, universally valid, insights? The second problem is that, when taken to its logical conclusion, constructionism leads to an 'anything goes' ideology, to 'radical cultural relativism' (Kagitcibasi & Berry, 1989, p. 519).

Spence (1985), recognizing the non-universality, the indigenousness, of many of psychology's theoretical concepts and empirical findings, and surmising that claims for universality can be upheld only in the case of 'many relatively basic phenomena', fears what she calls 'an extreme constructivist position' (p. 1285). Constructionism, says Spence, can lead to 'paralyzing nihilism' (p. 1285). As a remedy she proposes to counterbalance constructionism's relativism by adopting a simultaneous 'position of naïve realism' (p. 1285).

However, naïve realism, or common sense, is not a phenomenon that escapes culture's influence. As soon as we move beyond the level of natural practices such as collecting firewood or getting water, even common sense becomes filled with culture. The common sense of primitive agriculturalists is different from the common sense of industrial farmers, and theirs departs from the common sense of ecological peasants. Likewise, the common sense concerning, for example, the self or social interactions in, for instance, individualistic cultures or cultures with high power distance—as studied by Hofstede (1984)—is different from the common-sense view on this domain in collectivistic cultures or cultures with low power distance. As an aside, the etymological relationship of 'naïve', as in 'naïve realism', which means natural and spontaneous, and 'native', which means local and indigenous, is well documented. (See, for example, Partridge, 1966, p. 428.)

Is there not something else with which to counterbalance contemporary constructionism? There is a naïveté which is not local, an indigenousness, a nativeness, which is not territorially specific, and whose realism is global, worldwide; a naïve nativeness which, therefore, contains universals and represents a scientific rather than a naïve realism. I have in mind the human body.

By returning to the human body, I hope to find a counterbalance to a culturally relativistic psychology. In this body, then, we must look for aspects that are at the same time *universal* and *variable*. Only such '*universal variables*' will allow for a psychology which is both universal and open to the cultural variability of behaviour. The human body is no doubt instinctually underdeveloped, but this does not mean that it is empty. It is exactly because of its instinctual underdevelopment that each human body has to develop a self. The human body becomes filled with a self, a self that is embodied: a *corps-sujet*. Let me elaborate on this.

Enter the Monozygotic Twin: Body and Self

I start with Wonham's famous 'Internal Model Principle of regulator theory':

> A regulator for which both internal stability and output regulation are structurally stable properties must utilize feedback of the regulated variable and incorporate in the feedback loop a suitably reduplicated model of the dynamic structure of the exogenous signals which the regulator is required to process. (Wonham, 1976, p. 735)

Humans too must incorporate a sufficiently complex model of their 'exosystem'. But because their exosystem changes continuously, the internal model must be revised constantly. And such revision has to be executed in the terms of human beings' regulatory capacities. This may be evident.

However, since these regulatory capacities are themselves variable, a human being's internal model of the exosystem must include a model of a human being himself or herself. In such a model, which combines both the dynamic structure of the external system and the dynamic structure of the internal system, regulatory practices can be tested in a risk-free, imaginary, internal way. Thus the self is an 'as-if' system, a safety system, which human physiology evokes by necessity. Otherwise, the organism could be destroyed in its first reaching-out to the environment. Let me make more concrete this non-Cartesian, body-inclusive view of thinking.

For Giambattista Vico (1668–1744), the human sciences must begin 'where their subject matters began', that is, in the open field of history (Vico, 1744/1968, p. 104) and not in the darkened room sought out by Descartes. In that room, Descartes, living in a war-ridden Europe, expected to find a baseline from which to criticize 'the large number of falsehoods . . . accepted as true' and dividing people (Descartes, 1641/1984, p. 24). Setting aside 'all images of bodily things' (p. 24), Descartes succeeded in suggesting that thinking-detached-from-the-body is the baseline for being a human.

For Vico, the first humans, 'whose minds were not in the least abstract . . . because they were entirely immersed in the senses', made their attributions and shaped their environment 'by virtue of a wholly corporeal imagination', a *corporatissima fantasia* (pp. 117–118). In this imagination, which is 'nothing but extended or compounded memory', humans can step over 'the things found at their feet' (p. 75) in order to put them into new and usable relationships.

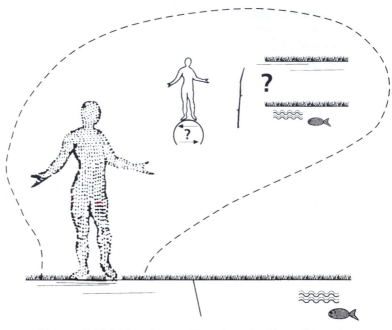

FIGURE 2. Thinking the non-Cartesian way (drawn by author; human figure from *Orbis Sensualium Pictus* by Johann Amos Comenius, 1658, p. 88).

For us, who are, in the words of Vico, 'detached from the senses ... by abstractions' brought about by our languages and the art of writing (p. 118), a visualization of early humans in the open field may be to the point. Imagine a group of early *homines erecti* searching for their way in a new environment (see Figure 2). The panorama is full of sensory and motorial challenges, some of them a matter of life and death. For instance, the green matter under their feet is grass, but a few feet further on, that green could be duckweed covering a morass. Some time ago one member of the group suddenly disappeared in such surroundings. In case of doubt this group will stop and start what could be called 'as-if' behaviour: If that green covers soil, then ...; but if that green covers water, then ... To free themselves from this double situation—or to get beyond this *doubt* (which is etymo-logically the same term as *two* or *double*)—they must discover what this matter is as a matter of fact.

They can do this by doing-as-if-they-walk, or shuffling, or by replacing their feet with a stick for the exploration of the area in front of them. Such factual, or imaginary, or conceptual behaviour is executed in a factual, or imaginary, or conceptual *risk-free* space, which for brevity's sake can be called mind. In such an exercise space, however, an image of the actor himself or herself must be included: human regulatory capacities tend to be in a state of flux and must be themselves brought into the picture, at least at regular intervals, for monitoring.

According to James (1890, p. 330), the self is 'the most puzzling puzzle with which psychology has to deal'. I am not inclined to disclaim the enigmatic character of the self; experientially, neurologically and philosophically the self is no doubt a problem. But I think that we can gain courage from the fact that the self is a biological necessity, a natural datum as it were. Seeing the self as biological, and given that human biology is the same the world over, leads us to look for universal self-aspects.

Universal Self-Aspects

What could be a minimal set of tasks for a subjectifying body that stands upright and is able to walk in an unknown environment, in which the green under the feet is grass, but in which the same green, some steps further, could be duckweed?

- A first task for each self is to define its *boundary*, that is, to contrast itself with the non-self, with objects and with other selves.
- A second task is to *evaluate* the situation: is it good, is it bad, is it neutral?
- A third task is to decide upon *activity* or non-activity.
- A fourth task is to preserve successful activities from the past and to abandon non-successful ones in order to perform effectively in the present, with a view to the future. That is, the self must develop a *time orientation*.
- A fifth self-task is to define the range of the activity-*space*. Where do the situations begin which I may overlook, which I may judge as lying beyond my scope?

Universal but Variable

These universal self-tasks or self-aspects per se cannot explain the variability of culture, nor can they account for differences in self-conception. But it so happens that these universals are at the same time *variables*: each task can be performed in several different ways. Consequently, more or less stabilized preferences for one or more of these task options can develop in cultures and in self-systems.

(1) To begin with, the self/non-self boundary can be conceived as sharp or vague. Thus, a self-definition can be individualistic or collectivistic. Spence (1985), for one, as already noted, brings out the contrast between the western sense of self, with its 'sharp boundary that stops at one's skin and clearly

demarks self from nonself', and the Japanese self, which, 'more permeable and more diffuse at its boundaries' (p. 1288), identifies itself with various groups.

(2) The options of the evaluative universal coincide with the polarities of the evaluative factor thoroughly studied in the worldwide project on connotative meaning by Osgood and associates (Osgood, Suci, & Tannenbaum, 1957). This evaluative factor is defined by such bipolarities as good/bad, pleasant/unpleasant and valuable/worthless. The midpoint of these polarities represents irrelevance of the adjectives or their equal applicability. Thus, the options of this task are: good, good and bad, neutral, and bad.

(3) Activity can be implemented in an active and in a passive mode. This dimension has a rich research tradition as well, as illustrated by Rotter's 'Internal–External Locus of Control' project. (Rotter's 1966 monograph on this theme was the most cited article in social sciences from 1969 to 1977; Strickland, 1989, p. 3). But here, once more, is an example of the ethnocentric bias of North Atlantic psychology, for there is at least one form of control other than internal and external control. No doubt, people can have a feeling of control—that is, a feeling of order—by controlling or by being controlled. This feeling of order, however, can also be attained by accommodating to existing realities, by aligning oneself with the situations at hand. When doing so, one is not controlling, but neither is one being controlled. Rothbaum, Weisz and Snyder (1982) have labelled this type of activity 'secondary control' and Weisz et al. (1984) have shown that in Japan secondary control has assumed 'a more central role in everyday life than in our culture' (p. 955). That is exactly why it took psychology, as a western institution, a century before it conceptually recognized this participative mode of activity. So the activity-universal has at least three options: activity, passivity and participation.

(4) As far as time orientation is concerned, two main types can be distinguished: the linear and the cyclical experience of time. In the linear version, time is experienced as an irreversible process, whereas in the cyclical version it is experienced as a series of events, repeating themselves, as the text of a never updated illuminated news trailer. But both in linear and in cyclical time, the now is distinguished from the not-now, while the latter is usually divided into a past and a future. Thus the time-orienting task has at least three options—past/present/future—and six if we take into account the cyclical and the linear versions.

(5) The space-orienting task has at least two options: small and large. For example: 'This house/neighbourhood/valley is my/our world' vs 'I/we have got the whole world, outer space included, in my/our hands'. There is a billion dollar difference between a Buddhist who is happy when pointing at the moon, and a westerner who is not happy before he or she can walk on the moon.

Culture as the Answer to the Combinatorial Explosion of Self-Options

According to the view presented here, the human biological system, *from* which and *for* which culture is produced, is not empty. It is filled with universal variables. Given 5 tasks with 2, 2, 3, 3 (or 6) and 2 options, respectively, there are theoretically 72 (or 144) self-types. Because culture is an orienting system for at least two actors, it is also a *co-orienting* system. For an actor with 72 (or 144) possible selves to co-orient himself or herself with another actor who also has such a number of possibilities is a formidable task. Culture saves us from this combinatorial explosion of selves. Culture makes the choice for us; it reduces by way of norm formation the alternatives to a manageable set and it presents this set as self-evident, as natural and more or less indisputable.

Cross-Linguistic Evidence for Self-Universals

The foregoing analysis which led to the identification of universal self-variables could be seen as subjective, armchair musing, as an exercise in the phenomenology of an actor's entering into new environments or unknown situations. Are there other sources of evidence for the universality of these self-variables?

There is at least one such source. If these variables are universal, and if self-constructing is a co-orienting process, that is, a process dependent on communication, and if speech is to a great extent the pre-eminent vehicle for transmitting culture, then we may expect that these universal variables or variable universals are reflected in every natural language. Although the world's languages are strikingly different in their grammatical means of expression and in the relative ease with which certain concepts can be encoded, one might test the hypothesis that all languages have primary, that is, relatively easy, non-complex provisions for encoding the different options of the self/non-self experience, of the activity and the evaluative universal, and of locality and time.

One of Bruner's (1990) conclusions from the vast research on language acquisition is that 'certain communicative functions or intentions are well in place before the child has mastered the formal language for expressing them linguistically' (p. 71). Bruner, in his search for a 'biology of meaning', hypothesizes the existence of a protolinguistic system, 'some sort of precursor system that readies the prelinguistic organism to traffic in language' (p. 69). Referring to the work on first-language acquisition based on the (content-oriented) semantic relations categories of case grammar, Bruner concludes that in the first stage of speech children's principal linguistic interest is in semantic relations such as *agent-and-action, action-and-object, agent-and-object, action-and-location* and *possessor–possession* (p. 78).

This conclusion provides support for the behavioural centrality of at least some of the aforementioned self-universals. The Self/Non-self-, the Activity-, and the Space-universal are clearly implicated. As for the Time-universal, Bruner suggests that children also start mastering early the linguistic devices for connecting the sequences they recount, for example, by the use of temporals like 'then' and 'later' (p. 79).

Evidence for the primogeniture of the Evaluative-universal comes from psychology's emotion research. In multidimensional scaling studies of emotions typically two bipolar dimensions are found: (un)pleasantness and (in)activation (e.g. Dittmann, 1972; Plutchik, 1980b; Watson & Tellegen, 1985; Wundt, 1905). They are found in non-western groups as well (Russell, Lewicka, & Niit, 1989), even when indigenous emotions are presented, that is, emotions that are supposed to be culturally specific, such as the Japanese *tukeagari*, which refers to 'feeling puffed up with the sense of self-importance' (Markus & Kitayama, 1991).

Thus, evaluating seems to be a robust universal as well and probably even precedes the development of other more cognitive universals. 'Cognitions', notes Plutchik (1980a, p. 12), 'have largely evolved in the service of emotions.' Although actors possess a rich repertory of means for the non-linguistic, voluntary or involuntary, expression of emotions to self and others—for instance, electrical skin phenomena, gastrointestinal motility, eye blink and eye movement—it is likely that the different modes of evaluating also enter quite early into the actor's linguistic system, just as Bruner's 'protolinguistics'.

Evidence for the existence of universal, 'well-movitated and fairly easily definable semantic/pragmatic "core" notions' stemming from 'primordial and universal patterns of thought and action' (Slobin, 1990, p. 236) can also be found in Slobin's cross-linguistic research project on early language acquisition. Slobin offers strong data for the thesis that there is a *universal child speaker*, apparently equipped with species-common, culturally and linguistically unspecific language acquisition strategies. It is only after this universal language acquisition period that the child speaker learns the typical distinctions which tend to be grammaticized in the mature version of his/her native language. For example, a mature speaker of Spanish who intends to say that 'The boy saw that the dog fell' must mark aspects of the actions— 'seeing' and 'falling'—which are not distinguished in English. In mature Spanish one says 'El niño veía que se caía el perro'. And this means, literally, 'The boy saw [imperfective; meaning: 'had been busy with seeing'] that the dog fell [perfective]'. Language-specific distinctions or aspects like these are not directly given in the protolinguistic experience of the child speaker, nor can they be easily pointed out by ostensive reference. According to Slobin (p. 236), they must be learned through linguistic devices themselves. They are, I would add, locally and historically negotiated, agreed linguistic 'consensuals', not indicative of a universal 'biology of meaning'. At any rate, Bruner's assumption of a protolinguistic system seems to receive support from Slobin's finding that there is 'a striking commonality in the content and functions of children's early speech across languages and cultures' (p. 234).

What is of interest here is the parallel between the elements of the protolinguistic system and the elements of the universal self-system described earlier. This parallel might suggest a common origin that the protolinguistic and the selfing-system have. Bruner is looking for a 'biology of meaning' and my starting-point is also biology. However, by amending Wonham's 'Internal Model Principle', I have defended the thesis that human biology, by reason of evolutionary survival, must develop an imaginary space wherein images or concepts of both the actor and the environment can interact in a risk-free way. To put it differently, human physiology must develop a self. The human body has to become 'subjectified'. And this universal subjectifying body or embodied selfing process is, I suggest, the common denominator of language acquisition and self-construction. Both processes operate from the same starting-point: the far from empty human body, the *corps-sujet* with its universal variables.

An Objective Stance against Relativism: The Body's Na(t)ive Realism

When Spence (1995) says that 'the Japanese character differs profoundly from the American one' (1985, p. 1287), I agree with her. There is sufficient evidence that the Japanese favour a vague, non-clear-cut self/non-self boundary, at least as far as other Japanese are concerned. The impact of an independent vs an interdependent construal of the self, for example, on individual experience, including cognition, emotion and motivation, has been richly documented in a recent article by Markus and Kitayama (1991). Yet at the same time I disagree with Spence. Why?

Self-options are biologically given. A culture can—and must—restrict the potential combinatorial explosion which they entail. And in so doing, culture enters the body. The body is not only the place where culture takes off, it is also its *landing place*. Our self is not something that hovers around our skin. Moreover, our body is the complex, the most integrated system in the universe. When placing the emphasis on a particular option, a culture or a self cannot annihilitate the other options of the universal in question. Overemphasizing a specific option automatically causes an increase in importance of the 'opposite' option(s). After a working day, with its accent on the active mode of the Activity-universal, the other activity options—passivity and/or participation—check in nearly automatically.

At the level of cultures this counterpoint phenomenon is visible also. Wertheim (1974) and Risseeuw (1988) note that all societies incorporate conflicting value systems, 'of which the opposing, contradictory values, dormant in relation to the dominant values, can, under certain conditions, gain in momentum and operate as a force leading to emancipatory movements or even revolutions' (Risseeuw, 1988, pp. 198–199). For instance, the growing criticism of North Atlantic individualism, and the collapse of authoritarian–collectivistic systems in Central Europe—both of which over-emphasize one of the self/non-self boundary options—can be seen as indicative of the complementary or antagonistic structure of our self-defining process.

The Japanese might appear to be different from North Americans, yet at the same time they are not. We are—indeed—brothers and sisters under the skin, but not because of the fact that our lungs, stomachs or kidneys are the same. Such universals cannot explain behavioural variability. We are—notwithstanding all cultural differences—akin to each other because there are body-bound self-universals which produce communality alongside specifics. These specifics, however—due to locally specific accentuations of certain modes—never wipe out with impunity the adjacent modes of a universal.

In her plea for counterbalancing individualism, Spence (1985) refers to Bakan's *The Duality of Human Existence* (1966). In this book Bakan develops the thesis that every living organism possesses two fundamental and antagonistic 'senses': a sense of self, or agency, and a sense of selflessness, or communion. The idea that people's mental life is governed by great polarities is quite old. It is, for example, part and parcel of traditional Chinese thinking. In classical Greece it was Heraclitus who proposed as a general principle the 'unity of opposites'. The Chinese paradigm focuses upon a dynamic principle of order, called *tao*. *Tao* is based on the all-pervasive polarities of *yin* and *yang*. Aristotelian thinking, dominant in western science, psychology included, conversely specified that opposites cannot be present in the same thing, at the same time and in the same respect (cf. Marková, 1987). And so Heraclitean thinking passed into disuse. But the Chinese–Heraclitean point of view never wholly disappeared. Freud in his 'Instincts and Their Vicissitudes' (1915/1957) advanced the notion that 'mental life as a whole is governed by *three polarities*, the antitheses Subject (ego)–Object (external world), Pleasure–Unpleasure, and Active–Passive' (p. 133). Such thinking in terms of fundamental opposites also prevails in the research on emotion to which I have referred earlier. Time after time it has been shown that our emotions can be described in terms of universal variables like (un)pleasantness and (in)activity. (Markus and Kitayama recently found a third polarity: ego-centred vs other-focused emotions: 1991.)

Constructionism, as a paradigm for psychology, is feared because of its inherent cultural relativism. It can lead to 'paralyzing nihilism' (Spence,

1985, p. 1285), to an 'anything goes' ideology. As a remedy, Spence proposes a position of 'naïve realism', of common sense. But, as I said earlier, as soon as we move beyond the level of simple, everyday practices, common sense becomes imbued with cultural particularities. But what about the naïve realism of the human body? Not the physiological body, but the subjectified body. Is this not the 'objective ... stance' psychologists who 'attempt to rise above their own culture' (Spence, 1985, p. 286) should reach for?

This stance is not objective and value-free, as Spence would like. It is value-laden. But the question of value-free science—that precious prescript—is not at stake here. Value-free science means: do not produce scientific insights for the sole benefit of a restricted group, for westerners, the gentry, the ministry, political parties or factions thereof. A reorientation towards the values of the subjectified body does not violate the prescript to be objective and value-free; after all, humanity is definitely an interest group, but it is not an arbitrary one.

How can we turn this body into a criterion for value judgements about cultures and about selves? If the human body is not only the starting-point of culture production and self-construction, but also the landing place of these activities, and if, moreover, this body is governed by intrinsically related polarities (or tripartite and plurimodal universal variables), then cultures or self-concepts which overemphasize certain options at the expense of others are less optimal than they could be. The new field of psychoneuroimmunology, as sketched by Maier, Watkins and Fleshner (1994), offers a promising research framework for this thesis. Thus, it is not only by undernourishment, institutionalized killing or ecological misbehaviour that cultures and selves can hurt the body.

Concluding Remarks

In reply to Sumner's statement, 'The mores can make anything right', the sociologist Park said: 'But they have a harder time making some things right than others' (quoted in Redfield, 1957, p. 160). Cultures and self-conceptions can be viewed as answers to the combinatorial explosion of options. These answers are arrived at through the reduction of alternatives. However, the third partner in this process is the human body, with its long-standing evolutionary history.

If we regard the relations between body, self and culture as dialogical relations (Hermans & Kempen, 1995), the dimension of power in dialogue, or symmetrical vs asymmetrical relationships, can be brought into the open. For a symmetrical conversation of these partners it will be necessary that psychology, with its rich grammar for the study of culture and self, develop a voice for the body.

References

Bakan, D. (1966). *The duality of human existence*. Chicago, IL: Rand McNally.

Baumeister, R.F. (1987). How the self became a problem: A psychological review of historical research. *Journal of Personality and Social Psychology, 52*, 163–176.

Berger, P.L., & Luckmann, T. (1966). *The social construction of reality: A treatise on the sociology of knowledge*. Harmondsworth: Penguin.

Bruner, J. (1990). *Acts of meaning*. Cambridge, MA: Harvard University Press.

Comenius, J.A. (1958). *Orbis sensualium pictus: Omnium fundamentalium in mundo rerum et in vita actionum*. Noribergae: Michaelis Endteri.

Cushman, P. (1990). Why the self is empty: Toward a historically situated psychology. *American Psychologist, 45*, 599–611.

Cushman, P. (1991). Ideology obscured: Political uses of the self in Daniel Stern's infant. *American Psychologist, 46*, 206–219.

Descartes, R. (1984). Meditations on first philosophy. In J. Cottingham, R. Stoothoff, & D. Murdoch (Eds. and Trans.), *The philosophical writings of Descartes* (Vol. 2, pp. 3–62). Cambridge, MA: Cambridge University Press. (Original work published 1641.)

Dittmann, A.T. (1972). *Interpersonal messages of emotion*. New York: Springer.

Freud, S. (1957). Instincts and their vicissitudes. In J. Strachey (Ed. and Trans.), *The standard edition of the complete psychological works of Sigmund Freud* (Vol. 14, pp. 117–145). London: Hogarth Press. (Original work published 1915.)

Geertz, C. (1973). *The interpretation of cultures*. New York: Basic Books.

Geertz, C. (1984). From the native's point of view: On the nature of anthropological research. In R.A. Shweder & R.A. LeVine (Eds.), *Culture theory: Essays on mind, self, and emotion* (pp. 123–136). Cambridge: Cambridge University Press. (Original work published 1974.)

Gergen, K.J. (1985). The social constructionist movement in modern psychology. *American Psychologist, 50*, 266–275.

Ginsburg, G. (1985). Taking talk seriously: A revision of the field [Review of: Shotter, J. (1984). *Social accountability and selfhood*. Oxford: Blackwell]. *Contemporary Psychology, 30*, 872–874.

Guisinger, S., & Blatt, S.J. (1994). Individuality and relatedness. *American Psychologist, 49*, 104–111.

Harré, R. (Ed.). (1986). *The social construction of emotion*. Oxford: Blackwell.

Harré, R. (1988). Two ethnocentric views of culture and identity [Review of: Baumeister, F. (1986). *Identity: Culture change and the struggle for self*. New York: Oxford; Weigert, A., Smith Teitge, J., & Teitge, D. (1986). *Society and identity: Toward a sociological psychology*. New York: Cambridge]. *Contemporary Psychology, 33*, 50–51.

Harris, M. (1993). *Culture, people, nature: An introduction to general anthropology*. New York: Harper.

Heelas, P. (1981). Introduction: Indigenous psychologies. In P. Heelas & A. Lock (Eds.), *Indigenous psychologies: The anthropology of the self* (pp. 3–18). London: Academic Press

Hermans, H.J.M., & Kempen, H.J.G. (1995). Body, mind and culture: The dialogical nature of mediated action. *Culture & Psychology, 1*, 103–114.

Hermans, H.J.M., Kempen, H.J.G., & Van Loon, R.J.P. (1992). The dialogical self: Beyond individualism and rationalism. *American Psychologist, 47*, 23–33.

Hofstede, G. (1984). *Culture's consequences: International differences in work-related values*. Beverly Hill, CA: Sage.

Howard, G. (1991). Culture tales: A narrative approach to thinking, cross-cultural psychology, and psychotherapy. *American Psychologist, 46*, 187–197.

James, W. (1890). *The principles of psychology* (Vol. 1). New York: Holt.

Kagitcibasi, C., & Berry, J.W. (1989). Cross-cultural psychology: Current research and trends. *Annual Review of Psychology, 40*, 493–531.

Kluckhohn, C., & Morgan, W. (1951). Some notes on Navaho dreams. In G.B. Wilbur & W. Muensterberger (Eds.), *Psychoanalysis and culture: Essays in honor of Géza Roheim* (pp. 120–131). New York: International Universities Press.

Lock, A. (1981). Universals in human conception. In P. Heelas & A. Lock (Eds.), *Indigenous psychologies: The anthropology of the self* (pp. 19–36). London: Academic Press.

Maier, S.F., Watkins, L.R., & Fleshner, M. (1994). Psychoneuroimmunology: The interface between behavior, brain, and immunity. *American Psychologist, 49*, 1004–1017.

Marková, I. (1987). On the interaction of opposites in psychological processes. *Journal for the Theory of Social Behavior, 17*, 279–299.

Markus, H.R., & Kitayama, S. (1991). Culture and self: Implications for cognition, emotion, and motivation. *Psychological Review, 98*, 224–253.

Markus, H.R., & Nurius, P. (1986). Possible selves. *American Psychologist, 41*, 954–969.

Marsella, A.J., DeVos, G., & Hsu, F.L.K. (Eds.). (1985). *Culture and self: Asian and western perspectives*. New York: Tavistock.

Osgood, C.E., Suci, C.J., & Tannenbaum, P.H. (1957). *The measurement of meaning*. Urbana: University of Illinois Press.

Partridge, E. (1966). *Origins: A short etymological dictionary of modern English*. London: Routledge.

Perloff, R. (1987). Self-interest and personal responsibility redux. *American Psychologist, 42*, 3–11.

Plutchik, R. (1980a). A general psychoevolutionary theory of emotion. In R. Plutchik & H. Kellerman (Eds.), *Emotion: Theory, research, and experience: Vol. 1. Theories of emotion* (pp. 3–33). Orlando, FL: Academic Press.

Plutchik, R. (1980b). *Emotion: A psychoevolutionary synthesis*. New York: Harper.

Redfield, R. (1957). The universally human and the culturally variable. *Journal of General Education, 10*, 150–160.

Risseeuw, C. (1988). *The fish don't talk about the water: Gender transformation, power, and resistance among women in Sri Lanka*. Leiden: Brill.

Rothbaum, F., Weisz, J.R., & Snyder, S.S. (1982). Changing the world and changing the self: A two-process model of perceived control. *Journal of Personality and Social Psychology, 42*, 5–37.

Rotter, J.B. (1966). Generalized expectancies for internal versus external control of reinforcement. *Psychological Monographs, 80*, 1–28.

Russell, J.A., Lewicka, M., & Niit, T. (1989). A cross-cultural study of a circumplex model of affect. *Journal of Personality and Social Psychology, 57*, 848–856.

Sampson, E.E. (1985). The decentralization of identity: Toward a revised concept of personal and social order. *American Psychologist, 40*, 1203–1211.

Sampson, E.E. (1988). The debate on individualism: Indigenous psychologies of the individual and their role in personal and societal functioning. *American Psychologist*, *43*, 15–22.

Sampson, E.E. (1989). The challenge of social change for psychology: Globalization and psychology's theory of the person. *American Psychologist*, *44*, 914–921.

Sampson, E.E. (1993). Identity politics: Challenges to psychology's understanding. *American Psychologist*, *48*, 1219–1230.

Shweder, R.A., & Bourne, E.J. (1982). Does the concept of the person vary cross-culturally? In A.J. Marsella & G.M. White (Eds.), *Cultural conceptions of mental health and therapy* (pp. 97–137). Dordrecht: Reidel.

Slobin, D.I. (1990). The development from child speaker to native speaker. In J.W. Stigler, R.A. Shweder, & G. Herdt (Eds.), *Cultural psychology: Essays on comparative human development* (pp. 233–256). Cambridge: Cambridge University Press.

Spence, J.I. (1985). Achievement American style: The rewards and costs of punishment. *American Psychologist*, *40*, 1285–1295.

Strickland, B. (1989). Internal–external control expectancies: From contingency to creativity. *American Psychologist*, *44*, 1–12.

Vico, G. (1968). *The new science of Giambattista Vico* (T.G. Bergin & M.H. Fisch, Trans.), Ithaca, NY: Cornell University Press. (Original work published 1744.)

Watson, D., & Tellegen, A. (1985). Toward a consensual structure of mood. *Psychological Bulletin*, *98*, 219–235.

Weisz, J.R., Rothbaum, F.M., & Blackburn, T.C. (1984). Standing out and standing in: The psychology of control in America and Japan. *American Psychologist*, *39*, 955–969.

Wertheim, W.F. (1974). *Evolution and revolution: The rising waves of emancipation*. Harmondsworth: Penguin.

White, G.M., & Kirkpatrick, J. (Eds.). (1985). *Person, self, and experience: Exploring Pacific ethnopsychologies*. Berkeley: University of California Press.

Wonham, W. (1976). Toward an abstract internal model principle. *IEEE Transactions on Systems, Man, and Cybernetics*, *6*, 735–740.

Wundt, W. (1897). *Vorlesungen über die Menschen- und Thierseele* [Lectures on the human and animal mind] (3rd rev. ed.). Hamburg: Leopold Voss.

Wundt, W. (1905). *Grundriss der Psychologie* [Outlines of psychology] (7th improved ed.). Leipzig: Wilhelm Engelmann.

ACKNOWLEDGEMENTS. For their comments on an earlier version I wish to thank Thom Bezembinder, Hubert J.M. Hermans, Melissa M. Monfries and Peter J. Naus.

Part III
SEXED AND GENDERED BODIES

5

'Loving the Computer'
Cognition, Embodiment and the Influencing Machine

Elizabeth A. Wilson

ABSTRACT. Cognitive psychology has been founded on a model of the mind as an information-processing machine. This paper is not concerned with the arguments for or against modelling the mind on computers, as these arguments are already well rehearsed in the literature. Instead I am interested in what the relation between computer, cognition and the thinking man promises or guarantees. Specifically, I am concerned with how cognition comes to be constituted through certain dominant fantasies of embodiment that the computer metaphor promotes. To what extent does psychology's computational machinery prescribe a disembodied cognition? And in what ways is such a prescription of cognition indebted to the logic of a masculine morphology? The paper draws on Turing's classic essay 'Computing Machinery and Intelligence', Atkinson and Shiffrin's early model of human memory, Irigaray's formulation of sexed morphology and Tausk's analysis of the influencing machine in paranoid delusions to argue that at the heart of cognitive theories we find the body of the thinking man.

In principle, it is possible to be a cognitive scientist without loving the computer; but in practice, skepticism about computers generally leads to skepticism about cognitive science. (Gardner, 1987, p. 40)

Introduction

There is very little written about psychological processes in a contemporary scientific context that does not in some way invoke either the computer or the brain. On the one hand it may be that the mind is considered analogous to a digital computer—a highly complex, but essentially rational and logical information-processing machine (e.g. Newell & Simon, 1972; Pylyshyn, 1984). On the other hand there is a wealth of neurological research that has been able to cortically map certain psychological functions (e.g. Luria, 1973; Sperry, 1982); although this approach has been more concerned with topographical localization than with a theory of the mind per se. Broadly speaking, we can say that there are two general approaches to a contemporary scientific study of the mind: the *computational*, which takes the mind to be the logic-driven manipulation of symbolic information; and the *neurological*, where psychological capacities are located in circumscribed cortical areas.[1]

Traditionally, these two approaches to psychology have taken separate and divergent research paths. Neurological data have had little impact on cognitive theories of memory, perception, attention, etc., and cognitive theory appears to have had little relevance to empirical work on brain structure and function (see Churchland, 1986). More recently, however, these two different paths have been converging: bringing neurological data to bear on cognitive theory, and vice versa, this conjunction of interests has produced a domain that I will call the *neuro-cognitive sciences* (but is sometimes referred to as cognitive neuroscience or computational neuroscience). A hybrid field that can no longer be contained within traditional disciplinary boundaries, neuro-cognitive science encompasses a wide range of cognitive and neurological research (e.g. Baron, 1987; Churchland & Sejnowski, 1992; Gluck & Rumelhart, 1990; Kosslyn & Koenig, 1992). What differentiates this hybrid domain from either of its constituent traditions is the view that neither neurology nor cognitive theory, taken separately, can furnish us with an adequate account of psychology. Connectionist theories and models of psychological processes are exemplary of this neuro-cognitive approach: merging both cognitive theory and neurological constraints, connectionism offers a psyche that differs radically from earlier cognitive theories and traditional neuropsychological accounts (Rumelhart, McClelland, & the PDP Research Group, 1986).

This paper offers a critical account of one of the traditions (cognitive psychology) that contributes to this new neuro-cognitive field. It is not my aim to adjudicate on the weaknesses and strengths of contemporary cognitive psychology in order to determine the value or the level of its contribution to this new hybrid domain. Rather, it is my goal to disclose some of the theoretical presuppositions of the cognitive tradition in psychology, so that we may ascertain to what extent these presuppositions are rewritten and carried through into the 'new' neuro-cognitive sciences. In particular, I am interested in the early work in this area: I focus on the precognitive (Turing, 1950) and early cognitive texts (Atkinson & Shiffrin,

1968) that have been crucial in the development of cognitive psychology. As such, this paper is an interrogation of the ground of the neuro-cognitive sciences.

Specifically it is a *feminist* interrogation of this ground. I have argued elsewhere (Wilson, 1995) that feminist interventions into psychology have been restricted by a certain political orthodoxy. This orthodoxy, which contains feminist questions in psychology to matters of sexism and bias, has suppressed the possibility and the urgency of a number of other kinds of feminist projects—projects which target the seemingly sexually neutral ground of psychological theory. While it has been traditional for feminists to inquire into the authenticity of reported sex differences in cognitive abilities (e.g. Hare-Mustin & Marecek, 1980; Maccoby & Jacklin, 1974), my aim is to inquire into the nature of cognition itself. What do scientific notions of cognition presume? What exclusions are necessary to enforce these presumptions? It is my argument that the problems central to cognitive accounts of sexual difference (e.g. are men cognitively oriented to spatial tasks and women to verbal tasks?) are not simply inscriptive over, or secondary to, an otherwise innocent domain (cognition). Rather questions of sexual difference are the very mechanisms that constitute that domain in general. If feminist interventions into cognitive psychology are to continue to have effective political purchase, then we may need to reorient our critical focus. While projects that concentrate on issues specifically coded as sexed (or sexist) remain vital, we could also begin to focus our attention on that which is coded as sexually neutral. In short, we could examine this process of sexual codification itself: we must refuse the disjunction between sexed and unsexed knowledges and relocate the sexually neutral at the very heart of masculinist authority. In so doing, feminist criticism in psychology may begin to suspect that what purports to be sexually indifferent in psychological knowledges (e.g. psychophysical processes, cognition, the laws of learning, the vicissitudes of neurological function) is deeply implicated in masculine interests and desires, whether or not such sexed interests implicate the category 'women'.

In this paper, issues of embodiment as they are argued in contemporary feminist theory (specifically here, Irigaray, 1985a, 1977/1985b), are the place from which I assess the apparently neutral ground of cognitive theory. I argue that computationalism in psychology proceeds, and is successful, not because of the veridicality of the computer metaphor, but because what is presupposed about embodiment in this metaphor fits with certain masculinist presumptions about psychological functioning. Specifically, I argue that there is a particular masculine morphology that informs theories of cognition, for which the computer has become an ideal site of projection. Cognition as neutral or dispassionate computation is a masculinist ruse of the most beguiling kind.

The Computer and Cognitive Psychology

The rise of cognitive psychology goes hand-in-hand with the rise of a more broadly based cognitive science.[2] This 'cognitive revolution' has been felt acutely in psychology. The increasing importance of a cognitive paradigm in psychology since the 1950s has been attributed to a variety of causes; the most popular of these being the decline of behaviourism's theoretical and experimental hegemony, the advances in computer technology and the consequent development of an information-processing model of cognition (Gardner, 1987). It is this latter development that concerns me here.

Cognitive psychology has been founded on, and continues to be dominated by, a metaphor of the mind as an *information-processing machine*. By offering the first sustained argument (within psychology) for the modelling of psychology on computational processes, and differentiating such an approach from psychodynamic, behaviourist and neurological accounts, Neisser (1967) is usually seen as the founder of cognitive psychology:

> A book like this one might be called 'Stimulus Information and its Vicissitudes.' As used here, the term 'cognition' refers to all the processes by which sensory information is transformed, reduced, elaborated, stored, recovered, and used. It is concerned with these processes even when they operate in the absence of relevant stimulation, as in images and halluci-nations. Such terms as sensation, perception, imagery, retention, recall, problem-solving, and thinking, among many others, refer to hypothetical stages or aspects of cognition. (p. 4)

In such a framework, there is a one-to-one mapping between human thinking or cognition and the computation of a machine: both the mind and the computer 'accept information, manipulate symbols, store items in "memory" and retrieve them again, classify inputs, recognize patterns and so on' (Neisser, 1976, p. 5). Many cognitive psychology textbooks figure this information-processing model textually: the chapters of texts are explicitly laid out, in a systematic progression from the sensible to the intelligible, to follow the transition from perception and sensation, to memory and attention, and to the higher order processes of language, problem-solving and reasoning (e.g. Best, 1992; Lindsay & Norman, 1977; Neisser, 1967). The cognitive revolution in psychology has been overwhelmingly successful. Like behaviourism before it, cognitive psychology now dominates the domain of scientific psychology to the exclusion of any other approach: psychology has become cognition.

In this paper I do not become overly involved in the arguments for and against modelling the mind on computers, as they are already well rehearsed in the literature: Churchland (1986), Dreyfus (1979, 1992) and Searle (1980) all argue against the computer metaphor, although for different reasons; while Pylyshyn (1984), Fodor (1981) and Haugeland (1985) give strong support for the essentially computational nature of mind. My position is not one of scepticism about the computer or cognitive science per se, instead I wish to explore my suspicions about the relation between these two. What is there to love in the computer? What particular attributes make it the desired object for cognitive psychology? What will be at stake is not whether computational theory adequately *describes* the mind, but rather how the mind is constituted through the idea of computation. To what extent does the idea of the computational mind prescribe a rational, discrete and disembodied cognition? How rigorously does such an imperative need to be policed? And in what ways is the contemporary scientific understanding of cognition indebted to a masculine morphology?

I start by considering cognition generally: if this analogy between the computer and cognition is taken seriously, then the problematic of a thinking machine becomes a central consideration. Turing's (1950) test of what could constitute a thinking machine, and thus thinking in general, provides an introduction into the basic presumptions in computational theories of cognition. Specifically it allows us to examine the investments in (dis)embodiment that motivate cognitive science. Following this, I look at one exemplary cognitive theory and model in cognitive psychology: Atkinson and Shiffrin's (1968) theory of memory. Here we see how cognitive theory is often at odds with the empirical models produced to support it: there seems to be an irreducible, interpretative activity in cognitive models that exceeds the serial and disembodied logic of traditional cognitive theory. Here Derrida's formulation of the trace assists us in rethinking the nature of cognitive processing. Finally, I draw on Tausk's (1919/1992) analysis of the influencing machine, and Irigaray's (1985a, 1977/1985b) notion of morphology to examine the masculinist desires hidden in these dominant and problematic understandings of cognition.

Turing, Embodiment and Sexual Difference

> We need not be too concerned about legs, eyes etc. (Turing, 1950, p. 456)

Alan Turing's (1950) paper on computing machinery and intelligence provides a foundation for the information-processing model of cognition, and an illustration of some of its central presumptions. I pursue Turing's test as it discloses its investments in keeping a distance from the corporeal, and in particular from sexual difference. In this seminal paper, Turing outlines a methodology for assessing the question 'Can machines think?': this test (the so-called Turing test) is simply a game of imitation, wherein the conditions for a thinking machine are met when its responses to a set of problems cannot be differentiated from those of a thinking man.[3] The Turing test, then, lays down the parameters within which all subsequent scientific formulations of cognition have been made (Haugeland, 1985).

The test is set up, initially, using three people—a man (A), a woman (B) and an interrogator of unspecified sex (C). The interrogator is in a separate room from the man and the woman, and it is his or her task to determine which of the two is a man and which is a woman on the basis of their (written) answers to certain questions (e.g. 'What is the length of your hair?'). It is A's task to confuse the interrogator (and thus he may lie), and B's task to help (although her truths will be indistinguishable from A's lies). The test proper comes into play by swapping the man (A) with a machine. If the interrogator makes the same sort of judgements, deductions and guesses after this swap as before, that is, if the interrogator is unable to distinguish the machine's answers from the answers of a man, then this particular machine is said to have passed the Turing test. The machine whose behaviour is indistinguishable from the intellect of the man is the machine that thinks.

This idea of cognition is curiously behaviourist (Block, 1990): thinking is simply the behavioural imitation of a man who is presumed to possess certain intellectual capacities. Nonetheless, certain cognitivist axioms about the logical, serial and computational nature of thinking are being articulated here, and by proposing a working definition of human and machine thinking that 'satisfies nearly everyone' (Haugeland, 1985, p. 6), Turing's test has laid the philosophical foundation for most cognitive research that has followed. My goal here is not to discuss these cognitivist axioms directly, but rather to investigate a set of hidden presumptions that render such axioms coherent. Consequently, it is the *method* of Turing's test rather than its intended results that interests me. There are two points to be noted here, and both relate to the disembodied nature of the 'thinking' that Turing promotes.

(A) Cognition and the body. The Turing test is conducted via written or couriered information between the players: there is no bodily, visual or aural contact between the participants. Very early in the paper, Turing (1950) impresses upon us that this arrangement has the particular advantage of being able to draw 'a fairly sharp line' (p. 434) between a man's physical capacities and his intellectual capacities. That is, by separating the players bodily, Turing claims to be able to test a purely intellectual exchange:

> No engineer or chemist claims to be able to produce a material which is indistinguishable from the human skin. It is possible that at some time this might be done, but even supposing this invention available we should feel there was little point in trying to make a 'thinking machine' more human by dressing it up in such artificial flesh. The form in which we have set the problem reflects this fact in the condition which prevents the interrogator from seeing or touching the competitors, or hearing their voices. (Turing, 1950, p. 434)

The thinking that Turing promotes need not be dressed up in flesh. We can know the mind directly, without detour through flesh (real or artificial): we need not see, hear or touch our respondents in order to access their cognitive processes. Grosz (1994) notes that this desire to draw a sharp line between mind and body lies at the heart of traditional Cartesian dualism. No less than Descartes, Turing fancies that we can know the mind without recourse to the body. However, as with the original Cartesian formulation, it is unclear that any such sharp separation of cognition (*res cogitans*) from flesh (*res extensa*) can be made. We must remember that the cleavage between mind and body is not a singular act—it is not a moment that can be definitively and finally enacted. Rather it is a division that always threatens to collapse, or to expose its internal machinations, and must therefore be continuously drawn and redrawn. We can follow this instability thus: in the first instance, the Cartesian–Turing system drains the body of cognitive effect, abandoning it to the mechanism of the reflex arc. A mere conduit for sensation, the body appears to be little more than a system of physiological levers and pulleys. Yet as the body becomes the repository of brute sensation, we see that this is the moment necessary for the production of the mind as pure intellectuality—the essence of the cognizing self. For Descartes and Turing equally, cognition is realized via the constraining and expulsion of flesh: cognition is a discrete, knowable object, subject to its own particular logic and laws, not by virtue of its internal, natural consistency as an object, but through its continual refusal of the flesh. The constitutive paradox here is evident: the autonomy of cognition is compromised by an irreducible and perpetual debt to the body. It is only when the body is fabricated as a benignly non-cognitive entity that Turing's fantasy of a discrete cognitive domain and of pure inter-cognitive communication can be entertained. The sharp line between cognition and flesh reveals itself to be an unstable boundary across which an osmotic balance (mind over body; inside against outside) must be perpetually maintained.

This fantasy of intellectual sovereignty and non-bodily cognitive communion to which the expulsion of the flesh gives rise is a powerful and constitutive one that is repeated again and again in computational cognitive theory. We can find a similar desire for a definitive separation of cognition and the flesh at the very end of Turing's paper. Here Turing embarks on flights of fancy about the possibility of producing a child-machine and educating it in a manner similar to that of a human child. Turing advises us that as far as the education of this computer-child is concerned, we need not be concerned with legs, eyes or the body in general: indeed he proposes a learning method that does not presuppose any sensibility or feeling in the machine. In this educational regime where bodies and sensibility are dispensable, rewards and punishments would become directly intellectual: in radical opposition to the behaviourist paradigm that Turing is drawing on, learning (like cognition in general) bypasses the body altogether. Somewhat surprisingly, Turing supports his argument for the optional nature of legs, eyes, etc., to the cognizing child-machine by comparing its education to that of Helen Keller: as if the deaf, blind and mute body is no body at all. A more careful consideration of the education of Helen Keller would perhaps demonstrate that she was completely dependent on her seemingly non-cognitive body (particularly her hands) for thought and communication, and this would return us to a more careful and sophisticated understanding of the relation of cognition to flesh.

This desire to separate body from cognition, sensibility from intellec-tuality, is the scene within which the Turing test becomes coherent: indeed, it is the *only* scene within which it is coherent. If the Turing test is the cornerstone of contemporary cognitive theory, then we can see that the scientific study of thinking has been premised on the expulsion of the corporeal, even as it must always return to the body as its touchstone for intelligibility. As we shall see below, it is not simply that Turing *chooses* to make a separation between mind and body, which would presuppose that we could simply choose otherwise and reinsert the body back into the field of cognition. More significantly, it would appear that the very idea of cognition requires an expulsion of the body from the psychological domain. We find that this raises complex and difficult questions about the nature of our political interventions into cognitive psychology.

(B) Cognition and sexual difference. There is a subtle but important transition in the players in Turing's game. Specifically, there is a double displacement of the female player and the corporeality she comes to represent. The Turing test starts with a comparison between the intellect of a man and a woman. This coupling is displaced, and the test proper is enacted through a comparison of the absented man and the machine that has replaced him—the female participant becoming peripheral to the main focus of the test. This displacement is enacted a second time, later on in the paper, when Turing—without explanation—replaces the female respondent with a man. What was initially a differentiation between a man and a woman, and then between a man and a computer (the female respondent having been sidelined), is now streamlined further by ridding the test of the female respondent altogether. She is replaced by a male respondent, and the test is now a direct comparison by the interrogator between this man and a computer. Once this change has been effected Turing (1950) considers 'the ground to have been cleared and we are ready to proceed to the debate on our question "Can machines think?"' (p. 442). But by what means has the ground been cleared, and to what effect?

It would seem that the reason why Turing fine-tunes the test in this way is that the female participant has become excessive and distracting to the goals of the test. Turing has introduced sexual difference at the beginning of the test as a question of significance, yet he removes it at the point it begins to encroach on the definition of cognition itself. We could ask why this comparison between the sexes was chosen over some other difference: what is it about the difference between a woman and man that makes it a self-evident and natural choice for Turing's game? Rather than simply being an arbitrary choice, it seems to me that deliberations over sexual difference are (hidden) at the very core of theories of cognition.[4] That is, Turing enacts cognition through an embodiment that can be shared by a computer and a man but not by a woman (as I argue in more detail later on, computation and the masculine are iso-morphic—they share the same morphological structure). The ground of cognition is cleared (and thus forged) by removing the sexual specificity of the female body. With Irigaray (1977/1985b) we could argue that the Turing test is less a dispassionate and logical process than it is a hom(m)osexual exchange between man and his self-same computer. It is the management of the body of the female respondent that allows this exchange between computer and man to occur: Turing's cognitive economy emerges from the movement of the female respondent's body in and out of the field of cognition.

My focus, however, is less on the love of the computer per se (e.g. that there is a narcissistic or masturbatory relation between men and computers, or amongst men through computers) than it is on the product of that love: cognition. Cognition is rendered manifest at that moment when the female participant becomes the receptacle for the corporeal and is expelled outside the hom(m)osocial pact of thinking beings. This process is not simply incidental to the constitution of cognition, rather this containment of the corporeal to the feminine, and its subsequent displacement, are the very means by which cognition is produced. We can say, then, that cognition is the projection of the masculine desire to be free of the body: while ostensibly an anti-dualistic attempt to mechanize the mind (Newell & Simon, 1972), cognition is simply a reinstantiation of the Cartesian desire for the kernel of man to be pure intellectuality.

The theories of cognition that now dominate cognitive psychology owe much of their coherence to Turing's test. However, these theories also have a number of other historical determinants, most of which overlap with the historical precedents that led to the development of artificial intelligence, and all of which take the processes of mind to be isomorphic with the laws of a binary logic. For example, George Boole, a 19th-century British mathematician, devised a formal system (developed further by Whitehead and Russell) wherein components of thought could be substituted with algebraic symbols which were subject to certain irrevocable principles of logic. Importantly, he considered that any one of these components of thought could be deemed either true or false and thus expressed as either a 1 or a 0 (a presence or an absence). This allowed the much later development of the binary code (based on the binary digit) that served as the foundation for 20th-century computing science (Gardner, 1987; Newell & Simon, 1972).

Under the influence of logical positivism (especially Carnap), McCulloch and Pitts (1943/1988) applied this same binary principle to the neuron. A neuron could be conceived as a logical proposition: either true or false, either firing or not. The firing of successive neurons could be considered isomorphic to the flow of logical deduction from proposition to proposition in an argument:

> The 'all-or-none' law of nervous activity is sufficient to insure that the activity of any neuron may be represented as a proposition. Physiological relations existing among nervous activities correspond, of course, to relations among propositions; and the utility of the representation depends upon the identity of these relations with those of the logic of propositions. To each reaction of any neuron there is a corresponding assertion of a simple proposition. This, in turn, implies either some other simple proposition of the disjunction or the conjunction, with or without negation, of similar propositions, according to the configuration of the synapses upon and the threshold of the neuron in question. (McCulloch & Pitts, 1943/1988, p. 21)

It was this sort of work, combined with the advent of electronic calculating machines, that brought together the neuron, electricity and logic and ensured the dominance of rationalist, logic-driven and disembodied theories of mind. As such, computational theories of mind are implicated in a binary tradition that hierarchizes and differentially values its terms. Turing's test presents cognition not as a neutral term in a politically and historically innocent philosophy, but as the privileged term in a philosophy that already names the (female) body inferior and non-psychological. We can consider the dualistic division of mind from body, cognition from affect, and intellect from sensibility to be isomorphic with the binary relations of true or false, on or off, present or absent, all or none; and a critique of one necessarily implicates the other. Turing's division of cognition from the flesh, and McCulloch and Pitts' all-or-none logical neuron, are simply different manifestations of the same philosophical economy.

Atkinson and Shiffrin: Embodying Cognitive Theory

The theory of cognition articulated by Turing and others has been extremely influential in psychology. Nonetheless, the relocation of cognition within explicitly empirical contexts (which I take to be a process of *situating* or *embodying* cognition) has effected a crucial shift in its formulation. Once positioned within particular empirical models, cognition becomes more active and interpretative than the clean logic of Turing, Boole, McCulloch and Pitts would have anticipated. My goal here is to show, briefly, how the

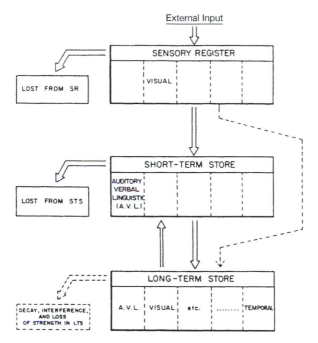

FIGURE 1. Structure of the memory system (Atkinson & Schiffrin, 1968, p.93)

neat, logical and systematic cognition that is explicated in the philosophy of cognition becomes somewhat disorderly and uncontainable once instantiated as a theory of memory. We will find that there is a certain excessive, interpretative element to cognition as articulated in these empirical models that disrupts the attempts to produce a contained, locatable and rational mind. The more any particular model of cognition is made to approximate human thinking, the more difficult it is to maintain the projective fantasy of cognition as an autonomous, logical process.

In psychology, the information-processing model holds that the processes of human cognition are isomorphic with the logical processing of information found in a computational program. According to Matlin (1989), human cognition can be understood as the *acquisition*, *storage* and *retrieval* of information. Information is assumed to move through a sequence of mental operations in much the same way that data are processed by a program. For Wessells (1982) the relation between information processing and human cognition is one of equivalence: 'cognitive psychology is the science of human information-processing' (p. 1).

Perhaps the exemplary information-processing model in psychology is Atkinson and Shiffrin's (1968) classic, but now outdated, multi-store model of memory (see Figure 1). Drawing on the flow diagram paradigm brought from information theory to psychology by Broadbent (1958), Atkinson and Shiffrin model human memory processes through a distinction between structure (which is analogous to computer hardware) and control processes (analogous to computer software). Briefly, information is assumed to enter the information-processing system via the senses, and these sensory data are immediately recorded by the *sensory register*. Information is held in this register for only a very short period of time (up to a few hundred milliseconds). Information is either lost entirely from the system or it is transferred to the next stage—*short-term store* (or working memory). As in the sensory register, information is held here only for very short periods of time, although it can be retained longer than in the sensory store especially if the information is rehearsed. From here information is either lost from the system or it is transferred to the last stage—*long-term store*, where information can be stored permanently.

The flow of information between stores is not a process of passive conduction (where the information is carried along as if on a conveyor belt); rather information moves between stores as an effect of serial copying:

> Note that by information flow and transfer between stores we refer to the same process: the copying of selected information from one store into the next. This copying takes place without the transferred information being removed from the original store. The information remains in the store from which it is transferred and decays according to the decay characteristics of that store. (Atkinson & Shiffrin, 1968, p. 94)

It is in this description that we can see perhaps the most important, but also the most volatile aspect of theories of cognition: cognition is an active process. This activity of a cognitive system was one of the key differences between the old behaviourist paradigm of psychological processing and the new cognitive models (Neisser, 1967). Where previously the organism and its behaviour were the mere effects of stimulus–response associations, cognitive models posit a system that actively transforms the information presented to it. As Atkinson and Shiffrin suggest, information is not passively carried through the cognitive system, rather it is transformed at every stage through the processes of selection, copying and transfer. These processes are in turn controlled by other cognitive systems already in operation: language, attention, socially and culturally specific systems of beliefs and expectations. The information that is selected and copied is always a function of what is already deemed to be important by the cognitive system as a whole.

The status of the trace in such a cognitive system clearly demonstrates the actively interpretative nature of these processes. Where early cognitive *theory* presumed a discrete and autonomous trace that is manipulated according to logical rules, early cognitive *models* in psychology produced a trace that is manufactured by the vicissitudes of transformation and interpretation. As information is copied and transferred through different memory stores, the cognitive trace (or the mark of processing) is continually being remade. In the sensory store,

> . . . a visual stimulus leaves a more or less photographic trace which decays during a period of several hundred milliseconds and is subject to masking and replacement by succeeding stimulation (Atkinson & Shiffrin, 1968, p. 95)

This 'more or less photographic' trace is then copied, transferred, copied and transferred before it reaches long-term memory. Traces in long-term store are then subject to interference and decay, and their accurate retrieval cannot be guaranteed. To this end, there is no one trace that persists throughout processing, and the trace which is laid down in long-term memory has an interpretative, rather than direct, relation to the original environmental stimulus. Any cognitive trace is always already a copy: first a copy, in the sensory store, of an external stimulus, and then a copy, in subsequent memory stores, whose 'origin' has long since decayed. In Atkinson and Shiffrin's model, cognition is a process built not on the logic of on or off, all-or-none, but on the vicissitudes of a transcriptive process without origin or end.

Derrida has already suggested how we might account for such a process. While both Derrida and cognitive psychology take the trace to be the origin of the psyche, the issue at stake here is *what sort of trace* each places at the origin. The trace of traditional cognitive psychology is a full and locatable presence. Even though it might not be directly observable, this trace is presumed to be a presence that exists as a discrete, definable and self-contained entity in the cognitive machinery. Indeed, this trace is the means by which that machinery operates—it is that which is transformed by the information-processing mechanisms. In a full and mature cognitive science, the vicissitudes of cognition will be reducible to the movements of such traces in the cognitive apparatus.

The Derridean trace, intimately tied to a critique of the Saussurian sign (Derrida, 1967/1974) and certain psycho-neurological texts (Derrida, 1967/1978), is another matter altogether. While also placed at the origin of the psyche, it is mobilized, explicitly, to contest both the notion of an origin, and the idea that any psychical entity or structure can be fully present, knowable and located. Occupying an undecidable space between cognitive presence and absence (being containable to neither, yet nonetheless resident in both), the Derridean trace unhinges a metaphysical psychology that relies on the distinction and opposition of presence and absence, on and off, inside and outside. When such a trace, neither fully present, nor completely absent, is placed at the origin of the psyche, the very notion of an origin and the structure of the psyche itself are radically contested. No longer a locatable site of certainty, the trace-as-origin is put under erasure. Derrida explicates the movements of this trace under the name *différance*:

> What is written as *différance*, then, will be the playing movement that 'produces'—by means of something that is not simply an activity—these differences, these effects of differences. This does not mean that the *différance* that produces differences is somehow before them, in a simple and unmodified—in-different—present. *Différance* is the non-full, non-simple, structured and differentiating origin of differences. Thus, the name 'origin' no longer suits it. (Derrida, 1972/1982, p. 11)

The Derridean trace is not an inert presence-identity which either causes or refutes cognitive presence. It cannot become an object of scientific inquiry; which is not to say that it is absent, enigmatic or immaterial. The trace 'appears' only by effacing itself: the only possible trace is the trace under erasure. Bennington (1991/1993) summarizes in a way that reminds us of Atkinson and Shiffrin's empirical model: 'Every trace is a trace of a trace' (p. 75). Any other notion of the trace simply repeats and perpetuates the traditional metaphysical desire for presence:

> An unerasable trace is not a trace, it is a full presence, an immobile and incorruptible substance, a son of God . . . (Derrida, 1967/1978, p. 230)

Bennington (1991/1993) comments further that the Derridean trace definitively rejects any interpretation of psychical elements as present atomistic features out of which larger and more complete psychical structures can be built (the name 'origin' no longer suits it). The trace, via Derrida (and as it is alluded to in Atkinson and Shiffrin, but never fully exploited), is not a solid and immobile substance from which larger structures could be built, nor is it the determining origin to which a system may be reduced. The trace, as *différance*, exceeds the expectations and delimitations of an empirical trace: the trace of traditional cognitivism is the result of an obstruction or congealing of the processes of *différance*.

While empirical models push us further towards a recognition of cognition's interpretive nature, cognitive theory in general fails to fully capitalize on this recognition. While every psychological model of memory since Bartlett (1932) establishes the essentially reconstitutive and interpretive processes of memory, cognitive theorists still insist on placing a non-interpretive, logic-driven process at the centre of their models. Atkinson and Shiffrin acknowledge the interpretive nature of cognitive processing, but the full theoretical implications of this remain repressed in their work. This remains a widespread disavowal in contemporary cognitive psychology. Cognition is not the product of a binary and restrictive logic, it is a process that is active, reconstructive, cultural, embodied, affective, non-conscious, non-unitary and over-determined. Cognition is a process which of *necessity* is embodied as the active interpretation of sensory information through pre-existing internal states and pre-existing external systems. These processes are not peripheral or secondary to an essentially logic-driven process, *they are the very mechanisms of cognition itself.*

The traditional logic of cognitive theory is disrupted when the processes of cognition are embodied in systems of memory, in a broader cognitive network, and in social, interpretive systems. The fantasy of cognition as an autonomous, logical, disembodied process cannot be sustained once efforts are made to explicate this process in empirical contexts. If the tradition of information processing has been unable to reliably predict, explain or simulate anything but the most basic (and, frankly, uninteresting) aspects of human psychology (as Neisser, 1976, has argued at length), this is not because this science is not yet fully developed. The difficulties here are not empirical, they are philosophical: the limits of these cognitive models are reached because they pursue an inert and disembodied psyche. Powerful as such models are, they will always be exceeded by their own internal and interpretive processing.

Morphology and the Influencing Machine

The information-processing model assumes that cognition is autonomous, logical and disembodied: affect, culture, flesh and sexual difference are exterior to the essence of the thinking man. Miller and Gazzaniga (1984) note that this division between cognition (knowing), conation (willing) and affection (feeling) is inherited from the western philosophical system within which contemporary cognitive science operates, but they make no move to render such a division problematic. Likewise, Gardner (1987) considers this division benign, and more methodological than constitutive:

> Though mainstream cognitive scientists do not necessarily bear any animus against the affective realm, against the context that surrounds any action or thought, or against historical or cultural analyses, in practice they attempt to factor out these elements to the maximum extent possible. . . . This may be a question of practicality: if one were to take into account these individualizing and phenomenalistic elements, cognitive science might well became impossible. (p. 41)

Gardner is indeed correct to suppose that the body, culture and the affective realm would make *this particular* cognitive science impossible: the cognition that lies at the centre of this particular cognitive science, the cognition of the disembodied intellect, would indeed be incapacitated by these 'peripheral' concerns. That these 'peripheral' concerns must be explicitly and repeatedly excluded from the cognitive domain suggests that their relation to a clearly delineated cognition is not one of secondariness, but rather one of foundational importance. These exclusionary practices show that other types of cognitive systems, and other types of cognitive science, may be possible; but they are possible only at the cost of the primacy of cognition as an affectless, logical and disembodied process. We are left to ask whose cognitive science is this? Whose desires does it privilege?

I have argued here that this process of containment and exclusion is constitutive of cognition. Embodiment and interpretation are not simply missing or forgotten ingredients that could, perhaps, be added back in—their exclusion is the necessary condition for the coherence of cognitive science as we now know it. Our political and epistemological responses to cognitive science need to acknowledge the constitutive effects of this corporeal exclusion, but this should not be our only concern. We also need to examine what these processes of exclusion attempt to cover over: that is, that cognition has divested itself of only a certain kind of embodiment. Cognition's apparent disembodiment masks a more fundamental embodiment: the masculine body, disavowed, is at the core of cognitive theory. Cognition *is* embodied, but only via a *masculine* morphology masquerading as neutrality itself. It is the desires and projections of a masculine corporeality that are the motive force within theories of cognition.

In order to fully develop such an analysis, we need to detour through Luce Irigaray's formulation of the imaginary and morphology. Irigaray draws her use of the imaginary from a number of different sources, but predominantly from psychoanalysis (Lacan and Freud) and phenomenology (particularly Merleau-Ponty). The Irigarayan imaginary borrows both the notion of unconscious fantasy from Lacan's mirror stage and the phenomenological accounts of conscious imagination and imaging. Exceeding the distinction between the conscious and unconscious, the imaginary, as used by Irigaray, is a lived and dynamic assemblage of psycho-corporeal parameters within which the subject is constituted (Grosz, 1989; Whitford, 1991). For Irigaray, unlike these earlier psychoanalytic and phenomenological accounts, the imaginary is always sexed, and thus also marked by morphology:

> [Irigaray] conceptualizes the imaginary in terms of sex, either male or female: the imaginary either bears the morphological marks of the male body, whose cultural products are characterized by unity, teleology, linearity, self-identity, and so on, or it bears the morphological marks of the female body, characterized by plurality, non-linearity, fluid identity and so on. (Whitford, 1991, p. 54)

For Irigaray, no knowledge is ever sexually neutral: it will always carry the inscription of the sexed imaginary from which it has emerged. By naming man as the common force behind universal scientific truth, Irigaray (1985a) suggests that scientific pursuits are vitally connected to the male imaginary: 'That which purports to be universal is equivalent to the ideolect of men and to the male imaginary' (p. 77). Dispassion is thus revealed to be fervently masculine, and neutrality to be the exemplary masculine partiality. The principal characteristics of this male imaginary bear the marks of a phallic morphology: 'production, property, order, form, unity, visibility, erection' (p. 77). This male imaginary operates through the domination of stability and solidity, at the expense of difference, reciprocity, exchange, permeability or fluidity (Irigaray, 1977/1985b). In a word, it is phallo-centric.

It is my contention here that cognition without a body, driven by logical constraints, and separated from the contaminating influence of sexual difference, is the product of a male imaginary and is isomorphic with a masculine morphology. Irigaray (1977/1985b) has argued that there has been 'a complicity of long standing between rationality and a mechanics of solids' (p. 107). That is, rationality operates in an economy respectful only of containment, fixity and certitude. Theories of cognition have been thoroughly subordinated to this economy. The classical theories of discrete cognitive traces inside fixed cognitive spaces have manufactured cognition as an exemplary object of masculine desire: this computation of locatable traces in fixed locales guarantees a mind that is discrete, reasonable, knowable, containable and safe. The coagulation of trace-as-*différance* has been the key to this cognitive production. The fixed and lifeless trace that we have found installed at the heart of computational discourses is the projection of a phallic morphology: an immobile and solid body.

To say that cognition is constituted through a masculine morphology is not to imply that there is some fundamental masculinity that pre-determines all cognitive possibilities: it is not to say that cognition or thinking, in general, are somehow essentially masculine. Instead it is to argue that there is a certain, sexed structure to cognition that remains masked. In particular, it is to insist that this sexed structuration is possible only through the repression of a feminine morphology. Cognition is the product of a phallic economy of containment, reserve and conservation that operates at the expense of the psyche's interpretive mobility. Irigaray (1977/1985b) reminds us that psychical systems have never been neutral, but are always indebted to a disavowed masculinity that ingests, represses or excludes other morphological forms:

> Thus if every psychic economy is organized around the phallus (or Phallus), we may ask what this primacy owes to a teleology of reabsorption of fluid in a solidified form. ... From there to standardizing the psychic mechanism according to laws that subject sexuality to the absolute power of form. ... For isn't that what we are still talking about? And how, so long as this prerogative lasts, can any articulation of sexual difference be possible? *Since what is in excess with respect to form—for example, the feminine sex—is necessarily rejected as beneath or beyond the system currently in force.* (Irigaray, 1977/1985b, pp. 110–111)

If cognition has indeed been produced according to the demands of a male imaginary and morphology, then this will shatter our confidence in the neutrality of cognition and propel us towards a number of political interventions into cognitive psychology's authority. Our goal, however, is not to posit an 'Irigarayan' cognition that is fluid and indeterminate, and that somehow avoids the violences and repressions of this phallic solidity: there is no natural or pre-discursive psychical fluidity to which our formulations could return. The return of the repressed is never a revelation of an unaffected innocence, and we will not be able to so easily escape the constraints of this phallic certitude. Instead our goal is to disrupt the containment and certainty of this neutral cognition, and, through the small and unlikely movements and ruptures that appear (as in Atkinson and Shiffrin), begin a re-imagining of the cognitive. Such a politics seeks to open a mobility at the heart of cognitive certitude and location, and to pursue a lability and labiality that is no longer containable as cognition's repressed foundation.

In this way, feminist interventions into cognitive psychology will find themselves radically reoriented. Questions of cognitive differences or simi- larities between groups (boys vs girls; men vs women) will be displaced as our primary concern as cognition itself emerges as the hitherto unrecognized problematic. If cognition emerges through a series of masculine presump- tions and commitments, then feminist responses to cognitive theory need to be something other than the pursuit of a kind of cognitive androgyny, where cognition is rendered equally emotional and rational, equally passionate and logical. Perhaps our most pressing task at this point is to initiate a systematic interrogation of the philosophical system that disavows the bodily and masculine nature of cognition itself.

The love of the computer exposes the bodily nature of cognition. There is a fertile nexus here between morphology, technology and cognition that is worth pursuing briefly. It is no secret, nor does it appear to be cause for serious concern, that the mind was modelled on a series of different technological objects (e.g. hydraulic machines, the telephone switchboard, the hologram) before the computer emerged as the current darling of cognitive science (Gardner, 1987). Moreover, as the neuropsychologist Karl Lashley has astutely observed, there is 'a curious parallel' between the history of such theories and the delusions of paranoia:

> In Mesmer's day the paranoid was persecuted by malicious animal magnet-
> ism, his successors by galvanic shocks, by the telegraph, by radio, and by
> radar, keeping their delusional states up to date with the latest fashions in
> physics. (Lashley, 1951, in Cobb, 1960, p. xix)

If there is a link between technology and delusion, there is also a link between technology, delusion and projective fantasies of the body. Victor Tausk (1919/1992), in an accomplished psychoanalytic interpretation of the influencing machine in paranoid delusions, hypothesizes a close relation between the nature of the influencing machine and the patient's own body. An influencing machine is a delusionary device, usually located some distance from the patient (e.g. in another city), that the patient claims is influencing his or her thoughts and actions. Influencing machines are almost always mechanical, and at the time of Tausk's writing seemingly always operated by men. Tausk was fortunate enough to observe the genesis and transformation of an influencing machine in a young woman—a process which revealed the corporeal foundation of the influencing machinery. Initially manifest in human-like form, over the course of some weeks the patient's influencing machine became more and more mechanical until it lost any resemblance to her own body.

This transformation suggested to Tausk that every influencing machine is a projection of the patient's own body onto the world. Moreover, the libido motivating this projection has regressed to an infantile (genital) stage where the body is traversed by numerous erotogenic zones: thus the body projected is the fantastic body of the pre-Oedipal realm. This means that the influencing machine is both the projection of the entire body, and a projection of the genitalia. That the projection is overdetermined in this manner is explained by the fact that the libido invested in the influencing machine is the libido of the pre-genital stage where the whole body is polymorphously perverse—'I am wholly a genital' (Tausk, 1919/1992, p. 564).

That the body becomes a machine is a defence against this libidinal regression, and its infantile, genital determination:

> The patient obviously seeks not to recognize herself in the influencing machine, and thus, in self-protection, she disinvests it of all human features; in short, the less human the appearance of the delusion, the less does she recognize herself in it. (Tausk, 1919/1992, p. 552)

Without wanting to make too much of the similarities between paranoid delusions and the processes of scientific discovery, it is worth noting that the processes of projection and disavowal cannot be contained within the domain of psychopathology. We have already seen that the human computational machine is simultaneously a projection of a certain fantasy of embodiment (specifically the masculine fantasy to be free of the body), and a disavowal of that projection. Moreover, these fantasies and disavowals are made manifest by an imaginary which is grounded in a phallic morphology. A historical analysis of the metaphorical lineage from hydraulic machine to computer would no doubt find a certain similarity in these objects that make them so appropriate for the task of representing cognition: specifically, a certain disembodiment, a containable rationality, and a direct, observable and measurable cognitive cause and effect that requires no appeal to unconscious or infantile motivations—all of which we are compelled to recognize as morphologically phallic characteristics. Embodying a masculine infantile genital wish (for control, linearity, autonomy and passage in the world of men), the computational machine of cognitive theory is an influencing machine, of sorts. Disinvested of its bodily features, the computer serves a similar purpose to the paranoiac's machine: the machinery of cognitive theory expresses, in disguised form, a variety of masculine infantile wishes about the world and about the self. As Tausk (1919/1992) himself argued:

> The machines produced by man's ingenuity and created in the image of man are unconscious projections of man's bodily structure. Man's ingenuity seems to be unable to free itself from its relations to the unconscious. (p. 569)

Conclusion

Like the pathological symptom, which can never fully eradicate its own unconscious genealogy, the machinery of cognition will always betray its investments and desires. It is our task to exploit these moments of unconscious disclosure. The cognitive machinery of scientific psychology is neither innocent nor neutral. The desire to be free from the body, to be rid of sexual difference, and to create computer-children outside the constraints of flesh and femininity are, of course, the aspirations of a peculiarly masculine logic. The instantiation of cognition in empirical models likewise betrays an overriding concern with stasis, presence and solidity that I have named phallic.

Cognition is not impartial ground. Feminist interventions that are not sufficiently wary of the partiality of the field of cognition in general will find themselves unable to effectively challenge the authority of the questions that this field and the emerging neuro-cognitive sciences present to us. For this reason, the central political issue for feminists working in the cognitive domain may be less one of how to adjudicate over readily identifiable sex differences in cognition than it is a recognition that cognition itself is the product of a more subtle play of sexual difference. What we may find at the very heart of cognitive theories of perception, memory, attention, language and imagery is not a neutral and dispassionate science, but the affects and sensations of the body of the thinking man.

Notes

Figure 1 is from 'Human Memory: A Proposed System and Its Control Processes', by R.C. Atkinson and R.M. Shiffrin, 1968, in K.W. Spence and J.I. Spence (Eds.), *The Psychology of Learning and Motivation: Advances in Research and Theory* (Vol. 2, p. 93), New York: Academic Press. Reproduced with permission of authors and publisher.

1. A few words about terminology: I use the words *mind*, *cognition* and *psyche* separately and differently. I take the idea of *mind* to be indebted primarily to a traditional philosophy of mind, which has usually envisaged psychological processes in opposition to a static and conventionalized account of the body. I take *cognition* to be the contemporary scientific instantiation of mind: cognition

refers to the highly abstracted, and presumably logical, processes of thinking, reasoning, problem-solving, pattern recognition, etc. I use the terms 'mind' and 'cognition' to refer to the idea of psychology that is entailed in each of these traditions. I take *psyche* to be a rather old-fashioned term that has lost currency in many contemporary contexts. I use the term 'psyche' (calling on its lexical connection to psychoanalysis) where I am attempting to cut across the narrow understanding of psychology entailed by mind and cognition. Specifically I use the term to refer to the type of psychology that would be articulated through the more generalized and subversive notion of embodiment.

2. Most opinions on the birth of contemporary cognitive science converge on the date that the *Symposium on Information Theory* was held at MIT: September 1956 (Gardner, 1987; Newell & Simon, 1972). The program at this symposium included Newell and Simon's presentation of the Logic Theory Machine; Chomsky's new grammar based on information theory; and George Miller's influential paper on the capacity of short-term memory (the 'magic number seven'). This symposium was widely seen as having brought to fruition the promised new science that had been evident since the Lashley, von Neumann and McCulloch papers at the *Hixon Symposium* at the California Institute of Technology in 1948 (Jeffress, 1951). This new cognitive science brought together research and theory from cybernetics, computer technology, information theory, formal logic and neuropsychology to form an authoritative hybrid domain. In the 40 years since, cognitive science has influenced a wide range of disciplinary knowledges, and has emerged as a powerful interdisciplinary field.

3. The Turing test resurfaced in 1991, when Hugh Loebner (a sociology graduate, Founder of the Cambridge Center for Behavioral Studies and owner of a business that manufactures portable plastic-lighted disco dance floors) offered $10,000 to the first person who could write a program that would pass the test. The so-called 'Loebner Contest' is now an annual event, and is directed by Robert Epstein (a behavioural psychologist). No program has yet passed the test. See 'What's It Mean to be Human, Anyway?', *Wired*, 3.04, April 1995.

4. For further discussion concerning the relation of sexual difference and sexuality to the Turing test, see Halberstam (1991) and Helmreich (1995).

References

Atkinson, R.C., & Shiffrin, R.M. (1968). Human memory: A proposed system and its control processes. In K.W. Spence & J.T. Spence (Eds.), *The psychology of learning and motivation: Advances in research and theory* (Vol. 2, pp. 89–195). New York: Academic Press.

Baron, R.J. (1987). *The cerebral computer: An introduction to the computational structure of the human brain*. Hillsdale, NJ: Erlbaum.

Bartlett, F.C. (1932). *Remembering: A study in experimental and social psychology*. Cambridge: Cambridge University Press.

Bennington, G. (1993). Derridabase. In G. Bennington (Trans.) & J. Derrida, *Jacques Derrida*. Chicago, IL: Chicago University Press. (Original work published 1991.)

Best, J.B. (1992). *Cognitive psychology* (3rd ed.). St Paul, MN: West.

Block, N. (1990). The computer metaphor of the mind. In D.N. Osherson & E.E. Smith (Eds.), *Thinking: An invitation to cognitive science* (Vol. 3, pp. 247–289). Cambridge, MA: MIT Press.

Broadbent, D.E. (1958). *Perception and communication.* New York: Pergamon.

Churchland, P.S. (1986). *Neurophilosophy: Toward a unified science of the mind/ brain.* Cambridge, MA: MIT Press.

Churchland, P.S., & Sejnowski, T.J. (1992). *The computational brain.* Cambridge, MA: MIT Press.

Cobb, S. (1960). A salute from neurologists. In F.A. Beach, D.O. Hebb, C.T. Morgan, & H.W. Nissen (Eds.), *The neuropsychology of Lashley: Selected papers of K.S. Lashley* (pp. xvii–xx). New York: McGraw-Hill.

Derrida, J. (1974). *Of grammatology* (G. Spivak, Trans.). Baltimore, MD: Johns Hopkins University Press. (Original work published 1967.)

Derrida, J. (1978). Freud and the scene of writing. In *Writing and difference* (A. Bass, Trans.) (pp. 196–231). Chicago, IL: University of Chicago Press. (Original work published 1967.)

Derrida, J. (1982). Différance. In *Margins of philosophy* (A. Bass, Trans.) (pp. 3–27). Chicago, IL: University of Chicago Press. (Original work published 1972.)

Dreyfus, H. (1979). *What computers can't do: The limits of artificial intelligence* (Rev ed.). New York: Harper & Row.

Dreyfus, H. (1992). *What computers still can't do: A critique of artificial reason.* Cambridge, MA: MIT Press.

Fodor, J.A. (1981). *Representations.* Cambridge, MA: MIT Press.

Gardner, H. (1987). *The mind's new science: A history of the cognitive revolution* (Rev. ed.). New York: Basic Books.

Gluck, M.A., & Rumelhart, D.E. (Eds.). (1990). *Neuroscience and connectionist theory.* Hillsdale, NJ: Erlbaum.

Grosz, E. (1989). *Sexual subversions: Three French feminists.* Sydney: Allen & Unwin.

Grosz, E. (1994). *Volatile bodies: Toward a corporeal feminism.* Bloomington: Indiana University Press.

Halberstam, J. (1991). Automating gender. Postmodern feminism in the age of the intelligent machine. *Feminist Studies, 17*(3), 439–460.

Hare-Mustin, R.T., & Marecek, J. (Eds.). (1990). *Making a difference: Psychology and the construction of gender.* New Haven, CT: Yale University Press.

Haugeland, J. (1985). *Artificial intelligence: The very idea.* Cambridge, MA: MIT Press.

Helmreich, S. (1995). *Anthropology inside and outside the looking-glass worlds of artificial life.* Unpublished doctoral dissertation, Stanford University.

Irigaray, L. (1985a). Is the subject of science sexed? (E. Oberle, Trans.). *Cultural Critique, 1*(1), 73–88.

Irigaray, L. (1985b). *This sex which is not one* (C. Porter, Trans.). Ithaca, NY: Cornell University Press. (Original work published 1977.)

Jeffress, L.A. (Ed.). (1951). *Cerebral mechanisms in behavior: The Hixon symposium.* New York: John Wiley.

Kosslyn, S.M., & Koenig, O. (1992). *Wet mind: The new cognitive neuroscience.* New York: Free Press.

Lindsay, P.H., & Norman, D.A. (1977). *Human information processing: An introduction to psychology* (2nd ed.). New York: Academic Press.

Luria, A. (1973). *The working brain* (B. Haigh, Trans.). New York: Basic Books. (Original work published 1973.)

Maccoby, E.E., & Jacklin, C.N. (1974). *The psychology of sex differences*. Stanford, CA: Stanford University Press.

Matlin, M.W. (1989). *Cognition* (2nd ed.). New York: Holt, Rinehart & Winston.

McCulloch, W.S., & Pitts, W.H. (1988). A logical calculus of the ideas immanent in nervous activity. In W.S. McCulloch, *Embodiments of mind* (pp. 19–39). Cambridge, MA: MIT Press. (Original work published 1943.)

Miller, G.A., & Gazzaniga, M.S. (1984). The cognitive sciences. In M.S. Gazzaniga (Ed.), *Handbook of cognitive neuroscience* (pp. 3–11). New York: Plenum.

Neisser, U. (1967). *Cognitive psychology*. New York: Appleton-Century-Crofts.

Neisser, U. (1976). *Cognition and reality: Principles and implications of cognitive psychology*. San Francisco: CA Freeman.

Newell, A., & Simon, H.A. (1972). *Human problem solving*. Englewood Cliffs, NJ: Prentice Hall.

Pylyshyn, Z.W. (1984). *Computation and cognition: Toward a foundation for cognitive science*. Cambridge, MA: MIT Press.

Rumelhart, D.E., McClelland, J.L., & the PDP Research Group (1986). *Parallel distributed processing: Explorations in the microstructure of cognition* (Vols. 1–2). Cambridge, MA: MIT Press.

Searle, J. (1980). Minds, brains, and programs. *Behavioral and Brain Sciences, 3*, 417–424.

Sperry, R.W. (1982). Some effects of disconnecting the cerebral hemispheres. *Science, 217*, 1223–1226.

Tausk, V. (1992) The influencing machine (D. Feigenbaum, Trans.). In J. Crary & S. Kwinter (Eds.), *Incorporations* (pp. 542–569). New York: Zone. (Original work published 1919.)

Turing, A.M. (1950). Computing machinery and intelligence. *Mind, 59*(236), 433–460.

Wessells, M. (1982). *Cognitive psychology*. New York: Harper & Row.

What's it mean to be human, anyway? (1995, April). *Wired, 3.04*.

Whitford, M. (1991). *Luce Irigaray: Philosophy in the feminine*. London: Routledge.

Wilson, E. (1995). Knowing women: The limits of feminist psychology. In B. Caine & R. Pringle (Eds.), *Transitions: New Australian feminisms* (pp. 29–41). Sydney: Allen & Unwin.

6

Feminism, Psychology and Matters of the Body

Betty M. Bayer and Kareen Ror Malone

ABSTRACT. Psychology's renewed interest in the body, even within feminist theory, has brought with it several philosophical and theoretical challenges. These challenges stem mainly from questions about how to celebrate a return to the body when conceptions of the meaning of 'woman' have been tied historically to women's bodies. That is, for feminists, any return to the body requires a two-fold examination. It requires first an inquiry into the part of reigning epistemological assumptions in psychology's fastening of women's bodies to women's psyches, and its construction of women's psychological problems as rooted in their bodies. And, second, it necessi-tates attention to those ways in which women's bodies have confronted age-old mind–body splits. Only by this twinned appreciation of the body both as the site of oppression and as the possibility for emancipation can feminists move beyond repeating yet another variation of woman as body.

Art historian Nanette Salomon (1996) turns her feminist critical gaze onto that classical nude female figure, the *Venus Pudica*. Tracing this female nude form back to sculptor Praxiteles' Aphrodite, Salomon seeks to 'make strange' western art's manifold reproductions of this subject/pose/gesture of a female nude whose hand is placed over her pubis. To 'make strange' is to pose this female subject differently, to inquire into those conventions—social, cultural and historical—that solidify the pudica gesture as synec-doche for 'woman'. Despite the derivation of the word pudica from 'pudenda', whose meaning conflates shame and genitalia, the pudica pose, most commonly taken to mean 'modest pose', seems to resist any definitive resolution. This is because, as Salomon argues, the pudica gesture can be read both as one of pointing (to sexuality or powers of fertility) and as one of covering (in modesty, shame or fear). At the same time the pudica pose makes the female body matter sexually, it gestures towards an ambiguity surrounding female sexuality in that it recounts the 'enigma' or 'mystery' attached to women's bodies as encoded by oppositional dualisms. According to Salomon, these dualisms infuse representations of nude figures, with female bodies cast as 'attractive from without', as an 'external source for decoration', and as sexually specified by the pubis and male bodies as 'coherent and rational from within', as embodying an 'internally logical, organic unity' (p. 72). Here ambiguity emerges from coordinated constructions of the male subject 'as the subject par excellence' (Grosz, 1994, p. 191).

Repetitions of classical figurations in female and male nudes across centuries of paintings and sculptures effect a sedimentation of such sexed and gendered cultural historical meanings of bodies. That female reproductive organs or genitalia have come to make the female body matter, and that the female body has mattered differently, and often unequally through its assigned inferiority or lacks, from the male body, are considerations no less central for psychology as it seeks to recover the body in psychological discourse, theory and research. The hysteric's body, for example, has, from earliest medical history onward, been infused in different ways with the 'mysteriousness of femininity' (Evans, 1991). In its earliest rendition, hysteria was regarded as a case of the 'wandering womb', in medieval thought as body possession, in 19th-century understandings as a problem of women's 'reproductive apparatus', and in contemporary theory as an 'inner psychic conflict'. Each one of these constructions of hysteria has brought about an 'astounding metaphoric transformation: hysteria itself has become the tricky, oversexed, and deceptive woman its sufferers had previously been thought to be' (p. 2). Vestiges of these associations between female hysteria and the disordered or unruly body find their way into innumerable psychological theories on women's 'madness', 'sanity' or imperfections. As Martha Evans (1991) argues in her history of hysteria, 'woman is a mystery not only because she is the other sex, the object of knowledge, and crazy, but also because she is (a) body' (p. 3).

For Sigmund Freud (1933/1974), women's bodies posed not only an impasse to full psychosexual development, at least insofar as development of the super-ego went, but also a mystery about the nature of femininity. For other theorists, women's 'natural' maternal body was used to ground claims of their moral superiority (e.g. Erikson, 1964). Even contemporary feminist challenges to prevailing moral development theories have relied on women's reproductive choices or maternal thinking and practices to substantiate an 'equal' but 'different' voice or ethics of care (e.g. Belenky, Clinchy, Goldberger, & Tarule, 1986; Gilligan, 1982; Ruddick, 1989). The reproductive body has also been mobilized as the sociobiological currency driving men's heterosexual preferences for younger women (Kenrick & Keefe, 1992). And gender theories working to untie the body–psyche knot, such as psychological androgyny, carried within them the very baggage of 'sexed' bodies they promised to shed (e.g. Bem, 1974). From places in the social order through to psychological theories of inner life, the meaning of 'woman' rarely emerges bodiless on any number of gendered psychological intelligibilities.

To unsettle these meanings of the body is to take issue with their seemingly fixed effects: that is, to make the ambiguity surrounding constructions of the female body and sexuality matter differently. It is to transpose ambiguity as mystery into a question of the matter of the body, a transposition thoroughly revealing of ambiguity's doubleness in having its meaning secured through as well as obscured by hierarchical dualisms in knowledge/ power productions. Judith Butler (1993), in her feminist theorizing on 'bodies that matter', and to whom our title pays a certain homage, states the case this way:

> To speak within these classical contexts of *bodies that matter* is not an idle pun, for to be material means to materialize, where the principle of that materialization is precisely what 'matters' about that body, its very intelligibility. In this sense, to know the significance of something is to know how and why it matters, where 'to matter' means at once 'to materialize' and 'to mean'. (p. 32)

As feminists, we need to confront knowledge/power relations structured into materializations of the body while we seek to address possible intelligibilities encircling the question of what is the body. We need also to get behind the 'mystery of femininity' as not simply 'the mask of womanhood in and of itself', but rather a 'screen for what women have been assigned to hide' (Evans, 1991, p. 242). This is the poser, for theory in psychology, as elsewhere, has historically tied understandings of 'woman' to their bodies, meaning that any celebration of the return of the body raises questions about return *for whom* and *of what kind*. By revisiting recent critical scholarship showing the less-than-steady relations between mind and body, between gender constructions and sexed bodies, we can begin to rework psychology's inherited paradigmatic assumptions that have served to maintain a certain hold on women's embodied subjectivity.

Feminism, Epistemology and the Mind–Body Question

We thus bring this central problematic of how and why the body matters to psychology at a time of a seeming revival of bodily interests, and of, as Lee Quinby (1995) argues, ever-expanding analyses of a materiality–discourse nexus. In late 20th-century thought, the body enters theoretical treatises of subjectivity, sexuality, gender, race and class at that moment when 'knowledge' or 'reason' is said to be in crisis (Grosz, 1993). As a crisis generated, in many respects, by the body of Otherness, it stands to reason that traditional epistemological repudiations of the body are themselves coming under critical scrutiny. Renunciations of the body within western philosophy are in fact equally telling of the historically protean nature of the body, descrying the body as 'animal, as appetite, as deceiver, as prisoner of the soul and confounder of its projects' (Bordo, 1993, p. 3).

Separations between mind and body and the hierarchical ordering of mind over body haunt the history of western philosophical formulations of knowledge from Aristotle and Augustine through to Descartes and Kant (Alcoff, 1995). In early Christian writings, bodily senses and desires are rivaled in contests for a higher form of Truth or closeness to God: 'More and more, O Lord, you will increase your gifts in me, so that my soul may follow me to you, freed from the concupiscence which binds it, and rebel no more against itself' (Augustine, trans. 1961, p. 234). Augustine thus fixes the body as a source of sin, as weakness, as a measure against which the strength of his will towards God is knowable. Pleasures of the body are to be denied, bodily impulses quelled: 'the life of the body is coded as a negative stage to be transcended . . . [T]he sublation functions as a *denial*, a denial of the self, of the embodied self born of an earthly mother' (Lionnet, cited in Miller, 1994, p. 14).

Enlightenment science formulations of mind–body relations are also often given through ideas of struggle, conquest or contest, for if, as Linda Alcoff (1995) puts it, the 'real epistemological action was thought to occur in the mind', then the body had to be controlled (p. 3). Whether through acts of will or other means of transcendence of the body, such strivings towards disembodiment of different kinds were all attempts to purify the relation between knowers and known. The mind cleansed of bodily contaminations (sensuality, animality) was in the service of securing boundaries between objectivity and subjectivity, inner and outer space, self and world (Bordo, 1987). And, abjuring all associations with the body—emotion, nature, subjectivity—philosophical imperatives for transcendence reflected a 'flight from the feminine' into a restructuring of world/knowledge as masculine (Bordo, 1987, p. 5). Likewise,

> [t]he ideology of progress, which was so deeply entrenched in Enlight-
> enment thought, meant that the growth of a humane, rational and civilized
> society could be seen as a struggle between the sexes. . . . The very concept
> of progress was freighted with gender. (Jordanova, 1989, pp. 36–37)

Underlying this project's emphasis on dislodging the knower from time, place and circumstance are the subjective concerns attached to perspectivism, to knowers bound by location, viewpoint and history.

Feminist efforts are not just directed towards rescuing the feminine or the body from philosophical or theoretical obscurity. Instead, their efforts, alongside those who have identified racial, sexual and class specificities of prevailing epistemologies, have served to particularize theories of knowledge production. It follows that celebrations of the return of the body are similarly in need of specificity. While for some this return may hold little more than the promise of a union with that previously disavowed, for others it may offer an 'enjoyment of the unsettling effects that rethinking bodies implies for those knowledges that have devoted so much conscious and unconscious effort to sweeping away all traces of the specificity, the corporeality, of their own processes of production and representation' (Grosz, 1995, p. 2).

It is through the bodies of the Other that a counter-repudiation of sorts has been registered against the phallogocentrism of predominant epistemologies. But this call upon the body to put epistemological certainty at stake carries with it the matter of how the body itself, especially the bodies of Others, has been at risk. Contemporary exigencies such as AIDS, anorexia nervosa and violence against women, in combination with historical practices of strait-lacing, foot-binding and genital mutilation, are matters not outside of this turn to the body. In other ways, the bodies of Others have brought attention fully around to the self, to concerns with one's own body (Burroughs & Ehrenreich, 1993). Body and self also undergo transformations in American cultural–historical mergers of consumption, corporation and technology. Reproductive technologies, human genome projects, cosmetic body sculpt-ing, surgical re-sexing of the body, body piercing and tattooing bring about a different awareness of the 'fit' body (e.g. Kimbrell, 1992; Morgan, 1991). Bodies in pain, under regulation, as malleable and flexible artifact, social construction, social text or instrument of social control converge on our asking of *what is the body*?

To ask 'what is the body?' is, however, not to proclaim a 'crisis of the body'. Rather, in taking up the multiple deployments of the body in stirring up epistemological uncertainty, in disturbing notions of self-unity or self-contained individualism, and in wresting control over our own bodies, our appeal is to the at-times-recalcitrance of the body. Similar to feminist invocations of 'voice', 'experience', 'autobiographical acts', 'narrative' and 'testimony' as conscientious objectors to hegemonic strains of a universal, ahistorical and generalizable self and other (e.g. Code, 1995; King, 1994), so we see the body as issuing in its own challenges (e.g. Probyn, 1992). Together, they act as a set of forces resisting established hierarchical gender dualities and other axes of differentiation, such as sexuality, race, ethnicity and class, structuring relations between inner and outer, between self and other, and between self and world. Their assembly in the 'battle of the sexes' or the 'war over the body' is as much about material transformations in day-to-day contingencies as it is about bodily recognition in the symbolic order. The body as 'epistemological metaphor for locatedness' (Bordo, 1990, p. 145), as gesture of the 'explicit sexualization of knowledges' (Grosz, 1993, p. 188), thus emerges as a key agent in feminist efforts to 'make strange' or 'unfamiliar' the female subject in contemporary reclamations of the body (cf. Burroughs & Ehrenreich, 1993; Salomon, 1996).

Out of the Shadows and into the Light: Feminism, Science and Gender Dualisms

> Written on the body is a secret code only visible in certain lights; the accumulations of a lifetime gather there.
> (Jeannette Winterson, 1992, p. 89)

Feminist appreciations of how the body comes to acquire a particular sexed and gendered meaning have required not only a reading of the symbolic world but also a grasp of the body as itself a historicized entity. Unraveling the multilayered structures organizing the meaning of the body and the place of the body in women's oppression *and* in their emancipation has been an orienting principle of feminist projects. Fundamental to this project has been a critical examination of social, political and historical processes by which the body was called upon to ground arguments of 'natural' sexual differences. This kind of investigation brings within its scope analyses of epistemology, including relations between knowers and known and hierarchical dualisms instating the meaning of the body.

Most of us are by now familiar with the lengthy inventories of oppositional constructs indexing sex and gender. Lined up like so many pairs of complementary mates, dualisms twine around an extensive universe of such relations: mind/body, culture/nature, activity/passivity, reason/emotion, objective/subjective, public/private, order/chaos, independent/dependent, hard/soft, all of which were further organized hierarchically. The first term of each of these pairs has been granted positive connotations and aligned with men and masculinity; the latter terms, holding a lesser place in this hierarchy, have been encoded with negative values and so aligned women and femininity with negativity (Braidotti, 1994; Ferguson, 1993; Hekman, 1990; Wilshire, 1989). It is precisely the workings of these dualisms that have enabled psychology to hinge women's subjectivity to all manner of bodily functions, on the one hand, and to measure women's psychological and sexual life against a male norm, on the other hand (e.g. Benjamin, 1986; Weisstein, 1971). This scheme has translated as well into practices of exclusion of women from the realms of knowledge production and into a rationale for control over the bodies of women and others who were 'naturally' more given to bodily rule.

Of course these arrangements have had many schematic lives. Londa Schiebinger (1993), for example, argues that what has changed in these frameworks are basically ideas on the origin and attributes of sexual difference. Whereas ancient theories may have traced the roots of sex difference to cosmic principles of dualism, modern science's materialistic bent led anatomists and physiologists to probe the 'body as whole—each bone, organ, hair of the head, and nerve—for telltale signs of sexual differences' (p. 38). By regarding science and sexuality in the Enlightenment

as working hand-in-hand to buttress 'the doctrines of sexual complementar-
ity and republican motherhood . . . [in] emancipatory liberalism animating
the American and French revolutions', (pp. 38–9), Schiebinger shows how
deeply entrenched was the sexualization of science. For modern botanist Carl
Linneaus, as an illustrative case, classifications of plants were drawn along
the lines of (hetero)sexual differences and relations that coincided with
transformations in modern European science and in sexuality and gender.
Furthermore, Linneaus's designation of a class of animals as 'mammalia'
occurred at a time when, according to Schiebinger, men of medicine and
politics heightened attention around the importance of mother's milk and so
to infants' need of a mother's as opposed to a wet nurse's breast. Similarly,
in early 20th-century psychology, Hollingsworth (1916) identified those
'devices' such as law, education, art, illusion and other 'bugaboos' that
helped to turn 'social' into 'natural' facts about women's maternal instinct.

Steeped in the traditions of ordered oppositions or dualistic thinking and
of a privileging of the male over the female body, the body emerges as a
historicized entity that is thoroughly entwined with the workings of social,
cultural and political life. As Thomas Laqueur (1990) sees it, early one-sex
models, wherein female genitals were construed as an internally located
inversion of male ones, pointed up how 'ordered contrarieties', such as
fatherhood/motherhood, masculine/feminine, hot/cold, could be 'played off
a single flesh in which they did not inhere' (p. 61). That is, the bodies of
men and women did not mark these distinctions clearly but rather absorbed
shifting and varying differentiations of gender. Lasting over millennia, the
one-sex model's longevity, argues Laqueur, had little to do with the 'facts'
of sex or biology or with advances in science and medicine. Instead,
Laqueur proposes that its lifespan be read as an 'exercise in preserving the
Father, he who stands not only for order but for the very existence of
civilization itself' (p. 58). Shifts to a two-sex model were similarly wrought,
in that social, political and cultural upheavals ordered and organized sexual
specifications of the body (also see Schiebinger). Laqueur shows that power
and gender *sex* the body, that the body incorporates such differentiations,
which, while historically unstable, are nonetheless pressed into the service of
maintaining some normative model of the male body. This standard body
then stands as a reference point for a variety of dominant cultural ideals.

The reaches of such gendered embodiment are shown as well in ancient
through to contemporary accounts of conception, which, while loyal to a
characterization of the male 'seed' as the more vital component, shift and
change despite science's enhanced technological vision to 'see' sperm and
ova. Whereas in the 1950s the egg is depicted in passive terms and the sperm
in active ones (e.g. a 'sleeping princess awaiting the kiss of a prince' or
sperm as 'white knight'), this passivity and activity undergoes decade-by-
decade shifts that resonate more with changes in heterosexual relations than
in science (Martin, 1991). In a late 1980s documentary, *The Miracle of Life*,

the story of conception slides into a re-creation of the battle of the sexes through its reliance on metaphors referring to 'defense' and 'mission', in the case of the sperm, and 'entrapment', or 'a drawing inside', in the case of the egg. The possible activity or agency of the egg is embodied through metaphors reminiscent of the 'femme fatale' or engulfing, over-involved mother, a cultural–psychological pathologizing of the egg not unlike late 1980s' American popular films characterizing women as oversexed and dangerous (e.g. *Fatal Attraction*). In contrast, the agency of the sperm is given through military metaphors as well as through allusions to executive management.

As these studies suggest, gendered embodiment runs deep, and, although cast in the light of prevailing dualist thinking, there is at the same time some historical flux and symbolic drift in gender dualities. Caroline Bynum (1992) points up a kind of slippage in dualist systems in her study of medieval mystics where the lines become blurred between 'spiritual and psychological, on the one hand, and bodily or even sexual on the other' (p. 190). Coincident with a misogynist denigration of the body in its association of women and flesh with 'lust, weakness, and irrationality' were those medieval women mystics who, contrary to such doctrines, experienced bodily manifestations (e.g. miraculous lactation, stigmata, miraculous anorexia) and practiced bodily manipulations (e.g self-flagellation) that were taken to signify a union with God. As ascetics who often told of their union in ecstatic and erotic overtones, women mystics' testimonials speak to something being ' "switched on" by "the other" ' that is at once beyond and yet rooted in women's bodies. But even more than this, women mystics' celebration of their bodily union with Christ served to authorize a religious place for women, just as these 'newer' behaviors of the female body indicated that the body itself has a history constantly in-the-making.

Feminist and other cultural histories of science, medicine, botany and religion are revealing not only of the mutable nature of bodies but also of gender as more fluid, and more mobile and mobilizable, than those histories that adhere to more rigid and static framing of gender and gender dualities. In their use of cultural and social history as a wedge to prise open established hierarchies of gender dualisms, these studies first turn up the conflicting and complex layerings of knowledge and power relations that go into their making, and, second, loosen the grip of these arrangements on the sexed body as a 'natural' object. Through these analyses, life—biological, social, psychological—is brought forward as a multilayered embodiment of gender relations, and the body itself as historically a site of struggle or contest over gender meanings.

What feminists in particular have brought out of the shadows is a denaturalization of the body, one that casts light on the power relations circulating in and through the sexualization of science, of epistemology and of accompanying dualisms. This has been accomplished not simply by reinscribing the body as the site of oppression due to its repudiation in master discourses, but rather by seeing how women have used their bodies to counter the very disavowal of the body such discourses set up. Women's bodies have been pivotal to this critique, illuminating another set of complex layerings of the body through the doublings and redoublings of oppression and emancipation, discipline and rebellion, pain and pleasure, desire and desire denied.

Feminism, Psychology and the 'Body Politic'

Not unlike feminist efforts in psychology to rework the terrain of women as 'objects' by considering what might transpire when women enter theory and research as 'subject', questions of the body span out into the field of subjectivity, sexuality, control and power (cf. Suleiman, 1986). Set over against psychology as a complicit agent in the social control and regulation of women and their bodies, feminist psychologists have directed their attention to every level of psychological thought and practice (see Morawski, 1994). Often anti-foundationalist and anti-dualistic in aim, feminist challenges have sought to affirm and celebrate women's embodiedness and relational being, to revalue women's intuitive and spiritual powers, and to stir trouble with psychology's philosophical underpinnings. Following what Kathy Ferguson (1993) characterizes as praxis, cosmic and linguistic feminisms, the cross-lineages of feminisms in psychology can also be found in a shared concern with language, with 'the ways women and men take up and are taken up by language' (p. 155), and with women's bodies—'our reproductive experiences, our sexuality, our labor—as central both to knowledge and to politics' (p. 155).

To wit, as Susan Bordo reminds us, feminism has long been on to the body as a site of power struggle or political contest, and to an immediacy around the formulation of a 'personal politics' of 'culture's grip on the body'. Feminist inversions of the 'old metaphor of the Body politic' into a new one of the 'politics of the body' (Bordo, 1993, p. 21) strike a sympathetic chord with Foucault's (1977) 'political "anatomy"' or 'body politic'. For feminists in psychology, Foucault's tracing of psychology's genealogical history also proves relevant for how it throws into 'radical question' the 'space of interiority' (May, 1993). Once coupled with feminist critiques of knowledge and the body politic, it becomes possible to add that women's bodies have put into radical question the particularization of psychology's interiorizing of sexuality and subjectivity.

Where Foucault's work seems to be key to feminist scholarship is in his understanding of knowledge/power relations as productive, as multiply deployed, as operating through the technologies of culture, history and science at multiple levels, and as working through micro-level practices, such as self-surveillance or self-monitoring on, through and in the body (see Bordo, 1993; Quinby, 1994). If the model of power in discursive formations and changes is best understood as one of 'perpetual battle', as Foucault (1977) maintains, then it would seem that women have indeed put their bodies on the line. For example, depictions of women's 'unruly', 'disordered' or 'out-of-control' bodies as psychological manifestations of hysteria, anorexia nervosa, premenstrual syndrome, sexual promiscuity or frigidity might be alternatively cast as women's mobilizations of the body against the restraining edicts of science, including psychology (see Bordo, 1993). Evans (1991) makes just this kind of argument about hysteria. She states:

> As the paradigm for the repression of our subjection not only to our own bodies and their unruly sexual desires, but also to their link with social structures of meaning and power, hysteria has persistently confronted us with the splits and strictures of Western culture—the division we have decreed between body and mind, the fear of nature and attempts to overcome it—and the social assignment to one gender of bearing the burdens of those cultural sanctions. (p. 242)

Whether we read these psychological phenomena in this way or not, it remains the case that feminist psychologists need to think about the body fashioned in, through and by psychology. Prevalent amongst psychology's characterizations of women's bodies are those that link women's reproductive capacities with medical illness models and those that replay the 'archetype of the unreliable menstruating woman' (Ussher, 1989). Psychology's 'scientific' practices inscribe on women's menstruating, reproductive and sexual bodies diagnostic categories of 'premenstrual syndrome, postnatal depression and the menopausal syndrome' (Ussher, 1989, p. 136; also see Parlee, 1992). Psychology's discourses and practices not only homogenize and make normative women's bodies as a 'problem body', but they also make women's bodies seeable in this way. Any quick scan of psychology's theory and research on women and the body is revealing of psychology's emphasis on body image, body awareness, eating disorders, body dissatisfaction, low self-esteem, body-image distortions, depression, motherhood, body-image disturbances and sexuality, to name some of the more frequently invoked categories. In psychological theory and research, women's bodies materialize through their absorption of gender and sex differentiations, ones that mark them off as falling on one or the other divide of psychology's norms of an ordered or disordered psyche. The body emerges as women's 'problem' body instead of psychology's problem with or theoretical lacks on the matter of women's bodies.

Insofar as psychology makes of the body an object of perception through its interest in the visible as observable and hence knowable, it serves to transform the 'lived body' into the body as in the mind's eye (Radley, 1991). Take, for example, psychology's repeated use of a body-image questionnaire that asks women to choose from amongst nine figure drawings (body

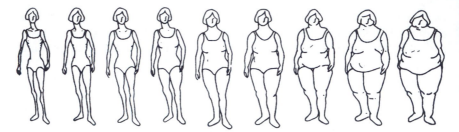

FIGURE 1. Nine figures drawings for body-image questionnaire.
From Stunkard, Sorenson, and Schulsinger (1983, p. 119).
(Reprinted with permission of author and publisher.)

outlines as found in Stunkard, Sorenson, & Schulsinger, 1983; see Figure 1)
the one that represents the desired (ideal) and the real (one's own) body. The
extent of the discrepancy between women's two choices is then translated
into a measure of women's psychological discontent or dissatisfaction with
their own bodies (e.g. Fallon & Rozin, 1985). This questionnaire is used to
point to women's dissatisfaction as residing in women's psyches in terms of
a perceptual distortion, a finding that is on occasion presumably validated
further through a comparison to the ideal female figure form selected by
men.

But this questionnaire, like the pudica gesture, can be thought of as both
pointing to and covering over what is now taken as women's normative
discontent. That is, psychology replicates and sediments further this gesture
of ambiguity around women's bodies as a site of sexual power and a site of
shame. The concealment, we would argue, is to be found, in part, in the
history enfolded within psychology's hinging of outer bodies to inner
psyches, and in how its fastening of one to the other relies on a particular
interpretation of gender dualisms. This conception encompasses psychology's loading of 'body image' with psychological issues around sexuality,
appetite, will and desire (see, e.g., Jordanova, 1989). In this concealment the
possibility of women's bodily enactments (e.g. hysteria, anorexia nervosa)
being viewed as resistance to control, constraint or regulation is surrendered
to psychological interpretations of the body–psyche relation gone awry.
Gender dualisms enable this construction by absorbing the signs of women's
resistance.

Cloaked as women's normative discontent with their own bodies, the
radical potential of women's body rebellions is erased, situating normative
discontent within women as opposed to within psychology and culture.
Concealed also are the historical traces of psychology's scrutiny of the
bodies of Others—from early anthropometric, phrenological and charactero-
logical researches, such as those by Galton or Sheldon, on face or body types
(Radley, 1991)—and of the negative encodings of Otherness. Such body-

image questionnaires not only regulate and constrain the body through classifying, sorting and ordering it, but they also effect a field of differentiations that invest and specify the meaning of the body. The historical traces of the use of body types to classify and categorize persons carry within them a repressed set of codes of social orderings around gender, race and class.

Psychology's discourse and practice, its measures, variables, categories, analyses and interpretations, bring about a kind of corporeality for women. This 'body talk', if you will, materializes bodies in ways that coordinate the body with psychology's language of self-governance: self-control, self-discipline, self-regulation, self-management, self-esteem, self-regard, and so on (see Grosz, 1995). The matter of the body is thereby given over to the matter of transcendence, issuing in, in its own way, what Mary Winkler (1994) refers to as a 'resurgence of a secularized asceticism and passion for control in our own culture' (p. 234). Popular self-help books of the 1990s, for example, resound with messages equating an overweight body with appetites and desires out of control, directing women to 'stop the insanity' through rigorous self-discipline and control (Perini & Bayer, 1995). Translating women's freedom into a matter of self-control, the body is positioned as in opposition to women's freedom; it is what women are to conquer. This version accomplishes a decontextualization of women's bodily struggles at the same time that it shifts responsibility to the level of individuals. In a curious twist of events, women's struggles with their bodies are brought back as a problem of their own doing and making.

This displacement sorely misses the possibility of women's bodily resistance to master discourses. To the extent that the struggle between bodily denial and desire is wrapped into the struggle for transcendence, and to the extent that these struggles are articulated through bodily regulation and control, women's bodies may be registering their own multi-leveled discontent. The contemporary body ideal of the hyper-slender female body, with its 'undressing' of more and more of women's bodies—a bare-bones look (Seid, 1994)—ushers into the politics of the body a 'new, "natural"' body. On the one hand, women's hyper-slender bodies renounce the markings (curves, breasts) and functions (reproduction) of a feminine body. On the other hand, these lean, trim and 'fit' bodies announce a body under rigorous self-control (see Bordo, 1993). Through these doublings of the meaning of the body, women's bodies evidence the contradictions and tensions surrounding a living out of a body that has been simultaneously feared and adored, desired and loathed, coveted and repudiated. A critical genealogy of the historicity of women's bodies, one that locates psychology along with culture and other institutions mediating the body, may enable feminist psychologists to reconceive the powers and pleasures of the body, and, in so doing, to bring women's desires, sexuality and subjectivity squarely within the matter of their bodies.

The Personal is the Political: The Body and its Desires

Still, the feminist task of articulating the ambiguous place of women's bodies as sites of both inscription and resistance proves to be as complex as the cultural layering of the body itself. If one examines its contemporary praxis, the alliance between feminism and the body may well appear, at first glance, uncomplicated. Pro-choice means control over our own bodies. Ending the threat of rape for women re-establishes the integrity of women's bodies and honors the autonomy of our (bodily) desires. But the significance of the body is even more deeply insinuated into feminism than these obvious instances allow. Consciousness raising, an icon of praxis within feminism, clearly implicates the body. It is presumed that through the experience of our bodies, women both express and empower themselves. The notion that the body and the experiential base it provides are natural allies of feminism is almost fundamental. Take this passage from Jennifer Allen (1993), which, although quite intricate, reveals a raw intimacy between feminism and corporeality:

> Phenomenological feminism is a beginning of 'seeing/making new patterns of perception'. Further exploration of the wild region in light of feminist experience necessitates a 'depth hearing': '*A hearing engaged in by the whole body.*' Our hope is to indicate an open-ended perspective from which we may begin to circle toward an inexhaustibly deep source of possibilities for experiencing and thinking otherwise. (pp. 253–254; emphasis added)

The 'lived body' is her methodology of emancipation. Still, how one conceptualizes this politics of the body is hardly simple.

Even Allen's seemingly direct appeal is marked by a particular manner of speaking intended to both evoke and demonstrate the 'wild region' of feminine corporeality. Her phenomenological approach requires rhetorical innovations which, in turn, imply a certain imbrication between body and text. The body, whether heard or read, does not simply translate. These discursive complications also interdict any simple correspondence between the experiential dimension and one's political aims. This slippage between discourse and materiality of the body (whether rendered in physical or experiential terms) intervenes in any feminist project that attempts to integrate the personal and the political—an integration that is particularly tantalizing for feminists in psychology. Thus, for example, standpoint feminists who employ women's (or girls') narratives, narratives that presumably reflect experience, must also develop a method of reading or interpreting such reports (Tolman & Diebold, 1994). The difficulty in articulating a non-ideological but nevertheless critical approach to women's experience and women's bodies motivates a number of significant feminist turns. Most fundamentally, it has led feminists to a consideration of the way in which the body and representation are enmeshed. A foundational inquiry into the categories of experience and the body undermines any pat security about the status of the knower (e.g. feminist researcher) as well as complacency about what is known (Dallery, 1994). The importation of the question of textuality itself challenges certain previous relations that have structured the interface between body/experience and sociality (whether oppressive or emancipatory); that is, easily assumed categories, such as alien vs authentic, can no longer be taken for granted. Within this shifting territory, feminism relentlessly pursues various modes of (re)configuring the body, its experiences, its desires and its relationship to representation.

Joan Scott (1992) argues that any undue reliance upon experience entails significant risks. It often positions experience as an unencumbered reference point where experience serves as mode of explanation and vehicle of change. The problem, here, is the problem that plagues any such decontextualization: experience itself cannot provide the position from which its categories are generated. Taken purely as autonomous systems, body and experience do not allow one to examine the social order that produces the identities and differences which are in fact the origin of those experiences. Experience (and the body from which it comes) falsely sutures a multiplicity of historically generated positions traversed by race, class and a multiform engendering. One does not fully comprehend the operation of such factors merely from the experience of those social influences and categories.

Far from being our companion in arms, the body may in fact lull feminists into a sort of methodological short-circuit wherein its status as origin gives birth to a number of problematic epistemological commitments. The body-as-experience may usurp the political aims of feminism (W. Brown, 1991). There can be no assertions of truth, not even those grounded in the body, that are not also assertions of power. Any such disingenuity in the name-of-the-body is easily perceived by those feminist groups whose bodies were somehow overlooked. Men may notice as well, most especially when it is their political privileges that are being usurped. Relinquishing the ties to the body may allow feminism to give up its 'preference for deriving norms epistemologically' and instead decide its aims and values purely within the political forum (W. Brown, 1991, p. 77). Other feminists could easily argue that relinquishing such a claim on the body would vitiate a radical investment of feminism itself as well as ignoring the historical link between women and their bodies.

A number of issues inherent in the theorization of the body are evident in feminist debates regarding rape. Often these debates turn on an unwitting choice of certain bodily significations as pregiven rather than considering the contextualization of such significations. Sharon Marcus (1992) suggests that some feminists have ignored the way in which so many rape discourses, feminist and conservative, exclude women from the 'community of violence'. In violence between equals, rape would be another violent act and a retaliatory response by women would be expected by both sexes. Instead, women are set up to be cast as passive and sexualized in the rape script. The very notion of bodily invasion portrays women as passive, the accentuation of the indignity of vaginal penetration sexualizes women (just as the penis as weapon sexualizes men). There is little current discourse that understands rape as an encounter between equals, even though such a framing might easily reduce the chances of being raped. The possibility of rape could be re-scripted as an assault within the grid of 'subject-to-subject' violence. This re-scripting, based on an analysis of exclusion, might open another line of resistance. Exclusion from the discourse of aggression, or 'subject-to-subject violence', perpetuates rape.

What is important in Marcus's observations for this paper is the manner in which her analysis depends on a particular reading of the body. Marcus, beginning with an 'omitted' term, opens our bodies to new significations. She proposes a body that is always in performance, one that is not set. Thus one should be able to transform how women experience their bodies in a rape situation, allowing for a wider spectrum of responses. Mary Koss (1993), the foremost psychologist in rape studies, also configures rape as a matter of the body.

> Women truly have no safe haven from victimization because they are vulnerable both within and outside their homes. In the company of those they know lies the potential of date, acquaintance, and marital rape as well as battering. . . . Thus, contemporary women in the United States live their lives under the threat of sexual violation, and this fear constitutes a special burden . . . (p. 1062)

Koss begins by situating women's bodies as needing (and lacking) safety, as deserving a haven. Koss would see a future in which women were free from the threat of rape; such freedom is a right of women (like the political right to a safe abortion). Note how this vision is conjoined with a certain construction of passivity, perhaps as a result of its coupling with the signifier 'woman'. In the passage, Koss constitutes a vulnerable body. The unfair vulnerability is echoed in the domestic metaphor of the home, a place which is safe neither outside nor inside. An absence of security is coded as sexual and as a sexual violation, evoking both gender and a certain notion of bodily integrity. This implicit horizon of understanding which defines Koss's feminine body is a textual construction pieced together from history. But the historical sedimentation is not questioned.

In calling attention to the divergence between Marcus and Koss, our purpose is not to favor one or the other view. Rather, it is to punctuate how the body is an inevitable tag-along to feminist discourse without, for all its self-evidence, determining exactly what feminists may or may not say about it. Oddly, without knowing *how* it will signify in a given discourse, we know that it *must* signify in any feminist discourse. It is the inside/outside of discourse. As part of the topology of speaking itself, the body bespeaks the oppression and illuminates the path to emancipation. The question of which body is what still remains.

Harry Berger (1987), in a comparison of the written vs the performed Shakespeare, renders any facile reliance on the lived body even more treacherous. He suggests that the body may merely be the most entrenched textual inscriptions within any given culture. The pre-existing interpellation of the body, its initial inscription, is repressed. This repression of an ideological inscription constitutes the body. The body is the return of the repressed, meaning that it is believed even as it deceives. In other words, the real trick of the body is precisely that it calls us to mistake appearances (experience) for reality.[1] Its recalcitrance signifies the most 'intractable political differences', for example, sex, race, affect. If Berger's view possesses merit, feminist flirtations with the body are risky business. It may prove an unreliable, even reactionary, consort.

Celia Kitzinger and Rachel Perkins (1993) argue that the conjunction of the public and private in feminism has misfired by falling into a non-political psychology of 'women's issues'. This criticism is well taken but it could be argued that this misfire is not a contingent case of feminist 'false consciousness'. Rather those 'private practices' that define the body within psychology and within feminism reflect centuries of codification that align bodily matters with the private realm. If this body is always complicated by this history as well as resistant to it, we should not expect bodily researches will automatically complement political agendas which have been initially founded on discourses grounded in the public sphere. For example, the notion of the body as a form of property opens numerous vistas of analysis and possible social change. Still, the ideas of property and contractual exchange as the sole metaphors for embodiment can blind one to ulterior aspects of the body, even as that body is imbricated in the social. One may discover aspects of corporeal comportment and sexuality that bear upon the political but are best rendered in terms of questions such as narcissism, sexual difference, fantasy, the impasses of representation itself. Can we address this issue without falling into an individualistic and privatized lexicon of clinical causes?

Unity or Disjunction? The Body in its Social Relations

In their pioneering anthology on psychology and gender, Rachel Hare-Mustin and Jeanne Marecek (1990) take up the difficult intersection between representation and the body by situating psychological representations of gender within their cultural context and along the axes of power. By entertaining such questions, they clearly challenge prevailing empiricist models. They also begin to sketch out a new territory of representation which points in postmodernist and constructionist directions. In this effort, an interesting conjunction is ventured as certain models of feminism and constructionism join forces. Feminists have always been aware that the body is deeply entangled in the social order, most especially as a sexed body. It is more than evident that the exclusion of women from the 'universal suffrage of man' is based on a bodily difference (Scott, 1995). The traditional (but nonetheless masculine) erasure of sexual difference motivates a keen suspicion that men are somehow invested, their very bodies are somehow invested, in the operation of reigning institutions of political and social power.

In the following quotation from Hare-Mustin and Marecek (1990), one sees how this entanglement between masculine corporeality (his desire) and more general structures of power is posited. Presuming that there is a workable analogy between the body and sociality, we can assume that this analogy also cuts both ways, affecting the terms in which we imagine women's bodies as well as those through which men's bodies are imagined. One might note how the authors attempt to articulate that relationship between discourse and the materiality of the body, taking from both constructionist paradigms and models of patriarchal power derived from feminism. The 'target' in both cases is that elusive field of effects between body and culture.

> Moreover, those who have power in an 'egalitarian' society have a vested interest in either denying their privileged position or legitimating it as natural, moral, or right. . . . In the nineteenth century, for example, the ideal of shielding women from sexual knowledge ensured female subordination to male sexual desires. Nowadays, women's sexual subservience is legitimated by what Wendy Hollway . . . and others have labeled the male sex drive discourse, the cultural belief that men have a barely controllable physiological need for sexual gratification. The legitimization of male power can also be seen when violent husbands justify their abusive behavior as disciplining their wives. . . . At a more general level, we suggest that psychology's emphasis on the differences between men and women also has supported the unwarranted scientific legitimization of masculine privilege. (Hare-Mustin & Marecek, 1990, p. 185)

We are not examining any of the compelling claims put forth in the above passage. What is significant, for our purposes, is the authors' effort to delineate a new domain of signification, defined by the power relations of the social arena as well as traversed by the complexity of bodily desire. The passage forges a link between embodiment (male sexual desire) and other forms of social power (suggested in references to psychology and imbalances in a supposedly egalitarian society). The authors' allusion to women's enforced innocence in the 19th century suggests a strong relationship between bodily knowledge and social power. It further suggests that male bodies, despite the duplicitous erasure of sexual difference, are somehow fulfilled in the social order. In the patriarchy, male desire and social power are mutually reinforcing. The feminine body functions as a distillation of effects attributed to the operation of power and knowledge; both of which are imputed to masculinity. Knowledge and power serve the masculine body. This proposition suggests that body, power and knowledge can coalesce, that there exists some point of transparency between the three terms.

There is, however, a complication introduced at certain junctures which we understand as a complication of the body. The elusive and incommensurate supplement that exists as body is one reason why, in many Lacanian and post-structuralist readings of the body, one confronts the annoying intellectual limit of not getting it (all . . . at once). The body also revises our usual ways of imaging how our politics and thinking mingle and it most definitely rebuffs the advances of any progressive linear narrative such as the discipline of psychology traditionally promotes. Regarding the subtle problematic of the body, Beverly Brown and Parveen Adams (1979) warn those who would combine a Foucauldian analysis with other approaches about how easily one can return to more traditional notions of the body:

> At its most radical, a combination of power and knowledge entails either a reduction of knowledge to power or, conversely, power to knowledge. In the first case, a theory becomes nothing but a series of effects of a supervening subordination and has no specificity over and above the concatenation of those effects. In the second case, power is nothing more than the differential distribution of that knowledge. More typically, however, these two analytically distinguishable forms are run together, so that the recovery of an original body is seen as both a retrieval of an eternal truth [knowledge] and a long lost power. (p. 42)

The difficulties described by Brown and Adams cannot, however, deter one from pursuing a precise understanding of the topography of body and sociality. Catherine MacKinnon (1987) cuts the Gordian knot in making the relation between the body and the body politic very explicit. Sexuality yokes domination to desire; it makes submission arousing. This arrangement ultimately leaves women out of the social circuit while at the same time seducing them into experiencing this exclusion-*cum*-enslavement as emotionally and physically gratifying. The interlocking network between the social and corporeal maintains the status quo of each. The system of patriarchy socially empowers men and this socially dominant position is mirrored in matters of sexuality and the body. With respect to both sexes, MacKinnon's radical feminism highlights, with unwavering clarity, the necessary continuum between (sexed) bodily desire and the social order, and the translation between these two orders as absolute and transparent. Many, in fact, have criticized MacKinnon for failing to accord to women's desires any autonomy (Cornell, 1993). Others plead for a more interesting reading of sexual desire, one that understands, for example, that in fantasy the various positions of subjectivity are not secure (Merck, 1993). In the social order, the positions of the subject can be much more clearly established.

Despite the severe determinism of her answer, MacKinnon attempts to answer a most difficult question, that is, how do bodily desire and oppression become complicit? She does not, as some do, take the nature of the body and its desires for granted. Radical feminists such as MacKinnon articulate a relationship between the body and its oppression through an analysis of the relationship between corporeality and representation, that is, fantasies and images of women in sex. The body in feminism, far from being passive or self-identical, gets itself mixed up and contaminated by, at least, two ulterior inquiries. The initial set of concerns articulates the question of the body. The second set addresses the question of representation (images, fantasies, signifiers) and the body. Both inquiries forfeit a body that possesses any essential constitution.

Many of these issues intersect at a point where the body and the Symbolic Order meet. The Symbolic Order, as used in Lacan or cultural studies, is comprised of the words, images, laws and customs 'given' to us through our induction into culture. This induction is not just a matter of cognitive framing or responding to the demand characteristics of roles, or even (simply) a transgressive, performative occupation of partial and contested identities, a view that can be reduced to ironic role-playing. Rather the imbrication of body and text is complexly layered. One can trace the manner in which historically sedimented reality and its subtexts construct and intersect to produce the current ambulatory corporeality. One can also ask how operations of representation structure human desire, and, by implication, the body that experiences desire. The latter task obviously asks us to understand with some precision the nature of the Symbolic Order and how it orders bodies. One thereby opens the analysis to the ways in which the Symbolic brings forth bodies. The Lacanian understanding of infantile sexuality is exactly this bringing forth wherein infantile sexuality is the social organization of the body rather than vice versa (Brown & Adams, 1979; Lacan, 1989).

Lacanians interested in feminism (Copjec, 1994; Ragland, 1994) take up the question of sexual difference as a matter of our relationship to the Other as both object of love and medium of representation, seeing in the impasses of that ontogeny the dissatisfaction that fuels desire and maintains the gender masquerade. The masquerade is called heterosexuality, but in fact it obscures our encounter with the Other (brings out the usual binaries). From a more Foucauldian/Derridean direction, Judith Butler (1993) plays with the operation of iteration and reiteration in the materialization of the body and in its relationship to identity and exclusion. The difference between Butler's books *Gender Trouble* (1990) and *Bodies that Matter* in part reflects her reconsideration of the cost of representation. We are not simply occupants of a symbolic designation but bound through symbolic exclusion to the very signifiers that materialize our being.

In stark contrast to constructionist views of whatever stripe, many in feminism view embodiment as that which will engender a long-desired transformation of the Symbolic Order. Embodiment is the possibility of 'freeing' women's desires (Dempster, 1988). This was the position announced earlier by Jennifer Allen, who turned to phenomenology to tease out such a body. In spite of such appeals, one cannot evade the same dilemma faced by MacKinnon, that is, women's forced choice between a corporeality whose referent is the patriarchal social order, and locating some trace that allows a critique of that order. But a different answer locates the body in a manner that diverges sharply from the more 'top–down' social vision of bodily inscription. Women must turn to our bodies and our corporeal suffering in order to distinguish the elusive difference between women's true desires and those aspects of femininity that are patriarchally orchestrated. Unless one can locate this often repressed difference/trace which resides in our corporeal being, women possess no place from which to be oppressed. Towards this end, Marcia Germaine Hutchinson (1994) advocates guided imagery and regression therapy. One sees, in her work, a very specified notion of the body that is essential to her entire feminist project.

> So what does it mean to have a healthy body image? As we embrace a new notion of beauty, we will enjoy our bodies, their roundness, curves, lines, and planes—and their unique idiosyncrasies. We will revel in our bodies' strengths and femaleness. We will eat in a way that nourishes us, and that honors the signals and needs of our bodies. We will exercise in order to increase energy. . . . We will explore physical movement in order to feel more fully alive and embodied. (Hutchinson, 1994, p. 167)

This interesting passage demonstrates how the function of the body became so utterly complicated. If a radical constructionism would foreclose any point of resistance by subsuming all desire into a patriarchal vortex defined by its political and economic parameters, a too easy slide into the testimony of the body overlooks the degree to which even our most intimate moments are painstakingly choreographed by the Symbolic Other/Order. One must note two possible points where Hutchinson may find herself thwarted by the very body that she so carefully conjures. In her recourse to the healthy body, the author uses the body to forward various senses of unity. The body is supposed as ultimately unified, as a site over which women can gain sovereign control (it's mine, mine!). In addition, if one can so clearly demarcate the healthy body of a certain type of woman, one can as easily isolate the alien pathogenic agents, a move that repeats age-old dualisms. Patriarchy and its traumas become enclosed totalities.

What is most startling about Hutchinson's passage is that it is simply one imperative after another, for example, 'We will revel. . . . We will eat. . . .

114 SEXED AND GENDERED BODIES

We will exercise.' The performative invocation of language as the desire of the Other (here the author) is nowhere more evident than at this moment of emancipating our own female bodies. One can attempt to return to the body but the obstacle of representation always gets in on the act. We are then faced with the question of locating the place(s) from which the body speaks. Is this place simply defined as emanating from the voices of other women, from resistant readings of our own narratives, from regression therapy (Kuhn, 1988; Tolman & Diebold, 1994)?

The notion of temporality introduced in the very idea of consciousness raising introduces at least a minimal wrinkle into this feminist encounter with the body. For if the body emerges through a certain reflectivity on the contradictions between past and present, it is neither a simple cipher of the social, a plaything of the patriarchy, nor a thing in itself to which we can return. Rather, the body exists at a certain interstice created by a temporal pulsation; the body is not only a historical construction, it is the existence of historical contradiction. The body is where history fails. It is a reading at cross-purposes with itself. In this formulation, a number of annoying conundrums about the body become integrated. The body continues to serve as a site for critique and transformation but it also bears an amenable relationship to social representation; a body can cleave to representations, even oppressive representations, but this subjection is neither singular (the sites are multiple) nor without remainder. The question of the body now proceeds from rather different premises. At this point, representation and body collaborate by undermining one another. The body, for these feminist inquiries, slips.

Conclusion

Throughout this paper, we have appealed to 'the body' at the same time that we have registered our own complaints about any simple subscriptions to 'the body'. It is not our intent to sidestep this contradiction, for in many ways it is precisely this dissension between a general, integral 'body' and specific invocations of the body that has fostered critical rethinking of the body. That women have come to signify the 'body' and bodily interests is but one critical element. The other(s) reside with the multiplicity of bodies that are said to materialize 'woman'. Woman as the maternal body, as the vulnerable body, the victimized body, the hysterical body, the body with no desire of its own, the regulated body, the rebellious body, the thin body, and so on, all trace a line around 'the body' without necessarily delivering to us the meaning of 'the body'. Likewise, imagined or yet-to-be-realized bodies, in this or other worlds—the free body, the emancipated body, the not-fearful body, the healthy body, the full-citizen body, the strong body and the powerful body—introduce their own limits. Any return to the body thereby raises fundamental questions about what the body is and which body is to feature in contemporary psychological theory and research.

If one considers the endless repetitions of the binaries that structure both body and gender, it is evident that these binaries circle a certain failure in meaning. Are men more moral or more bestial, or are women? Histories give us competing answers to such queries, suggesting that the binaries that structure the body betray themselves through contradictions and perverse inversions. Far from representing reality, binaries are ideological glosses of impasses, multiplicities and broader power relations.

Whether examined from the perspective of feminism or from the historical context of the science of psychology, the question of the body seems to push any systematic appropriation to its own limits. One sees this unruly liminality in the dispiriting 'sex wars', namely the feminist disputes over pornography and desire that were so divisive within the movement. Outside of polemics, the body continually restructures feminist theory, both allowing and disallowing its fundamental relationship to experience and standing analyses of the cultural inscription of women's bodies. The real of the body is just as evident in the corporeal protestations and resignifications that feminine embodiment always poses to patriarchal thinking. Hysterical formations and medieval mysticism counter the hegemonic discourse that excluded, appropriated and denigrated their expression; Dora, for instance, walked out of Freud's office while transforming Freud's theory of the relationship of sexuality and representation (Rose, 1986).

Contrary to seeking a resolution to what is the body, we would countenance working with bodily contradictions as sites of creative genesis, as feminists for so long have done. The slow but growing awareness of the question of the body, and the increasingly sophisticated approaches to its conceptualization, owe a great deal to feminism. Whereas western thought typically traded on the body to supply its terms of consciousness, rationality and self-interest, the body has perhaps pushed feminism into *thinking* at the most dangerous borders of western epistemologies. There is no indication that the body will be inclined to persist within standard or traditional parameters. If feminism pursues the question of the body, it too may be edged beyond its usual boundaries. We would argue that the body, simply as a corporeal inscription of the multiple effects of history, representation and intersubjectivity, will extend beyond any provisions of the social order. The body is transitory, and its movements are within and between bodies, propelling history, culture and science—and maybe even the Symbolic Order—all the while being urged along by them. Clearly, then, the body is a signifying medium; as such, it incarnates reigning inscriptions, for example, gender. Just as clearly, the body may well be that temporal or signifying interstice that intimates a beyond to any signifying system (Stockton, 1992). But whatever it is, the body is never as univocal as psychology and the western epistemologies it recapitulates would have it.

Note

1. Lacanians would see this as the function of the Imaginary body that would stand
   in contradiction to the bodily subject as a response to the Real. In other words,
   one cannot untangle the question of ideology and the body without accounting for
   the registration of the body in the interlocked orders of subjective representation,
   the Real, the Imaginary and the Symbolic.

References

Alcoff, L.M. (1995). *Feminist theory and the problem of experience*. The Ann
    Palmeri Lecture, Hobart and William Smith Colleges, Geneva, NY.
Allen, J. (1993). Through the wild region: An essay in phenomenological feminism.
    In K. Hoeller (Ed.), *Merleau-Ponty and psychology* (pp. 241–256). Atlantic
    Highlands, NJ: Humanities Press.
Augustine, St. (1961). *Confessions* (R.S. Pine-Coffin, Trans. and Intro.). Harmonds-
    worth: Penguin.
Belenky, M., Clinchy, B., Goldberger, N., & Tarule, J. (1986). *Women's ways of
    knowing: The development of self, voice, and mind*. New York: Basic Books.
Bem, S. (1974). The measurement of psychological androgyny. *Journal of Clinical
    and Consulting Psychology, 42*, 155–162.
Benjamin, J. (1986). A desire of one's own: Psychoanalytic feminism and inter-
    subjective space. In T. de Lauretis (Ed.), *Feminist studies/critical studies* (pp.
    78–101). Bloomington: Indiana University Press.
Berger, H. Jr. (1987). Bodies and texts. *Representations, 17*, 144–165.
Bordo, S. (1987). *The flight to objectivity*. Albany: State University of New York
    Press.
Bordo, S. (1990). Feminism, postmodernism, and gender-skepticism. In L.J. Nichol-
    son (Ed.), *Feminism/postmodernism* (pp. 133–156). New York: Routledge.
Bordo, S. (1993). *Unbearable weight: Feminism, western culture, and the body*.
    Berkeley: University of California Press.
Braidotti, R. (1994). *Nomadic subjects: Embodiment and sexual difference in
    contemporary feminist theory*. New York: Columbia University Press.
Brown, B., & Adams, P. (1979). The feminine body and feminist politics. *m/f, 3*,
    35–50.
Brown, W. (1991). Feminist hesitations, postmodern exposures. *differences, 3*,
    63–84.
Burroughs, C.B., & Ehrenreich, J.D. (Eds.). (1993). Introduction. In *Reading the
    social body*. Iowa: University of Iowa Press.
Butler, J. (1990). *Gender trouble: Feminism and the subversion of identity*. New
    York: Routledge.
Butler, J. (1993). *Bodies that matter: On the discursive limits of 'sex'*. New York:
    Routledge.
Bynum, C. (1992). *Fragmentation and redemption: Essays on gender and the human
    body in medieval religion*. New York: Zone.
Code, L. (1995). *Rhetorical spaces*. New York: Routledge.
Copjec, J. (1994). *Read my desire: Lacan against the historicists*. Cambridge, MA:
    MIT Press.
Cornell, D. (1993). *Transformations*. New York: Routledge.

Dallery, A.B. (1994). The politics of writing (the) body: Écriture feminine. In A. Herrman & A. Stewart (Eds.), *Theorizing feminism: Parallel trends in the humanities and social sciences* (pp. 288–300). Boulder, CO: Westview.

Dempster, E. (1988). Women writing the body: Let's watch how she dances. In S. Sheridan (Ed.), *Grafts: Feminist cultural criticism* (pp. 35–54). London: Verso.

Erikson, E.H. (1964). Inner and outer space: Reflections on womanhood. *Daedalus*, *93*, 582–606.

Evans, M.N. (1991). *Fits and starts: A genealogy of hysteria in modern France*. Ithaca, NY: Cornell University Press.

Fallon, A., & Rozin, P. (1985). Sex differences in perceptions of desirable body shape. *Journal of Abnormal Psychology*, *94*, 102–105.

Ferguson, K. (1993). *The man question: Visions of subjectivity in feminist theory*. Berkeley: University of California Press.

Foucault, M. (1977). *Discipline and punish: The birth of the prison*. New York: Vintage.

Freud, S. (1974). Femininity. In J. Strouse (Ed.), *Women and analysis: Dialogues on psychoanalytic views of femininity* (pp. 91–115). New York: Dell. (Original work published 1933.)

Gilligan, C. (1982). *In a different voice: Psychological theory and women's development*. Cambridge, MA: Harvard University Press.

Grosz, E. (1993). Bodies and knowledges: Feminism and the crisis of reason. In L. Alcoff & E. Potter (Eds.), *Feminist epistemologies* (pp. 187–215). New York: Routledge.

Grosz, E. (1994). *Volatile bodies: Toward a corporeal feminism*. Bloomington: Indiana University Press.

Grosz, E. (1995). *Space, time, and perversion: Essays on the politics of bodies*. New York: Routledge.

Hare-Mustin, R., & Marecek, J. (1990). Beyond difference. In R. Hare-Mustin & J. Marecek (Eds.), *Making a difference* (pp. 184–201). New Haven, CT: Yale University Press.

Hekman, S.J. (1990). *Gender and knowledge: Elements of a postmodern feminism*. Boston, MA: Northeastern University Press.

Hollingsworth, L.S. (1916). Social devices for impelling women to bear and rear children. *American Journal of Sociology*, *22*, 19–29.

Hutchinson, M.G. (1994). Imagining ourselves whole: A feminist approach to treating body image disorders. In P. Fallon, M.A. Katzman, & S.C. Wolley (Eds.), *Feminist perspectives on eating disorders* (pp. 152–170). New York: Guilford.

Jordanova, L.J. (1989). *Sexual visions*. Madison: University of Wisconsin Press.

Kenrick, D.T., & Keefe, R.C. (1992). Age preferences in mates reflect sex differences in human reproductive strategies. *Behavioral and Brain Sciences*, *15*, 75–91.

Kimbrell, A. (1992, May–June). Body wars. *Utne Reader*, pp. 52–64.

King, K. (1994). *Theory in its feminist travels*. Bloomington: Indiana University Press.

Kitzinger, C., & Perkins, R. (1993). *Changing our minds: Lesbian feminism and psychology*. New York: New York University Press.

Koss, M.P. (1993). Rape: Scope, impact, interventions, and public policy responses. *American Psychologist*, *48*, 1062–1069.

Kuhn, A. (1988). The body and cinema: Some problems for feminism. In S. Sheridan (Ed.), *Grafts: Feminist cultural criticism* (pp. 11–24). London: Verso.

Lacan, J. (1989). Geneva lecture on the symptom. *analysis, 1*, 7–26.

Laqueur, T. (1990). *Making sex: Body and gender from the Greeks to Freud.* Cambridge, MA: Harvard University Press.

MacKinnon, C.A. (1987). *Feminism unmodified.* Cambridge, MA: Harvard University Press.

Marcus, S. (1992). Fighting bodies, fighting words: A theory and politics of rape prevention. In J. Butler & J.W. Scott (Eds.), *Feminists theorize the political* (pp. 385–403). New York: Routledge.

Martin, E. (1991). The egg and the sperm: How science has constructed a romance based on stereotypical male–female roles. *SIGNS: Journal of Women in Culture and Society, 16*, 485–501.

May, T. (1993). *Between genealogy and epistemology: Psychology, politics, and knowledge in the thought of Michel Foucault.* University Park: Pennsylvania State University Press.

Merck, M. (1993). *Perversions.* New York: Routledge.

Miller, N. (1994). Representing others: Gender and the subjects of autobiography. *differences, 6*, 1–27.

Morawski, J. (1994). *Practicing feminisms, reconstructing psychology,* Ann Arbor: University of Michigan Press.

Morgan, K. (1991). Women and the knife: Cosmetic surgery and the colonization of women's bodies. *Hypatia, 6*, 25–53.

Parlee, M. (1992). On PMS and psychiatric abnormality. *Feminism & Psychology. 2*, 105–108.

Perini, G., & Bayer, B. (1995). '*Out of our minds,' in our bodies: Women's embodied subjectivity and self-help culture in the 1990s.* Paper presented at the annual meeting of the International Society for Theoretical Psychology, Ottawa, Canada.

Probyn, E. (1992). Theorizing through the body. In L.F. Rakow (Ed.), *Women making meaning: New feminist directions in communication* (pp. 83–99). New York: Routledge.

Quinby, L. (1994). *Anti-apocalypse: Exercises in genealogical criticism.* Minneapolis: University of Minnesota Press.

Quinby, L. (1995). Sex matters: Genealogical inquiries, pedagogical implications. In L. Quinby (Ed.), *Genealogy and literature* (pp. 157–174). Minneapolis: University of Minnesota Press.

Radley, A. (1991). *The body and social psychology.* New York: Springer.

Ragland, E. (1994). *Essays in the pleasures of death.* New York: Routledge.

Rose, J. (1986). *Sexuality in the field of vision.* London: Verso.

Ruddick, S. (1989). *Maternal thinking: Toward a politics of peace.* Boston, MA: Beacon.

Salomon, N. (1996). The Venus Pudica: Uncovering art history's 'hidden agendas' and pernicious pedigrees. In G. Pollock (Ed.), *Generations and geographies* (pp. 69–87). London: Routledge.

Schiebinger, L. (1993). *Nature's body: Gender in the making of modern science.* Boston, MA: Beacon.

Scott, J.W. (1992). Experience. In J. Butler & J.W. Scott (Eds.), *Feminists theorize the political* (pp. 22–40). New York: Routledge.

Scott, J.W. (1995). Universalism and the history of feminism. *differences*, *7*, 1–15.

Seid, R.P. (1994). Too 'close to the bone': The historical context for women's obsession with slenderness. In P. Fallon, M.A. Katzman, & S.C. Wolley (Eds.), *Feminist perspectives on eating disorders* (pp. 3–16). New York: Guilford.

Stockton, K.B. (1992). Bodies and God: Poststructuralist feminists return to the fold of spiritual materialism. *boundary, 2*(19), 113–149.

Stunkard, A., Sorenson, T., & Schulsinger, F. (1983). Use of the Danish adoption register for the study of obesity and thinness. In S. Kety, L. Rowland, R. Sidman, & S. Matthysse (Eds.), *Genetics of neurological and psychiatric disorders* (pp. 115–120). New York: Raven Press.

Suleiman, S.R. (1986). (Re)writing the body: The politics and poetics of female eroticism. In S.R. Suleiman (Ed.), *The female body in western culture* (pp. 7–29). Cambridge, MA: Harvard University Press.

Tolman, D.L., & Diebold, E. (1994). Conflicts of body and image: Female adolescents, desire, and the no-body body. In P. Fallon, M.A. Katzman, & S.C. Wolley (Eds.), *Feminist perspectives on eating disorders* (pp. 301–317). New York: Guilford.

Ussher, J.M. (1989). *The psychology of the female body*. London: Routledge.

Weisstein, N. (1971). Psychology constructs the female, or the fantasy life of the male psychologist. In V. Gornick & B.K. Moran (Eds.), *Women in sexist society* (pp. 207–224). New York: American Library.

Wilshire, D. (1989). The uses of myth, image, and the female body in re-visioning knowledge. In A. Jaggar & S. Bordo (Eds.), *Gender/body/knowledge: Feminist reconstructions of being and knowing* (pp. 92–114). New Brunswick, NJ: Rutgers University Press.

Winkler, M. (1994). Afterword. In M.G. Winkler & L.B. Cole (Eds.), *The good body: Asceticism in contemporary culture* (pp. 232–238). New Haven, CT: Yale University Press.

Winterson, J. (1992). *Written on the body*. New York: Knopf.

7

Situated Knowledges of Personal Embodiment

Transgender Activists' and Psychological Theorists' Perspectives on 'Sex' and 'Gender'

Mary Brown Parlee

ABSTRACT. Academic psychologists' treatment of 'sex' as an ahistorical, pretheoretical notion in theories of 'gender' is compared and contrasted with knowledge produced by persons whose own gendered embodiment is outside binary gender/sex categories and whose moral agency is erased by theories depicting them as exceptions to a binary-based scheme. This latter knowledge, emerging from an activist community's reflections on its own personal/political praxis in relation to dominant social institutions and ideologies, has selectively incorporated, challenged and transformed gender/sex discourses in significant segments of medicine and academic disciplines other than psychology. Psychological theories continue to reproduce binary categories (and practices organized around them), in part because they incorporate only some of the implications of a social constructivist perspective, and in part because psychologists seem to theorize gender/sex in isolation from other knowledge-producing communities.

If the body functions as the repressed or disavowed condition of all knowledges (including biology), then providing new bases to rethink the body may share the unarticulated assumptions of these knowledges. Other forms of knowledge, other modes of knowing than those which currently prevail, will need to be undertaken. This means, among other things, not only contesting the domination of the body by biological terms but also contesting the terms of biology itself, rethinking biology so that it too is able to see the body in terms other than those thus far developed.
(Elizabeth Grosz, 1994, p. 20)

Discourse transmits and produces power; it reinforces it, but also undermines and exposes it, renders it fragile and makes it possible to thwart it. In like manner, silence and secrecy are a shelter for power, anchoring its

prohibitions, but they also loosen its holds and provide for relatively obscure areas of tolerance.
(Michel Foucault, 1976/1978, p. 101)

Secrets suck.
(Nancy R. Nangeroni, 1995, p. 17)

Anthropologists, sociologists and researchers in science studies have investigated how the theoretical knowledge of university-based producers of 'official knowledge' intersects with (mutually constituting, collaborating, contesting, colonizing, reflecting, accommodating) knowledge produced in other cultural sites (Haraway, 1988/1991; King, 1994; Latour, 1987; Martin, 1987, 1994). Here I want to consider how psychologists' theories of personal embodiment are related to other situated knowledges of bodies and persons: in particular, how academic psychologists' representations of gendered embodiment are related to representations in discourses of the 'transgender liberation' movement (Feinberg, 1992; more on terminology below).

Psychological Theories of Sex, Gender and Embodiment— From the Academy

During the past two decades feminism, AIDS, and lesbian, gay, bisexual and transgender activism have put 'the body' on the agenda of most academic disciplines (e.g. Feher, Naddaff, & Tazi, 1989; Jacobus, Keller, & Shuttleworth, 1990). Textual representations of bodily processes have been part of scientific psychology since its beginnings in 19th-century physiology. Unlike more historically minded and self-reflexive disciplines, however, Foucault's (1976/1978) history of sexuality and the conceptual resources it makes available have been largely absent from contemporary discussions within North American psychology. Nevertheless, Foucault's analysis of *bio-power* is important for psychologists' efforts to theorize embodied subjectivities as *both* material *and* cultural phenomena. In particular, Judith Butler's (1990) use of Foucault in her discussion of 'identity' and 'intelligible' genders has implications for one of the most sustained of these efforts: psychological discourses concerning sex and gender.

Contemporary psychologists' uses of the terms 'sex' and 'gender' vary greatly (Unger & Crawford, 1993). Specific proposals have been made during the past 20 years to standardize usage, but they seem either to have lost their initial acceptance (e.g. Unger, 1979; see Hyde, 1994) or to have been met with immediate rejection (e.g. Gentile, 1993; see Deaux, 1993). Nevertheless, I believe Celia Kitzinger (1994) is correct in saying there is a common thread among the varied uses: 'In most attempts to distinguish between "sex" and "gender", there is an assumption that "sex" is somehow prior—the anatomical or biological bedrock upon which gender differences are built . . .' (p. 505).

As Kitzinger points out, however: 'Alternative versions are possible, as in this account by Christine Delphy (1984, 144) which reverses the traditional formulation:

> . . . logically [N.B.] the hierarchy of the division of labor is prior to . . . the sexual roles which we call gender. *Gender in its turn created anatomical sex*, in the sense that the hierarchical division of humanity into two transforms an anatomical difference (which is in itself devoid of meaning, like all physical facts) into a category of thought.'[1] (p. 505)

In other words: human bodies differ in many ways, which are always, necessarily an admixture of biological processes and social history.[2] The socially significant classification of persons as 'women' and 'men' serves as a heuristic for searching out and selecting the particular biological differences which are grouped together under/as the contemporary western category 'sex'. (Laqueur, 1990, discusses changing conceptions of 'sex' in western scientific traditions; see also Tuana, 1989.) The Foucauldian argument is that *as the biological definition of sex becomes established in/ through social practices, traces of its dependence on a conceptually prior notion of gender become invisible.*

The analyses by Kitzinger and Delphy and by Foucault and Butler are similar in important ways. They assume gender and power are inextricably intertwined. They treat 'gender' *and* 'sex' as historically specific, socially produced categories (*effects*) rather than as prior givens, perhaps located in a trans-historical Nature or Culture, categories not needing to be theorized. They deconstruct and reconstruct the everyday (contemporary, western) understandings of bedrock-biological-sex and socially constructed gender that are reproduced in and by the work of most psychological theorists (e.g. Bem, 1993; Eagly, 1994; Harré, 1991a; Hyde, 1990; but notably not Kessler & MacKenna, 1978/1985).[3]

One theorist who has focused on sex and gender as part of his effort to develop a theory of personal embodiment is Rom Harré (especially 1991a). Because his work may be more familiar to readers of *Theory & Psychology* than the work of feminist psychologists cited above (and others), and because it is in some ways more developed theoretically, I use it as the starting-point for my discussion of situated knowledges of embodiment.

In Harré's (1991b) analysis of the necessity of personhood as embodied being:

> Continuity of consciousness is rooted in the singularity of a point of view founded on the robust material persistence of the human body as the

vantage point from which each person gains their perspective on the physical world. Moral continuity as an agent is more weakly related to personhood since one's claims to and disclaimers of responsibility are grounded in one's shifting location in a local network of positions. While one has only one body from which to survey the world, one has, at least in principle, many moral positions from which to act upon it. (p. 53)

Harré's psychological theory is similar in many ways to theories of subjectivity put forward by feminists in other academic disciplines and interdisciplines, most recently including Judith Butler (1990, 1993), Elizabeth Grosz (1994) and Allucquere Rosanne Stone (1995). They all reject Cartesian dualisms (of mind/body, reason/emotion). They treat the supposed interiority of 'mental states' (more or less explicitly along Foucauldian lines) as effects of power, as socially constructed. They produce a thoroughly constructivist account of embodied agency that includes even the 'I' (what Harré in his 1991b calls paper Self-1, 'the necessary singularity of persons'), eschewing recourse to a prediscursive 'I' (which Butler characterizes critically as a subject *mired* in but not *constituted* by discourse—1990, p. 143).

Such similarities suggest that the 'discursive turn' in psychology, to which Harré's work has importantly contributed, and postmodern feminist theorizing may be converging. For someone like me who believes both are engaged in fundamentally rethinking and remaking psychological knowledge, or more precisely academically certified psychological knowledge, this is a welcome development.

However, a feminist reading of Harré's theory for a corporeal psychology poses an obvious and central theoretical question. Is the 'one body' from which 'one' surveys the world always already a sexed body?

Careful reading of Harré's texts does not provide a clear answer. On the one hand, he speaks as if it were not. For example, 'One's idea of one's body as male or female is established very early in life' (Harré, 1991a, p. 77). '[A] person's body is just a cluster of attributes drawn from the whole range of properties characteristic of human beings' (Harré, 1991a, p. 17). But by 'one' and 'person' here he seems to be speaking of/from the perspective of the being who is becoming subjectively embodied as a female or male person (taking on 'male embodiment' or 'female embodiment' as it is discursively constituted in the local culture).

On the other hand, Harré (1991a) speaks as if, *from the point of view of the theorist*, bodies always come in female or male forms. For example,

Male and female bodies differ in two ways. Sexual dimorphism of the genital organs is sharply defined. (p. 43)

Based on the biological sex of the body, the distinctions of gender are loaded with practical and moral implications. I shall call this loading a 'social construction'. I shall be exploring the ways in which the categories of gender, 'man' and 'woman', are socially constructed on the basis of the identification of bodies as 'male' and 'female, the biological distinctions of sex. (p. 38)

Thus Harré, like other psychologists theorizing sex and gender whom I have read, explicitly articulates a 'social constructionist' stance with respect to gender.[4] But in these theoretical efforts a conceptual analysis of gender as a social construction is characteristically linked with a conception of biological sex that is ahistorical, fixed and binary (see also Kitzinger, 1994).

That is, the theories acknowledge (with different emphases) and attempt to account for the variability and fluidity of gender, the variety of combinations of social and psychological gender-related (gender-constituting) elements that can characterize embodied persons. But the basic conceptual framework of two-ness for descriptions—theoretically relevant analyses—of bodies as sexed seems to be firmly entrenched (see critiques by Birke, 1982; Fausto-Sterling, 1993; Kessler & MacKenna, 1978/1985). Empirical observations that do not fit the binary sex categories 'female' and 'male' are *noted* by Harré (e.g. 1991a, p. 46) and by other psychological theorists, but are treated *only with reference to the binary categories. They are conceptualized as theoretically insignificant noise* ('overlaps', 'anomalies', 'rare') *rather than as observations to be positively theorized in and of themselves.*

On pp. 38–39 of *Physical Being: A Theory for a Corporeal Psychology*, Harré (1991a) lays the groundwork for his conclusion that '"male" and "female" do seem to be body-kinds' (p. 45) with a general discussion of philosophical foundations for the practice of categorizing. Objects—a heap of stones, in his example—can be classified in different ways. Some classifications are animated by particular human interests: for example, a builder might separate stones according to shape, according to practical uses to which the stones will be put. Other classifications, such as the geologists' theoretical classification of stones into schist and granite on the basis of chemical composition, are, in Harré's view, 'rooted in natural differences, not in human practical interests'. These are 'natural kinds' because the choice of categories 'can be justified by reference of something other than the apparent properties of the stones [e.g. chemical composition]'.

In Harré's view, it is by this reference to something other than observable properties—the 'something other' being known (epistemologically constituted as such) within a physical theory—that the 'real essences' of material things are known. It is the real essence of an object that permits explanation of 'why the characteristics that make up the nominal essence are always found together'. In Harré's view, then, physical theories (in which by implication practical interests play no role?) trump practical interests in any contests concerning an object's 'real' essence, what can 'count as genuine'.

On pp. 44–45 in the same volume Harré applies these ideas about categorizing to sex and gender.

> Conceptual clarity in these matters can be assisted by thinking in terms of a double application of the overt–nominal/covert–real essence distinction. Chromosomal difference serves as the real essence of the distinction in sex;[5] the overt manifestation of which in complementary, and in principle visible, genitals is thus nominal. But since the genitals are usually hidden, their differences serve as the real essence of the public manifestation of sex differences, whether in tidied-up secondary characteristics [body hair, fat, height, etc., are *bimodally* distributed, shaped by cultural practices toward a dichotomous, *bipolar* distribution] or in manufactured tertiary [such as styles of clothing]. . . . To sum up: the model of nominal (overt) and real (covert) essence taken from the philosophy of chemical kinds can be applied to sex differences, provided that we are ready to deal *ad hoc* with the complexity of the double application of the overt/covert (displayed/hidden) distinction.[6] 'Male' and 'female' do seem to be body-kinds.

(The material in brackets condenses views expressed elsewhere in *Physical Being*. See Dupré, 1986, for a philosophical analysis which concludes 'male' and 'female' are not natural body-kinds.)

In an extended discussion of 'female' and 'male' body-kinds and gender, Harré writes:

> It is worth remarking that feminist reform of social restrictions on the activities of women could be based on the bimodality of actual distributions of powers and skills between the sexes: the distribution of all those characteristics that I have comprehended under gender overlap.
>
> One way of establishing a mere contingency of a correlation is to build up a repertoire of thought experiments in which other correlations among the relevant variables are shown to be possible. Suggestions for mappings other than the traditional one-to-one correlation between sex and gender have come from several feminist authors . . .
>
> [Harré then discusses four such suggestions; I quote only those for which he cites specific texts.]
>
> . . . 3) Post-feminists, like radical feminists, do not argue for the abolition of the masculine/feminine distinction, but for a dismantling of the social processes by which that distinction is rigidly mapped onto the biological dichotomy of persons embodied as males and females. Thus, it is argued, any human being can, and would, be enabled to adopt a masculine or feminine mode of life regardless of natural genital endowment. This is the position of authors like Davies (1990).
>
> 4) Finally, a fourth position has emerged, most notably as advocated by J. Kristeva (1981), if I have understood her somewhat delphic pronouncements aright. The radical and post-feminist positions remain in her scheme as necessary stages in personal/social development, to be transcended at a third stage when there comes to be a social order in which there are no dichotomous distinctions isomorphic with biological gender [*sic*].

> Could these alternative mappings serve as the foundations for possible ways of life?
>
> In considering the viability of the world conjured up in the Davies–Kristeva thought experiment, we are driven back to technical questions of sociobiology. . . . Discussion of this matter has been clouded by feminist political rhetoric and outbursts of moral indignation. The only works, among the many I have skimmed, that address the issue reasonably dispassionately are Tiger and Shepher's (1975) *Women in the Kubbutz* and Mary Midgeley's (1978) *Beast and Man*. . . .
>
> Having arrived at a fairly well-specified conceptual system for discussing body-kind judgments based ultimately on sex, as the doubly hidden real essence of body kind, the question of the mechanisms of the formation of gender identity out of sex can be raised. How do the mappings of social–cultural identified (man/woman) onto biological sex (male/female) come about? (Harré, 1991a, pp. 50–53)

(An early feminist analysis of the question can be found in Rubin, 1975.)

While several features of these passages seem to me to invite comment, I want here to draw attention to only two. (1) In these texts 'women', 'the sexes' and 'actual distributions of powers and skills between the sexes' are used as key (pretheoretical) concepts, as if their meanings are unproblematic and clear for both author and readers. (2) The conceptual system is honed through use of philosophical analysis, 'thought experiments' and, at key points, an extremely selective review of the scholarly and research literatures on sex and gender. These concepts and ways of knowing seem to pass unremarked within the parts of the academy inhabited by psychologists, but in other cultural locations, both outside the academy and within it in other disciplines, knowledge of sex, gender and embodiment is being produced through other modes of knowing, with quite different results.

Psychological Theories of Sex, Gender and Embodiment— From Transgender Activists

During the past two decades in North America persons whose gendered embodiment is outside conventional gender/sex categories have become politically consciousness of their shared identities and interests as 'outsiders' (see, e.g., Bolin, 1994; Bornstein, 1994; Feinberg, 1992; Woodhouse, 1989). Some of the social conditions triggering this new activist movement, and some of the political activities that comprise it, are suggested by a recent editorial by Jean Marie Stine in the magazine *Transgender Tapestry* ('Celebrating the Diversity of Gender Expression', 74, Winter 1995, p. 1):

> 1995 was a watershed year for the transgendered community . . . events that catalyzed the TG community as never before [include]:
>
> • The murder of Brandon Teena, a woman living as a man, by two bigots who first raped her when they discovered her 'secret'.

- The formation of TOPS (Transgendered Officers Protect and Serve for TG police, firefighters, military, etc.).
- The 1st FTM (female-to-male) Conference of the Americas for women living, dressing, or having surgery to become, men.[7]
- The American Psychiatric Association declar[ed] that transvestism is not a mental disorder, but simply a different gender orientation.
- 1st National Transgender Lobby Day, with members of leading trans-gender organizations including doctors, attorneys, psychologists, and others visiting their representatives in Washington DC.
- The death of Tyra Hunter, crossdresser left unattended by paramedics after a car wreck, when they opened her pants to discover she was a man.
- The formation of GenderPAC, the first TG political education fund.
- The successful fight to include the transgendered in the new Employ-ment Non-Discrimination Act coming up before Congress.
- The 1st International Conference on Gender, Crossdressing and Sex Issues.
- First transgendered celebrity to be selected as spokesperson for a line of cosmetics and to be featured in ads for other national products: drag queen superstar RuPaul.
- First National Gay and Lesbian Task Force Policy Institute conference to include the TG community.
- A tidal-wave of visibility for the transgendered—on television, in movies, magazines, newspapers, comics, and books.

Other activities and issues are covered in a recent issue of a less 'establishment' publication, *Gendertrash* ('A Canadian community & politi-cally oriented publication for transsexual and transgendered persons', 4, Spring 1995):

- addiction and recovery in the street transsexual community;
- racism and poverty in the transgender community;
- discrimination and violence against transsexual inmates in California prisons;
- outreach programs for AIDS education and prevention.

Transgender Tapestry, Gendertrash and the many other publications pro-duced by transgender activists (e.g. *Chrysalis Quarterly, Transsisters: The Journal of Transsexual Feminism, Hermaphrodites with Attitude, TNT: Transsexual News Telegraph. The Magazine of Transsexual Culture*) also carry listings of publications and newsletters, organizations, resources and services, conferences, fairs, events of interest to the transgender com-munity.

As these and other publications make clear, transgender activists work together, as the term 'community' implies, to challenge pathologizing medical discourses and public intolerance, discrimination, violence and harassment. But there are nonetheless political differences and alliances within the transgender community with respect to other aims, and political relations with feminists and/or lesbian, gay and bisexual activists are complex. In negotiations over aims, strategies and tactics, and in struggles to avoid the fragmentation and paralysis of 1970s-style identity politics, new understandings of sex/gender have emerged. This knowledge, emerging from a diverse, self-aware community's reflections on its own personal/political praxis in relation to dominant social institutions and ideologies, is strikingly different from psychological theories of gendered embodiment emanating from the academy.

At a minimum, transgender activists have found it necessary to move beyond such bedrock concepts of common-sense and scientific discourses as 'woman', 'man', 'female', 'male', 'lesbian', 'gay', 'straight'—simply in order to take into account the empirical variety of actual persons' embodied subjectivities.

For example, is a MtF (male-to-female) transsexual (TS) person who cannot be distinguished from a female by genital examination a woman who should be allowed to participate in 'women-only' spaces (women's bars, music festivals, women's centers, and the like)? Is someone who feels, acts and is socially accepted as a man and who has a vagina a man? Is a female who cross-dresses (CD) and looks and acts like a man at home, who dresses and is accepted as a woman at work, and who is married to a MtF TS woman a 'woman', 'man', 'gay', 'lesbian', 'straight'? What about someone who was raised as a girl, develops breasts and menstruates, and grows a full beard at 25, and is often addressed in public as 'sir'—is this person 'really' a woman as she feels herself to be? Is someone who at adolescence develops breasts and spreading hips and a deep voice and a beard 'female' or 'male'? Is their woman ('genetic' or not) lover 'lesbian' or 'straight'? If they feel their gender identity to be that of a 'third gender', what pronoun should be used to refer to them in conversations where they are present but not directly addressed?[8]

Activists with a commitment to acknowledging the perspectives and moral claims of others and to taking responsibility for their own actions have worked to find answers to such questions through political praxis, and this has involved rethinking—re-theorizing—sex and gender categories, developing new terms. One transgender activist comments: 'It seems that we . . . are preoccupied with what we should be called. We are constantly inventing and redefining the descriptive terms for our various manifestations' (Laing, 1995, p. 48).

As a political movement taking shape within the 'double-consciousness' produced by powerful medical/scientific discourses of 'normal' and 'natural' sex, gender and sexuality, activists who want to change dominant discourses of sex/gender and the subject positions they make available act as if language and labels matter. (Groups who do not want change also act as if language and labels matter.) The power to name is clearly important: whether a particular term comes from medical/scientific discourses or from within an activist community, who uses it and to whom, in what context—all are necessarily implicated in the constitution and reconstitution of social identities and relationships; all signal political alliances, aims and strategies; all confirm or deny claims to moral agency.

This means that psychologists writing about sex/gender/transgender necessarily make—I am making—not only linguistic choices but also, simultaneously, ethical and political decisions about their/my relationships with transgendered persons and the political aims and moral claims they have articulated.[9] In writing this section of my paper I wished there were some collective discussion among psychologists I could turn to similar to that occurring among anthropologists during the past decade, concerning the ethics of representational practices (Marcus & Fischer, 1986).[10]

Bearing in mind these considerations and also my own situation as a supportive outsider to what Leslie Feinberg (1992) has called the 'trans-gender liberation movement', I 'simply' offer a list of some terms I have heard and read used as self-descriptions by activists or as descriptions (often 'diagnoses') by medical professionals to refer to persons whose gendered embodiment is outside conventional gender/sex categories. They include: transgenderist, transsexual, transsexual, transsexual woman, transsexual man, transgendered woman, transgendered man, person with an intersex condition, third gender, cross-dresser, transvestite, transsexual lesbian, woman, man.

Collectively the heterogeneous movement has been referred to by activists as the transgender community, the gender community, TS/TG/TV/CD community, transpeople, gender-benders, gender outlaws, gender queers, gendertrash, gender gifted and (with irony) 'differently gendered'. While the meanings-in-use of many of these terms are constantly shifting, consolidating and opening up again, only the most linguistically/politically tone deaf and aggressive outsider would, for example, so overlook the importance of language as to use medical terms (e.g. transvestite) and community-based terms (e.g. cross-dresser) interchangeably in all settings (but see Sedgwick, 1988).

Riki Anne Wilchins, founder of the activist group, The Transexual Menace, has analyzed the significance of sex/gender language for trans-gender activists in a way I think is directly relevant to psychological discourses produced in the academy by Harré and by others:

> Let's accept from the outset that . . . all language, and especially naming, is about power: that is language is political in nature. A name reflects culture's need to identify and manipulate something—as distinct from other things around it—and the name selected invariably creates the very perception of difference it supposedly just names. . . .
>
> I do not believe in the term 'transsexual' much less 'transgender,' although I employ both on occasion simply to contest the oppression which comes with being socially identified as either one. But that isn't surprising,

> since I don't believe in 'male' and 'female' or 'man and 'woman' either. Certainly I believe in them as political accomplishments, cultural categories instituted to cause us to read the body in a specific way: promoting and sustaining the imperative that the most important thing bodies can do is reproduce. But I don't view them as the so-called 'natural facts' they are interminably and predictably proposed to represent. (I should add that I *do* support anyone's right to identify as any of these.)
>
> The point is that all these names reflect the political aims of a cultural regime which produces certain gender 'realities' for its own changing, and historically specific, needs. Such is the power of culture, acting through language, to create the perception of the 'real,' and apportion privilege according. Or rather, to apportion privilege, and therefore create the 'real *as* real,' as undeniable cultural fact.
>
> So, if we are to disrupt the regime, we must take control of language, take control of (corrupt) the definitions, disturb the structure. This brings us to a number of terms coming into increasing coinage in the 'gender' community, such as 'gendertrash,' one 'S' transexuals, 'genderqueer,' etc. (Wilchins, 1995, p. 46).

Given her analysis, where and how she positions herself in the moral order, and her reasons for theorizing, Wilchins selectively makes use of 'official' knowledge produced from within the academy to clarify further her own and others' situation:

> Feminist philosopher Judith Butler has pointed out that to define any categories, to create a grid of intelligible identities, you must inevitably case out and obscure others. These others become what she calls an 'abject' region: those identities which become unspeakable, even unthinkable, within the grid because there are no terms or names for them. So defining this grid means making decisions (in other words, having the *power*) to decide which kinds of gendered bodies 'matter' and which don't. But it is only possible to maintain this illusory grid, with its nice, neat ordering of two 'natural' sexes accompanied by two 'natural' ordered genders *because* all alternatives are blocked out and/or discarded. It is inevitably the outside (i.e. 'us'), in remaining outside, that makes the inside possible. Because once the outside intrudes, neatness and coherence immediately vanish and are quickly replaced with messy, disordered multiplicity.
>
> From this viewpoint, transgendered bodies and genders *are* that outside, and it is precisely by discarding us as 'gendertrash' if you will, by stigmatizing us or by delegitimating us off the grid as merely 'aberrant' or 'deviant' or (Virginia Prince here) 'defective' or 'pathological,' which enables the binary grid to appear as immaculate, uncontaminated, and 'natural'. (Wilchins, 1995, p. 47)

Thus from Wilchins' perspective Harré's psychological theory of gendered embodiment (again, like that of many other psychologists) simply reproduces with the cultural authority of science common-sense and medical discourses of sex and gender. It reproduces an 'illusory grid, with its nice, neat ordering of two "natural" sexes accompanied by two "natural" ordered genders'. And it can accomplish this in part '*because* all alternatives are blocked out and/or discarded'. Some perspectives are missing/occluded because some embodied persons have no moral weight, no recognized subject position in the academic psychological discourses through which 'sex' and 'gender' are constituted as objects of scientific knowledge. Real persons can be and are constituted as Other ('anomalies', 'unusual', 'rare') in these academic discourses because psychological theorists have the power to speak and name, at least to their colleagues and sometimes to other audiences, without effective challenge.

Wilchins' mode of theorizing explicitly connects with some theories (Theories) of sex, gender and sexuality produced in academic disciplines outside psychology. However, others in the transgender community are also producing theories (small 't') of sex/gender in a different mode, 'simply' by articulating and making visible identities rendered unspeakable and invisible within the binary grids of 'official' psychological discourses. This mode of everyday theorizing, Liz Stanley and Sue Wise (1990) have argued, is too often unrecognized or underappreciated by academic social scientists.

For example, the following reflections on masculinity and embodiment were recently posted on a publicly accessible email network on transgender issues. One criterion for assessing the adequacy of academic psychological theories might be how well they can comprehend such analytical accounts of personal experiences.

> For most of us who were born male and have a gender identity of 'not man' (which may [*sic*] mean 'woman') and who were socialized as a man simply because we had an outie between our legs, we had a very tough time. . . . But that doesn't mean that some of us weren't able to figure out how to pass as a man anyway. It may have been tough, but we learned how to fake it, how to live enough as a man to be successful. . . . I used to joke that 'I have the anatomy, the hormones, and the training, so I guess I'll be the guy.' . . . Being a man is a breeches role for me, like one of those Japanese girls who plays the leading man in the all-female theatre company. . . . we do what we can and what we need to do, and make our choices everyday— and choosing to be a man today is certainly an honorable and valuable choice.

The gender/gender-identity of the person who wrote this clearly cannot be comprehended by the scientific theories of 'transsexualism' ('a woman trapped in a man's body') promulgated by university-affiliated, research-oriented, physician-controlled gender clinics in the United States from the 1960s through the mid-1980s (Bolin, 1994). Nor does Harré's language of 'mapping' binary sex onto binary gender seem to provide much illumination. By contrast, research by transgender activists and by academics working outside positivist research traditions, using methods that allow transgendered persons to speak for and about themselves to researchers they trust, has begun to articulate—to theorize—much more more complex and varied gender identities than are comprehended or named within the binaries of medical/scientific discourses (e.g. Devor, 1989, 1993, in press).

Situated Knowledges of Sex, Gender and Embodiment: Contests and Collaborations

In *Flexible Bodies: Tracking Immunity in American Culture from the Days of Polio to the Age of AIDS* anthropologist Emily Martin (1994) begins with a desire: 'To avoid the idealized picture of science, which its practitioners would like to believe, that knowledge is produced inside and flows out' (p. 7). She sets out instead to describe scientists' activities in a world where others are also agents, where groups with various experience and expertise do not passively accept 'official knowledge' and its technologies but actively evaluate, selectively use, transform and challenge them in the course of producing other knowledges for their own purposes.

For a substantial part of the past 40–50 years, the flow of 'official' scientific knowledge of sex and gender does seem to have been primarily one way. Medical/scientific discourses (in which practical interests are said to play no role) have been able to trump other interests in any contests over what is 'real' in the sex/gender domain, what can count as 'genuine'. Because they are embedded in powerful social institutions and practices, these discourses also have political and ethical meaning.

For example, women athletes can lose their Olympic medals if medical tests determine they are not 'really' females (de la Chapelle, 1986). A clinician tells 'an outwardly normal girl' that she 'is actually a genetic male' (Wilson, George, & Griffin, 1981). Physicians prescribe long-term treatment with hormones to a boy who does not have a 'normal' penis (the 'real essence of the public manifestation of [his] sex' in Harré's analysis) (Money, 1974). Teams of medical specialists assemble with powerful technologies to resolve the 'medical emergency' that they cannot decide by looking at a newborn baby's genitals if the infant is 'really' female or male (Kessler, 1990).

During the past 10–15 years, however—partly in response to situations like these—transgendered and intersexed persons, constituted as 'objects' in medical/scientific discourses, have found voice in/as a social movement. Activists have begun, as Martin observed in another context, to evaluate, selectively use, challenge and transform the medical/scientific knowledge. New discourses, more reflective of the empirical complexity of sex/gender/ sexuality being theorized by transgender activists, have begun to leave organizational traces in some of the arenas where medical/scientific knowl- edge is produced.[11]

While the political and cultural activities that are reshaping discourses of sex and gender are the work of a relatively small number of activists, they resonate with (both draw from and stimulate) recent academic research on gender/sex in several academic disciplines other than psychology. These include in-depth historical and anthropological investigations of cultures with more than two genders and/or sexes (e.g. see Herdt, 1994); critical re-evaluation of traditional conceptualizations of such cultures (Whitehead, 1981); critical re-evaluation of biomedical conceptualizations of trans-gendered and intersexed persons (Fausto-Sterling, 1993); contemporary sociological investigations in collaboration with people whose relationships or physical appearance transcends/transgresses traditional sex/gender map-pings (Bolin, 1994; Devor, 1989, 1993, in press; Woodhouse, 1989). Transgender activists also draw upon and contribute to the theoretical work on sex, gender and sexuality being done in and from non-traditional interdisciplines and fields like feminist theory, lesbian, gay and bisexual studies, history of sexuality, and queer theory (Abelove, Barale, & Halperin, 1993).

How do psychological theories of sexed/gendered embodiment, Harré's and others', fit into this intellectual ferment? When viewed in light of knowledge produced by transgender activists, I think three features of Harré's theory of sex and gender stand out.

One is that it leaves the notion of 'gender' seriously under-theorized. It is therefore limited in its capacity to account adequately for the empirical complexity of sex/gender phenomena. This may stem partly from what US journalists refer to when speaking of editorial writing they don't like as the 'thumb-sucking' aspects of the enterprise: the intellectual nourishment seems to come from limited sources. 'Thought experiments' can be very useful in some contexts, and selective literature reviews are not uncommon in psychology, but when the 'experiments' have real-life instantiations, and when there is a large and sophisticated scholarly literature extant, conver-sation with other knowledge-producing communities is also likely to be productive for psychological theorizing.

Second, Harré's theoretical account does not seem to incorporate fully the implications of a social constructionist perspective for conceptions of biological sex (and, again, he is not untypical of psychologists in this respect). One result, on my reading, is a lack of clarity regarding issues central to theorizing gendered embodiment. For example, according to Harré, 'If female hormones in a male body can make room for doubt as to which gender a person really [sic] is, then biological determinism has overtaken social construction as the dominant process in the differentiation of people by gender' (1991a, p. 43). Does he mean to conflate, as this sentence seems to do, reference to biological events (hormones and their actions) with something called 'biological determinism'? What does 'deter-minism' mean in this context? 'Determinism' of what, exactly? Whose 'doubts' is he referring to? From what subject position does he think authoritative judgments can come regarding what gender an individual 'really' is?

These two features seem to me serious empirical and conceptual problems for a psychological theory of gendered embodiment, regardless of how one thinks about the ethics and politics of theorizing and the relationships among different knowledge-producing communities. However, a third feature of Harré's theoretical language for analyzing sex and gender, related to the other two, also becomes evident when it is considered in light of knowledge produced by transgender activists. It does not provide what Kenneth Gergen has called a 'generative' theoretical account of sex, gender, bodies, embodiment.

Generative theories, in Gergen's (1978) view, are those with

> ... the capacity to challenge the guiding assumptions of the culture, to raise fundamental questions regarding contemporary social life, to foster reconsideration of that which is 'taken for granted', and thereby to furnish new alternatives for social action. It is the generative theory that can provoke debate, transform social reality, and ultimately to reorder social conduct. (p. 1346)

(I would also characterize such theories as critical or feminist.)

Harré's theory instead seems to reproduce as scientific knowledge common-sense beliefs about gendered embodiment: that conventional (Western, contemporary) sex/gender categories are 'natural' and that individuals who transgress them are to be spoken of, thought of and treated as objects (pathological, rare, anomalous) rather than as persons with moral standing and agency. It reflects and reproduces the power of psychological discourse without fostering ethical reflection on this power or accountability for actions.[12] And so, as Mary Gergen (1995) has argued in a related context, it does not encourage (much less incorporate) reflexive consideration of the relationship between psychological knowledge and the desiring, knowing subject of psychology. Yet psychologists, the psychological community, are obviously situated embodied subjects of the knowledge they produce. A penumbra surrounding psychological theories of sex and gender, regardless of where or how the knowledge is produced, is surely the knower's positioning in the discourses and social institutions which normalize and police heterosexuality.

In her paper 'Situated Knowledges', Donna Haraway uses vision as a metaphor in linking embodiment of the situated, knowing subject with a reconstructed notion of objectivity (all quotes are from Haraway, 1988/1991, pp. 190–195):

> We need to learn in our bodies ... to name where we are and are not, in dimensions of mental and physical space we hardly know how to name. ... So ... objectivity turns out to be about particular and specific embodiment and definitely not about the false vision promising transcendence of all limits and responsibility. ... The only position from which objectivity

could not possibly be practiced and honored is the standpoint of the master, the Man, the One God, whose Eye produces, appropriates, and orders all difference. . . .

The moral is simple: only partial perspective promises objective vision. . . . [I]t is precisely in the politics and epistemology of partial perspectives that the possibility of sustained, rational, objective inquiry rests. . . . I am arguing for politics and epistemologies of location, positioning, and situating, where partiality and not universality is the condition of being heard to make rational knowledge claims.

Notes

1. Delphy's claim is about analytic strategies: how and why the analyst 'picks out' 'gender' and 'sex' as categories in social worlds, constructs them as objects in/ of formal theories; she is not offering a hypothesis about the chronology of historical events in a world where 'gender' and 'sex' have an already theorized status (see also Fausto-Sterling, 1987).
2. See, e.g., Birke (1992) and Hubbard (1990). This is *not* the same as saying that 'biological and social processes interact', a language which obscures dialectical relations in favor of more familiar concepts ('variables') and methods (Parlee, 1990).
3. Butler (1990) follows Foucault in showing how ideas about biological 'sex', about 'female' and 'male', are constructed under specific material, historical circumstances. The contemporary western belief that there are two and only two biological sexes (with perhaps some theoretically insignificant 'anomalies' or 'overlaps') is shown to be produced as 'truth' (a 'reality effect') by powerful medical and scientific discourses, including psychological theories. To say cultural ideas and practices constitute our current ideas of 'sex' is *not* to deny the material reality of bodies capable of what biologists call sexual reproduction.
4. The idea that gender is 'socially constructed' frequently becomes elided with the notion that gender is 'socially acquired' and/or that conceptions of what is a 'feminine' woman and a 'masculine man' vary across cultures and are therefore socially produced (see also Brod, 1987). When this happens a *constructivist analysis is not being carried through consistently*: 'girls', 'boys', 'women' and 'men' continue to be treated as ontological givens, as fundamental categories (used unquestioningly by the theorist) for analysis of the social world.

    To adopt a constructivist perspective on the social relations of gender within which 'women' and 'men' are constituted as such under particular historical circumstances is not, of course, to deny the material reality of actual human beings (Riley, 1987; Stanley & Wise, 1990).
5. 'Chromosomal differences' would be more precise (de la Chapelle, 1986; Fausto-Sterling, 1993), and 'chromosomal variations' would be a more apt characterization of the results of sex chromatin screening procedures. Neither phrase could be used in this context with the same rhetorical effect as 'chromosomal difference', however.
6. In mentioning a need to 'deal, *ad hoc*' with some of the complexities of sex and gender, Harré (1991a) may also be referring to what he describes in the

paragraph preceding this quotation as the 'recently discovered envelope-and-core anomalies, as I shall call them, which must be accommodated in any scheme. . . . It can happen that while the "core" of a human body is one sex, the "envelope" has not developed the sex characteristics to match it. The commonest pattern is a male core within a female envelope' (p. 45). Given the terminology employed, and absent specific citations, I do not know if Harré is referring here to what has been discussed in the medical literature as 'hermaphrodism' and 'pseudohermaphrodism' (Money, Hampson, & Hampson, 1955) or whether he is referring to accounts in the clinical literature of the experiences of persons seeking sex reassignment surgery (Stoller, 1975). For present purposes the relevant point is that Harré retains the two categories 'male' and 'female' to conceptualize phenomena which do not fit into either category and might therefore seem to require additional new concepts or revision of existing ones (see, e.g., Eicher & Washburn, 1986).

7. Most attendees at the FtM conference used men's names for themselves and masculine pronouns to refer to each other; some referred to the collective group as 'the guys' or 'men' or 'transgendered men' (H. Rubin, personal communication, 1995). The *Transgender Tapestry* editorial's use of 'women' does not fit the conference participants' social gender presentation or their (own sense of) gender identity.

8. Spending time with persons who seem genuinely not to care what pronoun is used in talking about them has made me very aware of how difficult it is to avoid 'doing gender' in daily life (West & Zimmerman, 1987).

9. For example, when psychologist Harré writes about a MtF transsexual woman, Renée Richards, using scare quotes around the pronouns 'she' and 'her', he is privileging his view of who counts as a 'woman' over Richards's (who presents herself socially as a woman). Reasoned and responsive arguments can be made for the different views of sex and gender reflected/enacted in different pronoun usage in such contexts, but in academic psychological discourses they can also be avoided through exercise of authorial power vis-à-vis the textually represented persons (Morawski & Steele, 1991).

10. The recent Special Feature in *Feminism & Psychology*, 'Representing the Other', edited by Sue Wilkinson (1996), seems likely to be an important beginning of such a dialogue.

11. At a recent meeting of the Society for the Scientific Study of Sexuality, plenary sessions on 'Genitals, Identity and Gender' and 'Female or Male, Both or Neither' reported new data to packed audiences. Speakers referred repeatedly to a 'new paradigm' as they described leading-edge medical thought and practice on transgender issues. Emblematic of the changed relations between at least some medical professionals and activists, most speakers at the conference were introduced with a recital of both their scientific and activist credentials.

Perhaps surprisingly, changes in binary, pathologizing discourses of sex/gender have come more rapidly in medicine than in academic psychology. This may be because medical researcher/clinicians necessarily work with activists who both challenge them and promote empathic insight. Practices (including theorizing) change as multiple perspectives are taken into account.

12. This is not just an 'academic' observation in the everyday, pejorative and quite often mistaken sense of 'academic'. Psychologists' theories about what constitutes the 'real' essence of gender have particular social resonance at a time when persons have been killed or left to die because their gender did not 'map' onto their sex in 'traditional' ways (Minkowitz, 1994).

References

Abelove, H., Barale, M.A., & Halperin, D.M. (Eds.). (1993). *The lesbian and gay studies reader*. New York: Routledge.

Bem, S. (1993). *The lenses of gender: Transforming the debate on sexual inequality*. New Haven, CT: Yale University Press.

Birke, L. (1982). Cleaving the mind: Speculations on conceptual dichotomies. In S. Rose & The Dialectics of Biology Group (Eds.), *Against biological determinism* (pp. 60–78). London: Allison & Busby

Birke, L. (1992). In pursuit of difference: Scientific studies of women and men. In G. Kirkup & L.S. Keller (Eds.), *Inventing women: Science, technology and gender* (pp. 81–102). Cambridge: Polity.

Bolin, A. (1988). *In search of Eve: Transsexual rites of passage*. South Hadley, MA: Bergin & Garvey.

Bolin, A. (1994). Transcending and transgendering: Male-to-female transsexuals, dichotomy and diversity. In G. Herdt (Ed.), *Third sex, third gender: Beyond sexual dimorphism in culture and history* (pp. 447–486). New York: Zone.

Bornstein, K. (1994). *Gender outlaw: On men, women and the rest of us*. New York: Routledge.

Brod, H. (1987). Cross-culture, cross-gender: Cultural marginality and gender transcendence. *American Behavioral Scientist, 31*, 5–11.

Butler, J. (1990). *Gender trouble: Feminism and the subversion of identity*. New York: Routledge.

Butler, J. (1993). *Bodies that matter: On the discursive limits of 'sex'*. New York: Routledge.

Davies, B. (1990). *Frogs and snails and feminist tales*. London: Allen and Unwin.

Deaux, K. (1993). Commentary: Sorry, wrong number—A reply to Gentile's call. *Psychological Science, 4*, 125–126.

de la Chapelle, A. (1986). The use and misuse of sex chromatin screening for 'gender identification' of female athletes. *Journal of the American Medical Association, 256*, 1920–1923.

Delphy, C. (1984). *Close to home*. Amherst, MA: University of Massachusetts Press.

Devor, H. (1989). *Gender blending: Confronting the limits of duality*. Bloomington, IN: Indiana University Press.

Devor, H. (1993). Toward a taxonomy of gendered sexuality. *Journal of Psychology and Human Sexuality, 6*, 23–55.

Devor, H. (in press). More than manly women: How female-to-male transsexuals reject lesbian identities. In V. Bullough & B. Bullough (Eds.), *Gender and Transgender Issues*. Amherst, MA: Prometheus.

Dupré, J. (1986). Sex, gender, and essence. In P.A. French, T.E. Uehling Jr., & H.K. Wettstein (Eds.), *Midwest studies in philosophy: Vol. XI. Studies in essentialism* (pp. 441–457). Minneapolis: University Minnesota Press.

Eagly, A.H. (1994). On comparing women and men. *Feminism & Psychology, 4,* 513–522.

Eicher, E.M., & Washburn, L.L. (1986). Genetic control of primary sex determination in mice. *Annual Review of Genetics, 20,* 327–360.

Fausto-Sterling, A. (1987). Society writes biology/biology constructs gender. *Daedalus, 116,* 61–76.

Fausto-Sterling, A. (1993, March/April). The five sexes: Why male and female are not enough. *The Sciences,* pp. 20–25.

Feher, M., Naddaff, R., & Tazi, N. (Eds.). (1989) *Fragments for a history of the human body: Part one.* New York: Zone.

Feinberg, L. (1992). *Transgender liberation: A movement whose time has come.* New York: World View Forum.

Foucault, M. (1978). *The history of sexuality: Vol. I. An introduction.* New York: Random House. (Original work published 1976.)

Gentile, C. (1993). Just what are sex and gender, anyway? A call for a new terminological standard. *Psychological Science, 4,* 120–122.

Gergen, K. (1978). Toward generative theory. *Journal of Personality and Social Psychology, 36,* 1344–1360.

Gergen, M. (1995). Postmodern, post-Cartesian positionings on the subject of psychology. *Theory & Psychology, 5,* 361–368.

Gros, E. (1994). *Volatile bodies: Toward a corporeal feminism.* Bloomington: Indiana University Press.

Haraway, D. (1991): Situated knowledges: The science question in feminism as a site of discourse on the privilege of partial perspective. In *Simians, cyborgs, and women: The reinvention of nature* (pp. 183–201). New York: Routledge. (Reprinted from *Feminist Studies,* 1988, *14,* 575–99.)

Harré, R. (1991a). *Physical being: A theory for a corporeal psychology.* Cambridge, MA: Blackwell.

Harré, R. (1991b). The discursive production of selves. *Theory & Psychology, 1,* 51–64.

Herdt, G. (Ed.). (1994). *Third sex, third gender: Beyond sexual dimorphism in culture and history.* New York: Zone.

Hubbard, R. (1990) *The politics of women's biology.* Brunswick, NJ: Rutgers University Press.

Hyde, J.S. (1990). Meta-analysis and the psychology of gender differences. *SIGNS: Journal of Women in Culture and Society, 16,* 55–73.

Hyde, J.S. (1994). Should psychologists study gender differences? Yes, with some guidelines. *Feminism & Psychology, 4,* 507–512.

Jacobus, M., Keller, E.F., & Shuttleworth, S. (Eds.). (1990). *Body/politics: Women and the discourses of science.* New York: Routledge.

Kessler, S.J. (1990). The medical construction of gender: Case management of intersexed infants. *SIGNS: Journal of Women in Culture and Society, 16,* 3–26.

Kessler, S.J., & McKenna, W. (1985). *Gender: An ethnomethodological approach.* Chicago, IL: University of Chicago Press. (Original work published 1978.)

King, K. (1994). *Theory in its feminist travels: Conversations in US women's movements*. Bloomington: Indiana Univ Press.

Kitzinger, C. (1994). Editor's introduction: Sex differences—Feminist perspectives [Special feature]. *Feminism & Psychology, 4*, 501–506.

Kristeva, J. (1981). Women's time. *SIGNS: Journal of Women in Culture and Society, 7*, 13–35.

Laing, A. (1995, Winter). Last words: A label by any other name might stick. *Transgender Tapestry, 74*, 48.

Laqueur, T. (1990). *Making sex: Body and gender from the Greeks to Freud*. Cambridge, MA: Harvard University Press.

Latour, B. (1987). *Science in action*. Cambridge, MA: Harvard University Press.

Marcus, G., & Fischer M. (1986). *Anthropology as cultural critique*. Chicago, IL: University of Chicago Press.

Martin, E. (1987). *The woman in the body: A cultural analysis of reproduction*. Boston, MA: Beacon Press.

Martin, E. (1994). *Flexible bodies: Tracking immunity in American culture from the days of polio to the age of AIDS*. Boston, MA: Beacon.

Midgeley, M. (1978). *Beast and man*. Ithaca, NY: Cornell University Press.

Minkowitz, D. (1994, 19 April). Love hurts [the story of the life and death of Brandon Teena]. *Village Voice*, pp. 24–30.

Money, J. (1974). Psychologic consideration of sex assignment in intersexuality. *Clinics in Plastic Surgery, 1*, 215–222.

Money, J., Hampson, J.G., & Hampson, J.L. (1955). Hermaphroditism: Recommendations concerning assignment of sex, change of sex, and psychologic management. *Bulletin of the Johns Hopkins Hospital, 97*, 284–300.

Morawski, J.G., & Steele, R.S. (1991). The one or the Other? Textual analysis of masculine power and feminist empowerment. *Theory & Psychology, 1*, 107–131.

Nangeroni, N.R. (1995). The Transsexual Empire: The sucking sounds of secrets [Review]. *SCHEMail: Transgender Wit, Wisdom, and Politics, 4*, 16–17.

Parlee, M.B. (1990). Integrating biological and social scientific research on menopause. *Annals of the New York Academy of Sciences, 592*, 379–389.

Riley, D. (1987). *'Am I that name?': Feminism and the category of 'women' in history*. London: Macmillan.

Rubin, G. (1975). The traffic in women: Notes on the 'political economy' of sex. In R. Reiter (Ed.), *Toward an anthropology of women*. New York: Monthly Review Press.

Sedgwick, E.K. (1988). Privilege of unknowing. *Genders, 1*, 102–124.

Stanley, L. (1990). Feminist praxis and the academic mode of production: An editorial introduction. In L. Stanley (Ed.), *Feminist praxis* (pp. 3–19). New York: Routledge.

Stanley, L., & Wise, S. (1990). Method, methodology and epistemology in feminist research process. In L. Stanley (Ed.), *Feminist praxis* (pp. 20–62). New York: Routledge.

Stine, M. (Ed.) 1995. Celebrating the diversity of gender expression. *Transgender Tapestry, 74*.

Stoller, R.J. (1975) *The transsexual experiment: Vol. 2. Sex and gender*. New York: Aronson.

Stone, A.R. (1995). *The war of desire and technology at the close of the mechanical age*. Cambridge: MIT Press.

Tiger, L., & Shepher, S. (1975). *Women in the Kubbutz*. New York: Harcourt, Brace, Jovanovich.

Tuana, N. (Ed.) (1989). *Feminism and science*. Bloomington: Indiana University Press.

Unger, R.K. (1979). Toward a redefinition of sex and gender. *American Psychologist, 34*, 1085–1094.

Unger, R.K., & Crawford, M. (1993). Commentary: Sex and gender—The troublesome relationship between terms and concepts. *Psychological Science, 4*, 122–124.

West, C., & Zimmerman, D. (1987). Doing gender. *Gender and Society, 1*, 125–151.

Whitehead, H. (1981). The bow and the burden strap: A new look at institutionalized homosexuality in Native North America. In S.B. Ortner & H. Whitehead (Eds.), *Sexual meanings: The cultural construction of gender and sexuality*. Cambridge: Cambridge University Press

Wilchins, R.A. (1995, Winter). What's in a name? The politics of genderspeak. *Transgender Tapestry, 4*, 46–47.

Wilkinson, S. (Ed.). (1996). Representing the Other [Special feature]. *Feminism & Psychology, 6*, 43–91.

Wilson, J.D., George, F.W., & Griffin, J.E. (1981). The hormonal control of sexual development. *Science, 211*, 1278–1284.

Woodhouse, A. (1989). *Fantastic women: Sex, gender and transvestism*. New Brunswick, NJ: Rutgers University Press.

8

Habitus: From the Inside Out and the Outside In

Caterina Pizanias

ABSTRACT. Examinations of the body have been productive sites for analyzing aspects of contemporary culture in general and issues of identity/ difference in particular. They have also become battlegrounds for position-claiming within both the public arena and disciplinary practices, that is, bodies claimed in/for/of *x* discipline. I believe it would be more productive if, in the future, we were to begin to examine bodies in relation to power regimes instead. Bodies—and art—have been found to occupy the middle ground, the space between disciplines, between the 'already given or said' in everyday life and knowledge alike. I have found navigational assistance for the spaces 'in between' in Bourdieu's sociology, especially his concepts of the *field* and *habitus*. This paper is an articulation of my present position—that of an itinerant academic—and my presentational/rhetorical strategies reflect my appropriation of the canonical texts of the field, tempered by the disposition of one desirous of occupying a 'social space' within the academic 'field' and 'the functioning ethos' of feminist politics. My narrative can be read as a feminist 'take' on Bourdieu and a presentation of interdisciplinarity as social practice. It can also be read as a demonstration of a 'habitus' at work, or as a practice of writing the body.

Thinking the present is always the most difficult task. (Rosi Braidotti in Butler, 1994, p. 35)

In 1963, feminist artist Carolee Schneemann performed in New York her piece *Eye Body*, where she established for the first time her body as visual territory, deploying her eroticized body in/as her work, making it a 'living representation', a gift to other women as a gesture of 'giving our bodies back to ourselves' (Schneemann, 1979, p. 194). Schneemann's focus on and use of her body in all subsequent work, her destabilizing of the conventionally accepted duality of subject/object, private/public, through the continuing shifting between the polarities, instead of making it easier for other feminists to re-examine the role of the gaze in self-inscription, brought on their ire: she was labelled 'narcissistic' and was left quietly out of the canon that was increasingly influenced by deconstruction and French (at least its North

American variation) psychoanalysis.[1] And even though in the subsequent years feminist artists continued to use the body in metaphorical and symbolic ways, in their creative and political excursions along the double axis of identity and location, Schneemann's radical intervention of the early 1960s could really be appreciated only after the outburst of body work that came out of queer communities in the 1990s: performance, video, film, still photography. The time had come, as Alexandria Juhasz (1994) so aptly described it, to move beyond deconstruction, to a position where 'the body must be specified back into existence, acknowledging the material effects of race, class, gender, weight, disease, and other body-rooted indices of privilege' (p. 14).

This paper is a case-study about the contributions made by lesbian photographer Susan Stewart to the emerging genre of body art; it traces the bumpy road that one of her works, *Lovers and Warriors: Aural/Photographic Collaborations*, has travelled to date. But above all, the paper—taking its cues from the artists whose careers I have been following—is an attempt to mix binaries that historically have been opposed, such as those of subject/object, empirical work/theorizing, private/public, autobiographical/objective, and so on. It is a 'counter-discourse' to the logocentrism and phallocentrism of the traditional social sciences, psychology, sociology, anthropology and others. Because of my interest in contemporary artistic phenomena and my commitment to record and analyze feminist body art, I have found it necessary to 'row out of turn', so to speak, by practicing a multi- or trans-disciplinarity which is allowed into my inquiries the embodied subjects of performance art. Further, because my 'feminism' implies commitment to structural changes, I have taken another 'spatial turn' by retaining Pierre Bourdieu's treatment of the *artistic field* as a mapping device of sorts—in figuring out the *positionings* contingent on constantly shifting social alliances. I have found 'space' for movement while speaking about women who are moving sites themselves. In the process, I hope to open up the 'in between' as a legitimate site for new intellectual and social possibilities.[2]

Undoubtedly, there are problems with Bourdieu's rendering of the artistic field, as evident in his continued emphasis on the role of art primarily among the dominant classes or his misrecognition of artistic success and/or the current avant-gardes.[3] There is also no doubt in my mind that it is counterproductive, at present, to examine the body in/of/for psychology or any of the other traditional social science disciplines. Feminism and other post-structuralist discourses have successfully shown that the scientific objectivity, that is, the disciplinary 'capital', of these same disciplines is nothing more than a cover-up for their male centeredness and their prefer-ence for textual rather than somatic bodies—a preference which renders them ineffective in dealing with contemporary issues faced by bodies that do not float abstractly but are instead weighted down by race, gender, sexuality, ethnicity, age, and so on, and prompted to action by desires, memories and love.[4]

Pierre Bourdieu—despite Loïc Wacquant's occasional redemptive renderings (e.g. Bourdieu & Wacquant, 1992)—has not shown interest in contemporary feminist issues, or issues of race, ethnicity or sexuality. Yet even though he does not appear to be interested in feminist concerns, his conceptual formulations are portable and feminist friendly, because they enable one to find the space(s) for resistance in the here and now. They have become the key, for this author, to the complexity, contradictions and unpredictability of the cultural politics of 'difference' taking place now within contemporary *fields*—disciplinary or artistic. In his essay on philosopher Martin Heidegger, Pierre Bourdieu spoke of discourse as being 'the product of a compromise between an expressive interest and a censure constituted by the very structure of the field within which the discourse produces itself and within which it circulates' (quoted in Robbins, 1991, p. 4). My project is such a product, a compromise between my interest in finding out how artistic value is produced and circulated in contemporary artistic fields and the censure of the fields within which my work is being produced and will likely circulate.

Scholarly inquiries are constructed in relationship with persons or texts in the field that have had a direct role in opening or closing doors, maintaining boundaries, creating or solving problems, unearthing findings and contradictions. Before I became seduced by the possibilities an embodied/engendered/diasporic *habitus* offers, I had committed myself to recording the work of contemporary women artists, to concentrating on synchronic tensions rather than diachronic breaks, to understanding agency as it plays itself out among agents who had no say in the establishment of a field and whose *dispositions* are orienting them to practices that have been/are seen as heretical, degraded, erroneous. My theoretical motivation at the present revolves around solving contextual puzzles—'thinking the present'—and to be of use to the community of women artists. The project at hand is to find out how to retain the heuristic power of the *habitus* while I grasp the ways in which representational politics and strategies are played out in contemporary fields—artistic and academic.

> For a woman to write as a woman, she must write self-productively—that is, autobiographically—so as to create herself as a writer as she writes. (Clough, 1992, p. 77)

In the early stages of my research, I had set out to develop a framework for an empirical study of an art world of painting. As I went along 'collecting' data, I realized that it was very difficult to find a balance between respecting received theoretical frameworks, on the one hand, and the integrity of the artistic field, on the other. The received 'tradition' was not giving. On the one hand, one was faced with the Howard Becker option; Becker, by appropriating the concept of the art world from the philosophy of art, had put forward a conventional, ahistorical sociology of art which contributes little to empirical research that wants to include persons and artifacts alike. On the other hand, Janet Wolff, caught in the endless debates with theoreticist Marxism, produced a conceptual account of the aesthetic which enabled her to argue both for *and* against its inclusion in the sociology of art. I kept asking myself: Could there then be a way out of Becker's conventionality and Wolff's aesthetic agnosticism?

The first hopeful sign came in 1991 with the publication of Ann Game's *Undoing the Social: Towards a Deconstructive Sociology*, in which she explores the possibilities of constructing a different kind of sociology, a sociology that concerns itself with the immediate, everyday life experience and its transformation. This book opened many doors for me: it allowed the incorporation of deconstructive theories and strategies from cultural and literary studies, practices which until then occupied interests parallel to my project at hand; it dramatically demonstrated the absence of real bodies from the social sciences texts; and it engendered in me the habit of juxtaposing authors and disciplines alike—it showed me the way to become multi-, inter-, cross-, trans-disciplinary. She demonstrates, and in the process convinces one of, the necessity to develop a 'methodology of multiplicity' (Game, 1991, p. 187), which may account for the different orders and ways of meaning coexisting in social worlds at any given time: 'We are written, our bodies are discursively produced; but we also write, in all practices, not only practices of knowledge. And in this writing, or practice of codes of the culture, there is a possibility of rewriting—rewriting ourselves' (Game, 1991, p. 189). But rewriting the self in contemporary social science discourses is much easier said than done: How is one to write the self in discourses that pride themselves in their detachment from the phenomena they study? How is one to write the 'body' in discursive practices that repress such crucial features of the objects of their study as their somatic and psychic aspects? How is one to do 'embodied theory' when the discourses are practiced by disembodied practitioners, committed only to eliminating 'errors' on their way to some sort of disciplinary if not final truth?

> *In this complexity of positioning there is room for movement.* (Game, 1991, p. 191)

Mapping out the complexity, marking the positionings, creating space for movement had to wait another 'turn'. This time it came as a result of my running across Loïc Wacquant's article 'Toward a Reflexive Sociology: A Workshop with Pierre Bourdieu' (1991). In it I discovered a 'different' Bourdieu than the one I had encountered in *Distinction* (1984) and the cursory references in others' work—mostly complaints about Bourdieu's

reductive and deterministic approach to sociology, his version and/or contribution to French structuralism, and other similar disciplinary sparrings.
Having read Wacquant's article after Ann Game's *Undoing the Social*, I
decided to give Bourdieu another chance, this time leaving aside his 'major'
sociological works and instead venturing into journals in anthropology,
philosophy, literary studies, politics and education. There, I found a
Bourdieu who appeared—however momentarily—to have overcome the
antinomies of structure/action, of micro/macro. His concepts of *field*, *habitus*
and *symbolic capital* began to provide a way out of my impasse. But before
I go on, I believe at this point a description of the field[5] and its affiliated
concepts is called for, so that the reader not familiar with Bourdieu's work
will be able to see how the field is a space of antagonistic relations
constantly changing, requiring of its *agents habituses* that are fluid and
contextual rather than the fixed, atemporal, ideal and homogeneous habituses
which are found in sociological discussions of Bourdieu's works.

The field is constituted by institutions, which are populated by agents who
are constantly striving for *prise de position* by taking various stances
according to their *habitus*, which refers to a system of acquired schemes that
become practically effective (a) as categories of perception and evaluation,
(b) as principles of classification, and also (c) as principles of organizing
social action. The field is a field of forces and struggles, a space of
competition for distinction, that is, there are constant struggles to (a) define
a position, (b) defend against it, and (c) distinguish it from those below. In
order to understand the practices of the field's agents, one needs first to
understand that they are the result of the meeting of two histories: the history
of the positions they occupy and the history of their dispositions. To attain
this understanding, one must first understand the strategies employed by the
agents of the field; a strategy is understood as an orientation of practice that
is neither wholly conscious or calculative nor mechanically determined, but
is rather the product of a 'sense' of whatever the particular 'game' of a field
might be.

If one reads Bourdieu not from the position of establishing distance from
his sociology, one may see him as posing new intellectual questions, as in
his call for the construction of temporalized theories, the role that an
embodied habitus may play in the hierarchization of a field, the relational
aspects of *prise de position* vis-à-vis the available capital at any given time
in any particular field. A disciplinarily disinterested reading of Bourdieu,
that is, a reading not for the purpose of settling scores, will show the
'arbitrariness of their [fields'] genesis', thus opening space(s) for movement
and change. As Derek Robbins (1991) has said, Bourdieu's many investigations and speculations 'cry out to be imitated or adapted in respect to
social phenomena outside France' (p. 179).

Despite calls for imitation and/or adaptation such as Robbins', or redemptive apologies such as those of Loïc Wacquant, disciplinary responses

to Bourdieu's work from within and outside France cover the gamut of vitriolic criticism, from Marc Angenot and Raymond Boudon,[6] to Raymond Morrow's metatheoretically neutral rewriting of canonical, largely digested education texts:

> The central aspects of Bourdieu's critical sociology can be conveyed in terms of three concepts: a) society is a *system of positions* understood as social *fields*, b) *habitus* as the mediation of *subjective* and *objective*, and c) *social* and *cultural reproduction* as a process of continuous restructuration that reproduces relations of power. (Morrow, with Brown, 1994, p. 139)

But the Bourdieu 'take' that brought me to another 'turn' was Chris Shilling's *The Body and Social Theory* (1993), a work in which he examines the 'body' within traditional sociological thought and in relation to contemporary body-related issues including death, diet and reproductive technologies.

It is a fascinating and useful book because it is reflexive while still firmly planted within the disciplinary boundaries of sociology. The introductory chapter is a Bourdieusian—albeit schematic—examination of the field of sociology. It is a field created by men (as is the case with all other traditional disciplines), reflecting their epistemological and ontological concerns/commitments, which in turn were affected by the 'intersection' of their personal biographies with the social concern of their day. In other words, they were embroiled in the nature vs society debate (with the body firmly ensconced within nature), and they wished to construct a field which was 'distinct and irreducible' to either the natural sciences or psychology. The result, as Shilling states, is the 'position of the body as an absent presence' (p. 24) in sociology, a position that is still largely the case, despite some changes which have occurred because of influences such as those of feminism, changing demographics or the rise in consumerism within western industrialized societies. Chris Shilling correctly points towards the male centeredness of the discipline but remains silent with regard to the hegemony of textuality in treatments of the body, despite the changes.

At first reading, Shilling's take on Bourdieu is more imaginative than those usually found in sociological accounts, and is quite similar to my own—especially his understanding of the 'body' in social reproduction as the 'bearer of symbolic value' and how the 'unfinishedness' of bodies allows room for creative playfulness. But a closer look reveals statements such as these: 'there is little room in Bourdieu's work for a phenomenological understanding of the body' (p. 146); 'in Bourdieu's work it is difficult to find a methodological justification for focusing on the bodies of women or ethnic minorities as they are affected by a society that is *patriarchical*, or *racist*, as well as capitalist in its central features' (p. 147). Granted, Bourdieu has nothing much to say about ethnic and/or female bodies, but are Shilling, or Bryan Turner, or Roger Brubaker (the authors he uses to support his opinion) any different? They only raise the issue in passing and they too cannot do or say much about ethnic and other women and their bodies, bounded as they are by the discipline's commitment to remain disengaged from the social. Are bodies, then—ethnic or not—to be left in their mystified unfinishedness in the name of 'methodological justification'?[7] Has the time come to rethink the limitations of disciplinary boundedness? How is one to exploit the portability of *habitus* without falling prey to the disciplinary 'snipings' surrounding 'correct' interpretation of Bourdieu's theories? After all, aren't these snipings but 'positionings' of a dominant subject for 'personal stakes'? Since Bourdieu's detractors' and commentators' 'stakes' were not my own, I saw no need to take sides with them. And as I increased my efforts to 'invent within limits'—to simultaneously resist and preserve socio-discursive practices—I found plenty of support within Bourdieu's oeuvre: 'if one is to have a bit of freedom from the constraints of the field, an attempt to explore the limits of the theoretical box in which one is imprisoned' (Bourdieu, 1993, p. 184), then one must push the limits. Innovative possibilities to rethink the *habitus*, to take yet another 'turn', to transform its use, to subvert the rules of the game, to find room for movement, came to me via the work of Peggy Phelan.

I was attracted to Phelan's book *Unmarked: The Politics of Performance* (1993) by its cover, a photograph of painter Alice Neel taken by Robert Mapplethorpe in 1984. Neel was the gracious white-haired woman in a house-dress who, during the first National Conference for Women in the Visual Arts of the Corcoran Gallery, in Washington, DC, in 1972, having used her allotted time to speak about her art, refused to leave the podium until she had decided that all she needed said about her art had actually been said. Her insistence to speak about her art on her own terms—not to be silenced before her time—both showcased the arbitrariness of conference rules and marked the thirst women artists have felt for speaking their minds publicly. Seeing Neel on the cover I took it as a good omen. Turning to the back cover I read:

> *Unmarked* is a controversial analysis of the fraught relation between political and representational visibility in contemporary culture. Written from and for the Left, *Unmarked* rethinks the claims of visibility politics through a feminist psychoanalytic examination of specific performance texts—including photography, painting, film, theatre and anti-abortion demonstrations.

Having bought the book and begun reading through its pages, I saw that Phelan wrote about artists whose work I've known, that she favored specific, local, analyses of performances rather than 'theoretical' discussions of the performative.[8] She, like Ann Game, told stories instead, thus displacing the oppositions between theory and fiction, fact and fiction. She too was walking the spaces-in-between, the complex positionings that Game had spoken about. In each of her chapters she raises doubts about the certainties we carry from sciences about the real, from our self-reflective moments about the self, from the relationship between words and the body. She writes: 'It is in the attempt to walk (and live) on the rackety bridge between self and other—and not the attempt to arrive at one side or the other—that we discover real hope' (Phelan, 1993, p. 174).

Phelan's most important contribution to my own project is her politically informed examination of the relationship between the given to be seen and the looker, the connection between 'the psychic theory of the relationship in between self and other and the political and epistemological contours of that encounter' (Phelan, 1993, p. 3). She stays long within this unexamined area of art and politics, making absolutely clear the failure of the theories and politics of art to detect and counter the accepted 'truth' that visibility does equal power; that representation is never complete, but instead carries within it 'excess' meaning which makes multiple and at times resistant and/or transgressive readings possible. Performance art for Peggy Phelan, like transformation or writing the body for Ann Game, enables one to recognize the gaps, the leaky holes that are our physical bodies: 'We are written, our bodies are discursively produced; but we also write, in all practices, not only practices of knowledge. And in this writing, or practice of codes of the culture, there is a possibility of rewriting—rewriting ourselves' (Game, 1991, p. 189).

Going back to Bourdieu's field after I had read Phelan and Game, the *habitus* burst open and became for me Phelan's 'unmarked', 'a configuration of subjectivity which exceeds, even while informing, both the gaze and language . . . having no particular home, no boundaries dictated by genre, the unmarked can be mapped across a wide terrain' (Phelan, 1993, p. 27). Isn't this a *habitus* in action, in the 'game', whatever the 'game' might be? Isn't this a *habitus* that includes those aspects of identity and praxis which are only partially surveyed in the standard social sciences' theoretical frames, the parts which are present as intuition, lived as the 'feel for the game' found in the excesses of artistic representations but always left out in mainstream theories? 'It is no accident, then, that the unconscious and the body are exclusions in discourses that give themselves the status of knowledge or science' (Game, 1991, p. 188). Pierre Bourdieu could benefit from reading these authors, if, of course, his interests were other than strictly disciplinary, if he were to look at contemporary artistic phenomena not from the detached *position* of a *dominant habitus*, a *habitus* that has consistently avoided the ambivalent spaces where race, gender, sexuality and ethnicity intersect in the social construction and lived experiences of individual and collective subjectivities, the spaces within which Ann Game and Peggy Phelan move. And it is here that I want to digress in order to take the opportunity to consider a case-study, an artistic event, so that my idiosyncratic appropriation of Bourdieu will make better sense.

> *I make a gift of my body to other women: giving our bodies back to ourselves.* (Schneemann, 1979, p. 194)

In 1993, the director of an alternative gallery in Vancouver[9] asked Susan Stewart—an established photographer and community activist—to show her recent work. Susan, who is a member of the lesbian collaborative trio Kiss & Tell, decided this time to go solo. She decided to mount an installation which explored issues of gender, marginality and the politics of photographic representation. The work was shown under the title of *Lovers and Warriors: Aural/Photographic Collaborations.* In her artist's statement Stewart wrote:

> Part of what I hope to accomplish with this work is to explore what a lesbian text might look like as it occupies a traditional form, in this case classical photography. The second part of this equation is the occupation of public space in a bid to overturn exclusion. Toward that end, I have enlisted the support and help of the women in these photographs, women whose stake in being visible is as urgent as my own.[10]

Over a period of 3 years prior to the opening, Susan Stewart collaborated with 25 women, culled mostly from within Vancouver's lesbian community, in an effort to create 'representations of lesbians by lesbians and in the process experience the empowerment that comes from being *seen* in a context we create and control'. Susan thought that all these women were strong, imaginative and knowledgeable, that they had a fascinating story to tell, that it should be recorded and shared. During the initial stage of the collaboration, Susan showed them samples of her previous work, and asked them if they were interested in working with her on this project. The women were free to choose how much of themselves they wanted to share, in guise or not, with street clothes, imaginative costumes, nude or painted bodies. During the stage of photographing, they began telling each other their stories and sometimes they put them on tape.

Once the photographs were processed, the women had control over which of their images were to make it to the gallery wall and what parts of their life stories were to become part of the audio tape that was to accompany the photographs. Some of the women opted to pull out of the project; others chose a single photograph; yet others created photographic constellations. The women were mostly lesbians, whose ages ranged from 19–50 years. Their roles represented the gamut of Vancouver's multi-ethnic community and their sexual orientation covered the range of homosexual practices: dykes, butches, femmes, bitches, transgendered, S & M practitioners, sex workers, women scarred by illness or violence. The end result was an installation of 75 black-and-white photographs 'classically' shot, processed and framed. An hour of narrative was available to visitors if they wished to listen. Susan Stewart in an interview told me: 'I felt there were lots of stories, little fragments I was interested in expressing among friends, who I

FIGURE 1. Falcon (series of two) from *Lovers and Warriors: Aural/
Photographic Collaborations* (photography courtesy of
Susan Stewart)

felt were remarkable people who are completely unrepresented culturally.
Putting it together, I thought, will be a fascinating mix.' The *Lovers and
Warriors* mix, though, failed to catch the fancy of others—except the
collaborators themselves, who apparently celebrated its opening in grand
and joyous style. The experience was not to be repeated and the show's
passing might have been left unrecorded if it was not for my own curiosity
to look into it. What might be the cause of such silencing, especially coming
after the critical success of Kiss & Tell's *Drawing the Line*, as an
installation, video and post-card book, and of *True Inversions*, as performance and video?[11] Remembering Phelan's admonition to 'remember the
undocumentable', to make sure the art has left 'a rack behind', I pressed on
(Phelan, 1993, p. 31).

I had never seen the exhibit nor heard about it before my first meeting
with Susan Stewart. I had wanted to meet with her to talk about her work in

FIGURE 2. Beth (series of two) from *Lovers and Warriors: Aural/
Photographic Collaborations* (photography courtesy of
Susan Stewart)

general and discuss what I thought were antinomies in her work; specifically, I wanted to know how or why such a political artist continued to work
within the parameters of classical, that is, modernist, black-and-white
photography. It was during our first meeting that I heard about *Lovers and
Warriors*, saw the photographs from the exhibit, and heard the story of its
short public life. At the end of that encounter I had partial answers to my
original question, had been totally seduced by the photographs, and had
become immanently curious: how could it be that these beautiful photographs had failed to leave their mark in the art world?

Some time later, I went back and asked if I could borrow the slides and
audio tape so that I might re-create a visit to the exhibit. Needless to say it
was far from what might have been in the gallery: between having to click
the slide projector and fight the street noises interfering with my listening to

the narratives, I found the experience disconcerting. At a much later time in the day, I went back to my private gallery and this time around the narrative took over—I found it very difficult to look at the photographs and listen to the stories. My third and last 'visit' was totally split: I listened first to the audio tape in its entirety and then I played back the slides. It was during this last viewing of the slides that I realized Stewart was forcing my 'glances' to compete with one another: my literal glance at the photographs—figuring bodies in fictive spaces in all their 'formal' gloriousness—and my 'glance' into the narratives—the actual voices of her collaborators speaking about the social regimes that organize and subordinate women's sexual bodies and the internal resistances/solutions to them from within queer communities. Stewart's decision to force the viewers to relinquish the desire to see all, with her introduction of the narratives to disrupt their faith in the 'truth' of the image, was very effective. As a theorist I understood her intervention. As a viewer I did not like experiencing the conflict, the discrepancies between the photographs and the narratives. This radical intervention to politicize photography appeared to have also backfired with the casual viewers/visitors during the exhibit. But what about the critics, the curators, could they not see—sooner or later—what the artist was doing? Could it be that the art establishment was not ready for such an assault—the political engendering—of one of their most durable and relatively 'cheap staples', photography? Was it not after all the same art establishment that had so readily consecrated and loaded with 'capital' Stewart's previous work? What might have changed in the 5 years that intervened between *Drawing the Line* and *Lovers and Warriors*? The photographs had, if anything, become better. What then? The obvious differences are those that occurred in the wider social field. *Drawing the Line* rode on the success of feminist studies, as well as that of the psychoanalytic–queer discourses within the academic and artistic fields. More importantly, it was an easier piece of work: it was presenting and celebrating lesbian sexual pleasures, fantasies and desires. *Lovers and Warriors* entered the public space after the 'Mapplethorpe' affair, after US and Canadian right-wing politicians discovered that bashing queers was good for political capital gains. But what about the gatekeepers of the art world, why did they remain silent on *Lovers and Warriors'* passing?

Mainstream art worlds have never been keen about performance/body art—like that of Kiss & Tell or Shawna Dempsey—with occasional exceptions when it was performed by men or by women artists who used the body as metaphor, as 'text', as is the case with such artists as Mary Kelly, Jana Starback, Cindy Sherman and Richard Prince. Had Susan Stewart ensconced her photographs within quotations from feminist psychoanalytic texts— favored authorial references among the art world's legitimators—then she would at least have been reviewed, and she might even have been used to bash the philistine politicians or general public. Transgressors of 'form' have been the 'darlings' of the art world. Art historian Howard Risatti (1990) has best described these transgressors and their reception:

> Cindy Sherman, Sherrie Levine, Richard Prince—their work critiques art, revealing its institutional nature and decontextualized position vis-à-vis society; but, unable to withstand the voraciousness of the 'system', it is simply absorbed as the latest art-world wrinkle—these after all are artists famous institutionally for being anti-institutional. (p. 9)

I am willing to wager that the most important reason Susan Stewart was not allowed to leave 'a rack behind' was not her transgression/violence towards the formalism of her photographs, but her violence towards the artistic field, the context of the gallery, that 'sacred' place controlled by the priestly caste of the field's gatekeepers. She was invited by them to show her work on the basis of her accrued artistic capital: MFA (Master of Fine Arts), good reviews, faculty position at an art school, and so forth. They would have allowed her to be 'another wrinkle' on the art world's face. But she was not content with that: she wanted to 'occupy the public space in a bid to overturn exclusion' and she succeeded—by 'walking out of step', by claiming for herself the position of consecrator, overturning the rules of the game, bringing the community to art. And what part of the community did she bring in? She brought in members from the social and sexual under-classes and created spaces for them—subject position spaces—to present themselves, tell their own stories, and not to be there as the object of artistic and/or scientific inquiries as had been the case before. They expressed their individuality in strong voices; they told stories of sexually taboo practices not in shame; they spoke of their gender differences posed as questions, left unfinished and thus threatening; and they showed their diverse social/sexual marginalities by appropriating the idealized classical artistic practices of 'high art'! They presented publicly private images of their 'bodies', per-formed their 'identities', and in the process experimented with ways of restructuring their own images of themselves and demystified gender as conventionally understood in classical photography. These many transgres-sions by Stewart could not go unpunished: uppity women artists and unruly genders are pushed back into their 'closets'.

> *The power of making visible and explicit social divisions that are implicit, is the political power* par excellence: *it is the power to make groups, to manipulate the objective structure of society.* (Bourdieu, 1990, p. 149)

Loïc Wacquant brought me to Pierre Bourdieu and it was Bourdieu's concept of *habitus* which has kept me committed to fieldwork. But it was my reading of Bourdieu against authors such as Ann Game, Peggy Phelan, Rosi Braidotti and a host of other feminists from within the disciplines of psychoanalysis, feminist theories of representation and critical ethnography, postmodernists of all sorts, who enabled me to engender the *habitus*, to think of it as 'unfinished' rather than the fixed, atemporal entity locatable in the homogeneous and abstract fields of artistic and disciplinary production.[12] It was they who helped me see and understand *habitus* as operating on many levels at once in the experience of bodies, in the ways in which gendering, sexing, classing and other social processes inform our 'dispositions' and in turn are expressed in the multiple, fluid and contextual configurations or criss-crossings of race, class, age, ethnicity, sexuality, and so on. It was through their influence that I acquired my 'tactical' understanding of the field and its affiliated concepts, an understanding which has allowed me to recognize the differential specificities of its agents in relation to the significance of the symbolic capital that 'really counts' at any given moment. It was this same understanding which prompted my quest into the rethinking, re-evaluating of our notions, understanding and use of bodily and disciplinary selves.

There is no doubt in my mind that if women and all others who have been left out of the stories of the 'founding fathers' in traditional disciplines are ever to be included in the discourses of art or the academy, then it is necessary to incorporate the activities of the agents (as embodied entities) in the disciplinary fields as well as those activities of the agents of the fields we study: academic writing—like art making—is always multiply motivated and never disinterested or disengaged. Redefining the field in all its material complexities is one thing, deploying this new understanding as/in a multi-disciplinary praxis, a praxis that draws from a lineage of 'sisters' which has understood the 'body in question' as 'a point of intersection, as the interface between the biological and the social, that is to say between the socio-political field of the micro-physics of power and the subjective dimension' (Braidotti, 1989, p. 97), has been another. I do not believe that any real changes have taken place within mainstream disciplines to account for the axes of power in relation to class, race, sexuality and other bodily markers. Even though routinely and mantra-like these concepts are referred to in order to prove the author's 'topicality' in contemporary discussions, the analyses they are found in do not bear any of the complexities and paradoxes that ensue if one seriously incorporates them.

Exactly 30 years after Carolee Schneemann's first performance piece, the *Eye Body*, in 1963, Susan Stewart and her collaborators in *Lovers and Warriors* in a similar manner established their bodies as visual territories of their own making, offering their sexualized bodies and telling lesbian stories simultaneously as subjects and objects. But during those 30 years one has to strain to see references to Schneemann's work within the traditional dis-courses of both body art and art criticism. She is an older sister in a lineage that has failed to take roots within the mainstream, because the 'fathers' of the art world, as those of the social sciences, have found this art dangerous and disruptive. Had a sorority succeeded to claim a position within the field, then *Lovers and Warriors* would not have fallen through the cracks either.

During the last 30 years women and queers of all races, classes and ethnicities have been telling stories of their 'difference', which have gone mostly unnoticed by mainstream disciplines still caught in the binarism of empirical work vs theorizing, where abstract theorizing is thought of as superior to dealing with empirical data and 'case-studies' soiled with the contradictions of a lived life.[13] Persons from the margins have been telling their stories, but they have not been allowed to become part of the disciplinary collective memory, because they are 'unruly', transversing disciplinary methods and structures, transvesting positions, sometimes as insiders of disciplinary knowledge and sometimes as outsiders. It is much easier to make references to Rabelais's 'carnivalesque'—Mikhail Bakhtin after all has already 'vested' it for us theoretically—than to sit down and make sense of 'carnivalesque' collaborations such as *Lovers and Warriors*, with its plurality of subject positions, multiple identities, acting out the paradoxes of the shifting subject/object of the gaze of self-inscription.

Like Game and Phelan, I have tried to show that works of art, like texts of all kinds, are social phenomena, fictions that are produced, read and received socially by embodied desiring persons. Doing theory is not unlike telling stories, stories which we have told in order to acquire a memory and identity, and in any case to accumulate the necessary and appropriate capital to consecrate the 'spaces-in-between' so that they reflect the margin's *memories, sights* and *loves*. Peggy Phelan (1993) said it best: 'all require a witness, imagined or real' (p. 5). The effort to think and speak of the body outside disciplinary bounds is not easy. But I strongly believe that the time has come for feminists to offer critiques, abandon the pose of neutral recorder of experience, upset the grounds of disciplinary boundaries, bear testimony to the disciplinary power differential, reverse the exclusions, and resist the disciplinary/institutional 'domestication' of embodiment. This paper has been a provisional working of such a task.

Postscript

Since the first publication of this paper, *Lovers and Warriors* with a slightly changed subtitle (*Lovers and Warriors: A Queer Ethnography*) has had successful showings at the Westwerk Gallery in Hamburg (May 1997) and at the Frauen-Kulturzentrum in Frankfurt (September–October 1997).

Notes

1. The problems that Schneemann's (along with Hannah Wilke's and others') use of her body created for feminist writers can be seen in such essays as the

    following: de Lauretis (1990), Jones (1991), Johasz (1994) and Pollock (1990, 1994).

2. The difficulty of practicing inter- or trans-disciplinarity, especially by persons in the margins of society and/or the academy, has been best articulated in the following works: Min-ha (1991), Spivak (1993) and Ward Jouve (1991).

3. How 'out of the loop' Pierre Bourdieu is vis-à-vis radical contemporary art production is clear in his latest book, *Free Exchange* (Bourdieu & Haacke, 1995), a self-indulgent 'man to man' talk between Bourdieu and New York artist Hans Haacke.

4. Peggy Phelan (1993) best describes this new way of theorizing in her book *Unmarked: The Politics of Performance*:

> The work of theory, under current economic conditions can only be, for most of us, a labor of love. Insofar as love is labor, a trying, an essay, it, like theory, cannot be anything but an offering, a giving of what one does not have, a description and transcription of what one cannot see or prove with visible evidence ... [the] looker, like the lover, desires an/other revision of memory, sight, and love. (p. 32)

5. Pierre Bourdieu's works that have influenced my work within and around artistic 'fields' have been the following: *Homo Academicus* (1988); *In Other Words: Essays Toward a Reflexive Sociology* (1990); *An Invitation to Reflexive Sociology* (Bourdieu & Wacquant, 1992); *The Field of Cultural Production: Essays on Art and Literature* (1993); 'Delegation and Political Fetishism' (1994a); and 'Structures, Habitus, Power: Basis for a Theory of Symbolic Power' (1994b).

6. For a sampling of the debates that took place around this issue, I refer the reader to Angenot (1984) and Boudon (1989).

7. Pierre Bourdieu on theory and methodology:

> For me, theory is not a sort of prophetic or programmatic discourse which originates by dissection or by amalgamation of other theories for the sole purpose of confronting other such pure 'theoretical' theories. ... [Scientific theory as I conceive it] has more to gain by confronting mere objects than by engaging in theoretical polemics that do little more than fuel vacuous metadiscourse around concepts treated as intellectual totems. (quoted in Wacquant, 1989, p. 50)

And on methodology:

> This scientific monster [presently] inscribed in the institutional and mental structures of the sociological profession, rooted in the academic distribution of resources, positions, and competencies, as when whole schools are based almost entirely on one particular method, and reinforced by the political demand for instruments of rationalization of social domination and it must be rejected. The trick, if I may call it that, is to manage to combine immense theoretical ambition with extreme empirical modesty. (quoted in Wacquant, 1989, p. 51)

For Canadian adaptations of Bourdieu's concept of artistic field, see Pizanias (1992, 1993).

8. Judith Butler's theories on the materiality of the body and the performativity of gender have become 'intellectual totems', as Bourdieu would call them, and have spawned a discourse within the discourses of the body. See her *Gender Trouble: Feminism and the Subversion of Identity* (1990) and *Bodies That Matter: On the Discursive Limits of 'Sex'* (1993).

9. Located on Canada's west coast, in the province of British Columbia, Vancouver is a large, multi-ethnic city. (The population of the city proper is just over half a million; with the surrounding metropolitan areas, it is about 1.7 million.)

10. All quotations from Susan Stewart are from private conversations or interviews with the author.

11. *Drawing the Line* is an interactive photo-installation, presented in such a way as to encourage the viewers to consciously think where one 'draws the line' between erotica and pornography. To date it has been shown to great receptions 16 times in 15 cities across Canada, the United States and Australia. *True Inversions* is a 30-minute video about imagery, censorship and lesbian sex, and it is used as part of a multi-media performance. Both are available by contacting Video Out, 1965 Main Street, Vancouver, British Columbia, Canada, V5T 3C1.

12. Support for this process has come from other women writers, such as Trinh T. Min-ha, Pratibha Parmar, Rey Chow and Gayatri Chakravorty Spivak, Judith Butler, Teresa de Lauretis and some men, such as Edward Said and Kobena Mercer. As a cultural sociologist who studies contemporary issues in order to locate the data I need for my work, I had to start collecting oral histories—albeit partial ones—in order to get the information I required. In the process of collecting 'data', I became fascinated with the writing strategies of classical ethnography: according to the maneuverings (i.e. methodological strategies) which were deemed appropriate, all traces of myself and the person I am writing about must be extricated from the text. I have to produce objective texts that say nothing much about the subjects of my study, my experiences with them, and other such 'subjective' pollutants. I am expected to repeat received theories, so that I can come up with some more abstractions that either screen or cover up the interesting and relevant data from the unpublished field notes. Traversing/transvesting location and identities has been my solution.

13. To wit: Ken Plummer's recent publication *Telling Sexual Stories: Power, Change and Social Worlds* (1995), where he considers the proliferation of sexual stories increasingly being told while at the same time he is opening the field of social sciences to persons and ideologies that were left mostly unmarked until now. Ann Game and other feminists would find good company in Plummer; he says, '[we] are always becoming, never arriving, and the social order becomes a vast negotiated web of dialogue and conversation' (p. 20). He understands power as flow, as process 'which shifts outcomes and distributes control and regulation . . . [it] weaves its way through embodied, passionate social life and everything in its wake' (p. 26). His whole book can be read as an illustration of engendered habituses. Stories, like their tellers, are increasingly out of their closets; the question that remains is, when will mainstream disciplines incorporate them in ways other than euphemisms?

References

Angenot, M. (1984). Structuralism as syncretism: Institutional distortions of Saussure. In J. Fekete (Ed.), *The structural allegory: Reconstructive encounters with the new French thought* (pp. 150–163). Minneapolis: University of Minnesota Press.

Boudon, R. (1989). *The analysis of ideology* (M. Slater, Trans.). Chicago, IL: University of Chicago Press.

Bourdieu, P. (1984). *Distinction: A social critique of the judgement of taste* (R. Nice, Trans.). London: Routledge & Kegan Paul.

Bourdieu, P. (1988). *Homo academicus* (P. Collier, Trans.). Oxford: Polity.

Bourdieu, P. (1990). *In other words: Essays toward a reflexive sociology* (M. Adamson, Trans.). Cambridge: Polity/Stanford, CA: Stanford University Press.

Bourdieu, P. (1993). *The field of cultural production: Essays on art and literature*. New York: Columbia University Press.

Bourdieu, P. (1994a). Delegation and political fetishism. In J.B. Thompson (Ed.), *Language and symbolic power* (G. Raymond & M. Adamson, Trans.). Cambridge, MA: Harvard University Press.

Bourdieu, P. (1994b). Structures, habitus, power: Basis for a theory of symbolic power. In N.B. Dirks, G. Eley, & S.B. Ortner (Eds.), *Culture/power/history: A reader in contemporary social theory* (pp. 155–199). Princeton, NJ: Princeton University Press.

Bourdieu, P., & Haacke, H. (1995). *Free exchange*. Stanford, CA: Stanford University Press.

Bourdieu, P., & Wacquant, L.J.D. (1992). *An invitation to reflexive sociology*. Chicago, IL: University of Chicago Press.

Braidotti, R. (1989). The politics of ontological difference. In T. Brennan (Ed.), *Between feminism and psychoanalysis*. London: Routledge.

Butler, J. (1990). *Gender trouble: Feminism and the subversion of identity*. New York: Routledge.

Butler, J. (1993). *Bodies that matter: On the discursive limits of 'sex'*. New York: Routledge.

Butler, J. (1994). Feminism by any other name [Interview with Rosi Braidotti]. *differences*, *6*, 27–61.

Clough, P.T. (1992). *The end(s) of ethnography: From realism to social criticism*. Newbury Park, CA: Sage.

de Lauretis, T. (1990). Guerilla in the midst: Women's cinema in the 80s. *Screen*, *31*, 6–25.

Game, A. (1991). *Undoing the social: Towards a deconstructive sociology*. Toronto: University of Toronto Press.

Jones, A. (1991). Postfeminism, feminist pleasures, and embodied theories of art. In J. Frueh, C.L. Langer, & A. Raven (Eds.), *New feminist criticism: Art, identity, action* (pp. 16–41). New York: Iconeditions.

Juhasz, A. (1994). Our auto-bodies, ourselves: Representing real women in feminist video. *Afterimage*, *21*(7), 9–14.

Min-ha, T.T. (1991). *When the moon waxes red: Representation, gender and cultural politics*. New York: Routledge.

Morrow, R., with Brown, D.D. (1994). *Critical theory and methodology*. London: Sage.

Phelan, P. (1993). *Unmarked: The politics of performance*. London: Routledge.

Pizanias, C. (1992). Making art in the 'global village'. *Canadian Issues*, *14*, 109–128.

Pizanias, C. (1993). Reviewing modernist painting and criticism in the Canadian prairies: A case study from Edmonton. *International Journal of Canadian Studies*, *13*, 139–169.

Plummer, K. (1995). *Telling sexual stories: Power, change and social worlds*. London: Routledge.

Pollock, G. (1990). Missing women: Rethinking early thoughts on images of women. In C. Squires (Ed.), *The critical image: Essays on contemporary photography*. Seattle WA: Bay Press.

Pollock, G. (1994). Feminism/Foucault—surveillance/sexuality. In N. Bryson, M.A. Holly, & K. Moxey (Eds.), *Visual culture: Images and interpretations* (pp. 1–41). Hanover and London: Wesleyan University Press and University Press of New England.

Risatti, H. (1990, January–February). Some questions on interventionist art. *Art Papers*, pp. 6–9.

Robbins, D. (1991). *The work of Pierre Bourdieu*. Boulder, CO: Westview.

Schneemann, C. (1979). *More than meat joy: Complete performance works and selected writings* (B. McPherson, Ed.). New Paltz, NY: Documentext.

Shilling, C. (1993). *The body and social theory*. London: Sage.

Spivak, G.C. (1993). *Outside in the teaching machine*. New York: Routledge.

Wacquant, L.J.D. (1989). Toward a reflexive sociology: A workshop with Pierre Bourdieu. *Sociological Theory*, *7*, 26–63.

Ward Jouve, N. (1991). *White woman speaks with forked tongue: Criticism as autobiography*. London: Routledge.

Part IV
SICK AND HEALING BODIES

9

The Body as a Selfing Device
The Case of Anorexia Nervosa

Cor Baerveldt and Paul Voestermans

ABSTRACT. Psychology's conceptualization of anorexia nervosa illustrates how the discipline deals with the body. On the one hand, there is an emphasis on the body as a physiological apparatus. On the other hand, specific approaches such as social constructionism stress the non-physiological body as something to which certain discursive meanings get attached. We propose to view the body as a producer of meaning in its own right, as a 'selfing device'. To this end we emphasize bodily communication as a continuous flow of co-regulated interaction. The body presents itself as the natural juncture of 'co-regulative skills'. The 'selfing process' involves multiple stylized bodily skills that testify to people's ability to take part in the life-world. Anorexia is seen as a disturbance of those skills.

Anorexia nervosa involves the body. The question is: which body? Is it just the biological apparatus or organism, as the body might be referred to, or the body as a means of expressing feelings and emotions and as a mode of self-presentation? Or is it a combination? These are the probing questions for this paper. Not just the patient is involved bodily. Anorexia also presents a case for psychology's involvement with the body. However, the body as such is hardly a subject-matter for psychology. Psychology is a science 'buried in thought', locked up in phrases, so to speak. Insofar as science is a matter of searching for explanations, being buried in thought is not a problem, of course, but if the scientific focus is merely on what people *think* or talk *about*, psychology is robbed unduly of much of its material. The body presents a psychological world of its own, to which the case of anorexia nervosa will give us some access.

The adjective 'nervosa', which was included in the diagnostic label of this eating disorder right from the outset (Brumberg, 1988), suggests a belief in a kind of 'nervous' basis. Nervous did not imply bodily (neural) processes. Mental processes were included under that label as well. So the dispute centred immediately on the bodily vs the mental basis of the disorder. It has remained this way until the present time in those literatures in which a materialistic stance on behavioural and psychological issues is played off against a mentalistic one. Social constructionist attempts to come to grips with anorexia nervosa have tended to circumvent this dualistic dispute by emphasizing that the body is a complex cluster of cultural constructions. In this case the medical and biological perspective on the body is enriched by one in which bodily states and functions are related to self and identity. In this paper we want to explore this new perspective in order to understand the role played by the body in ordinary ways of living. First, the social constructionist choice for the non-physiological body is discussed. The linguistic bias of social constructionism is criticized in order to explore the communicative aspects of the body in a much more refined way. In our view the body is a 'selfing' device. The neologism 'selfing' is used deliberately. Research on the self tends to ignore the process side of the self. The notion of 'selfing' attempts to capture the activities through which the person becomes a social and personal self. We argue that the body is important in that regard.

The Body in Social Constructionism

In contemporary psychological reflections on self and emotions, the body seems to play a minor role except in the age-old form of the 'soft machine, stuffed with tender little wires and tubes', to use an expression by the Dutch poet Leo Vroman (1957). Social constructionism unmistakably has something to say about the body, but rather polemically. Theories that assign an important role to the physiological body in the constitution of emotions and feelings are de-emphasized (Averill, 1980; Harré, 1986; Ratner, 1989). There is a difference in how physiology is played down, depending on whether the weak or strong, radical version of social constructionism is adopted (Armon-Jones, 1986; Terwee, 1995). Social constructionism in its 'weak' form does not deny the existence of a limited range of natural emotional responses. Yet proponents of this form seem to agree that human experience, including the experience of the body, can become meaningfully connected with a sense of self only within the context of a cultural system of beliefs and values (Armon-Jones, 1986; Hochschild, 1983; Sarbin, 1986a, 1986b). The 'strong' version of social constructionism denies the relevance of physiological processes altogether. Weak and strong constructionism alike try to limit the medical and biological usurpation of the body. All social constructionists argue that viewing the body from a medical or biological perspective can only limit the understanding of its role in the way humans live. But what, then, is this role? To put it more sharply, does the body have a role in the production of meaning? The answer to this question is pertinent to the way anorexia is dealt with.

One thing is quite clear as far as the social constructionist perspective on the body is concerned: by contesting that physiology is central to the process of experiencing, body and physiology are implicitly equated. The two are collapsed and functional electro-chemical bodily processes have no bearing on the production of meaning, save for the fact that these processes are seen as merely conditional. It is quite obvious that, once certain bodily parts or systems are damaged, behavior will suffer as well.

In order to avoid the immediate drawback of a purely mentalistic view of meaning, social constructionism emphasizes a non-physiological body. From this perspective, the states and functions of the body become a cluster of cultural instead of natural, that is, biological, constructions. The formative and rhetorical aspects of language have a strong bearing on these cultural constructions. Language in, for example, the form of emotion talk and emotion words (Heelas, 1981; Lutz, 1986, 1988) or as narrative plots and everyday story-lines (Gergen & Gergen, 1983, 1984, 1988; Sarbin, 1986a, 1986b) becomes the main locus of socially constructed meaning. Constructionists claim that these 'meanings' penetrate psychological life in all its facets. The body is a rather shallow participant in this scheme because it is introduced, for example, in the conception of an emotion as 'a bodily enactment of a moral judgment or attitude in accordance with the conventions of local dramatistic roles' (Harré, 1991, p. 142; Sarbin, 1986b). Put more generally, the structure and meaning of bodily conduct originate from discursively constructed cultural resources that provide the scripts carried out by bodily gestures and postures. As will be shown in a moment, this non-physiological, 'dramatistic' body, which is constructed discursively from cultural resources, has undergone an interesting fate that has had a strong bearing on anorexia nervosa.

Politicizing the Social Constructionists' Body

Since the appearance of Berger and Luckmann's book *The Social Construction of Reality* (1966), it has become understood among constructionists that meaning and knowledge are produced in social interactions. They have also stressed that meaning and knowledge are constitutive of those very same interactions. Social constructionists have tended to emphasize only this latter point. As a consequence, empirical research has been restricted mostly to the analysis of already produced texts (Sarbin, 1986a; Shotter & Gergen, 1989). More recently, however, a shift of focus has occurred. The emphasis is no

longer on culture as an already constructed linguistic order, but on the
production and maintenance of meaning and identity in the course of
everyday conversational interactions and discursive practices (Harré &
Gillett, 1994; Shotter, 1993, 1995). The dynamic and productive aspects of
linguistic interactions are put to the fore. This implies an emphasis on
conversation, conflicts, dilemmas and relations of power and domination
(Billig, 1987, 1988; Edwards, 1991; Potter & Wetherell, 1987). This
political variant of social constructionism brought about a renewed interest
in the human body. Feminist authors especially have used a constructionist
or discursive framework in order to show how people are classified by
reference to their bodies (Butler, 1990, 1993; Jaggar, 1983; Jaggar & Bordo,
1992). Seemingly biological or naturally given categories like male/female
and categories of sexual orientation such as 'homosexual', 'bisexual', 'gay'
and 'lesbian' are revealed as being entirely socially constructed. The
politicizing of the body goes along with an emphasis on the obedience of the
body to the scripts of the dominant ethic, be it the ethic of heterosexuality,
masculinity, femininity, but also of homosexuality, the submissive traditional female care-giving functions or dominant male public functions
(Kitzinger, 1987, 1992; Unger, 1989, 1992). With this emphasis on body
politics, the body is given a central place in psychological thought. Yet the
question can be raised whether this politicizing still adheres to the general
social constructionist perspective of a body to which meaning is added.
Moreover, in this political outlook the body becomes meaningful only
insofar as discursive meanings such as those depicted in the mass media or
in social scientific and psychological discourse get attached to it. To
exaggerate a bit, the body becomes a sort of mannequin which 'wears' the
signs of sex, power, status, and the like, and as such serves as the
battleground for body politics (Merwe & Voestermans, 1995).

In this overview we have lumped together all the social constructionists,
even though Harré, for example, is very different from Gergen and both
differ from Shotter, to name only the most prominent constructionists. The
point we are trying to make is that no matter what nuances can be seen in
their texts, the body remains an entity to which socially constructed
meanings are added. The question we want to raise now is: what are the
consequences of this theoretical stance for the understanding of anorexia
nervosa?

Anorexia Nervosa and the Mannequin Body: Gains and Criticism

A brief survey of the literature regarding anorexia nervosa shows that early
explanations tended to psychologize the syndrome, neglecting both its
cultural aspects and the body in its own right. Psychoanalytic explanations,

for example, interpret anorexia as the fear of oral impregnation and the rejection of female sexuality (Thomä, 1967; Waller, Kaufman, & Deutsch, 1940). From the 1950s onward, ego-psychological and object-relational interpretations of orality came to emphasize the process of separation from the mother in the development of solid ego boundaries. Anorexia was interpreted as the consequence of 'ego-weakness', which resulted in what Bruch (1974) has called 'a paralyzing sense of ineffectiveness'. During the 1970s ego-psychological approaches were broadened by positions that emphasized the social and cultural aspects of identity formation. Selvini-Palazzoli (1974) and Minuchin, Rosman and Baker (1978) assigned a central role to communication patterns within the family system that hinder the development of an autonomous sense of identity. The mothers of anorectics especially were depicted as frustrated, over-protective women who did not acknowledge their daughters' autonomy (Bruch, 1978; Selvini-Palazzoli, 1974). Later feminist-oriented authors like Lawrence (1984) and Chernin (1986) pointed to the social position of modern, highly educated women, in which they are forced to conform both to the modern demands of a career and to those of traditional care-giving and motherhood. In particular, the role of the mother was reinterpreted by representing her as a woman who had been pressed by societal demands to give up her own ambitions and exclusively dedicate herself to the family. Both mother and daughter were seen as victims of a patriarchal society.

Current research into the genesis of anorexia has given up, for the most part, the attempt to explain from a single variable. Instead it is assumed that anorexia has multiple causes (Garfinkel & Garner, 1982). Non-specific psychological factors like low self-esteem, perfectionism and social uncertainty all presumably contribute to the genesis of the syndrome. In most of these explanatory efforts the body plays a minor role. The non-physiological body appears on the stage most often as the cultural ideal of thinness, pressing women to keep trying to lose weight. On the basis of an investigation of *Playboy* centrefolds and Miss America Pageant contestants in the period 1959–78, Garner, Garfinkel, Schwartz and Thompson (1980) demonstrated that a shift occurred to a more slender standard. More recently, the same trend was found for the years 1979–88 (Wiseman, Gray, Mosimann, & Ahrens, 1992). Garner et al. suggested that the postwar increase in anorexia nervosa is partly due to these changing cultural ideals for beauty and success. Nevertheless, although the ideal of slenderness can probably throw some light on the question as to why so many women in our society are preoccupied with trying to lose weight, it falls short as an explanation of anorexia nervosa. It remains unclear how the cultural appreciation of the female body can penetrate into the subjective experience of the body to such an extent that it makes some women modify and even mutilate their own bodies. Moreover, the striking observation about anorexia is the fact that these women persist in their attempt to lose weight and yet continue to report that they feel fat. It is quite unlikely that the cultural standard of a slender female body continues to motivate them. Diaries and other ego-documents of anorectics (e.g. Dunbar, 1986; Macleod, 1982) show that the weight anorectic women set for themselves is constantly pushed downward, which suggests that they are striving for body control rather than aiming at some idealized body shape.

A central argument in feminist explanations of anorexia nervosa has been the politicizing of the body along the lines discussed above. Anorexia nervosa has been interpreted both as an over-identification with sex role stereotypes (Boskind-Lodahl, 1976) and as a symbolic protest against the social position of women in society, involving a dismissal of these very same stereotypes (Orbach, 1985). Both Orbach and Boskind-Lodahl state that the social judgment of fatness is inherently sexist. It reflects the dominant male discourse about preferred female body shape.

For Boskind-Lodahl the modification of the body is a symptom of social inadequacy and the lack of self-esteem due to social stereotypes of femininity. This perceived inadequacy and the fear of being rejected by their social environment cause some women to adopt a passive and accommodating approach to life and an obsession with appearance and body shape. At first, they try to lose weight in order to live up to the perceived preferences of men, but eventually slimming becomes a means of reducing fear and social uncertainty in general. Orbach considers the body a medium of communication, a way of expressing something which cannot be said in words. The anorectic's body carries a message, which should be read as a message of protest. Orbach explicitly uses the metaphor of the hunger strike to make this point.

Although both Boskind-Lodahl and Orbach emphasize that the body is a means of expression, it remains a mannequin and a battleground for body politics. In essence, the assignment of meaning takes place by an outside observer rather than by the anorectic herself. The message of protest has to be inferred from a political analysis. This means that the excessive slimming is in fact considered as symptomatic of a given social order, rather than as a way to communicate about, or to protest against, this social order. By politicizing the female body this way, the body as the expressive medium of a real person gets out of focus. The body becomes an arena of political dispute in which the anorectic herself doesn't take part as an individual (Lenning, 1990). Anorexia serves as the arena for 'identity politics' (Sampson, 1993), which takes place outside the psychological reality of the day to day practices of the anorectic herself that claim and sustain an identity in the course of everyday social interactions. Orbach persists in a view of the body as the bearer of meanings which are eventually produced in a discursive process. This process takes place without the anorectic being part of it. It acquires those meanings only within the context of a dominant sexist discursive order. In that regard the body merely represents the feminist challenge of that order.

Extending the Discursive Paradigm: The Body as Language

The body as mannequin and the body as an arena for body politics both fail to explain how the body serves as a meaning-producing device in its own right. If we want to come to grips with the role of anorectics as women who *are* bodies of flesh and bones and do not just *have* a body as a cluster of politicized meanings attached to it, the body as a communicative device needs to be understood. One attempt to do exactly that is the social constructionist extension of the notion of discourse in such a way that it includes the communicative use of the body. Harré and Gillett (1994) proceeded that way and contended that 'it is a main thesis of discursive psychology that episodes in which psychological phenomena are brought into being by the use of nonlinguistic signs should be analyzed as if they were through and through linguistic' (p. 99). The implications of this contention for social constructionists' dealings with the body become apparent from Harré's design for a 'corporeal semantics'. He noted that '[t]he human body is such that its states, conditions, parts and postures serve as signs. It is both a semiotic system in itself and made meaningful by a semiotic system' (Harré, 1991, p. 223)

The claim that some sort of linguistics can provide a model for psychology in which the body is included is not new. Birdwhistell (1952), for example, stated long ago that 'it has to become clear that there are body behaviors which function like significant sounds, that combine into simple or relatively complex units like words, which are combined into much longer stretches of structured behavior like sentences or even paragraphs' (p. 80). The idea of bodily conduct as a patterned sequence of structural units, analogous to those of language, is also found in the work of Scheflen (1964).

Kristeva (1968/1978) was the first to criticize Birdwhistell for reducing communication to the exchange of information. She was particularly apprehensive about the reduction of praxis—the way people are immersed in their daily doings—to representations. A comparable critique was given more recently by Radley (1991). He explained that the restricted attention to body movements as communicative acts leaves out the possibility for analysing bodily conduct as a cultural practice in its own right. To further clarify this point, Radley criticized the reduction of non-verbal behaviour to communication. He referred to the contribution of Wiener, Devoe, Rubinow and Geller (1972), who pointed out that in the studies of non-verbal behaviour the notion of sign is easily confused with that of communication. Body movements or other bodily signs signal a certain state of affairs, but this is not the same as communication. What Wiener and others attempted to convey is that as soon as bodily conduct, which 'tells' the onlooker something about the person, is treated as a communicative act, the body of that person becomes an integral part of what the receiver perceives. On the perceiver's side a kind of message is decoded. Of course, we do that frequently—read off other people's bodily signs and cast them in a linguistic form. But by doing so our focus is entirely on the observer's (receiver's) judgements of certain postures or gestures. Through these judgements bodily movements and non-verbal signs are turned into something language-like, into linguistic communication. However, postures and gestures are not necessarily discursively produced. That may be the case when there is a deliberate effort, as in sign language. Yet a propositionally organized or argumentatively structured message, which subsequently generates signs, need not always be present. This last assertion is crucial for a new understanding of the body as a selfing device or a meaning-producing device. The recipient's understanding of bodily signs as a communication or as carrying a message should not be projected onto the producer's mind, as if it was this mind which formed messages by bodily means.

Radley was right in criticizing the rather self-evident practice of viewing non-verbal communication as linguistic communication. It becomes linguistic only by a rather specific and separate process. The notion of communication is also misleading. The process of the production of signs should not be confused with the process by which they are turned into a communicative message by the recipient's interpretation. In order to demarcate the notion of communication, Wiener et al. asserted that the signs of the body can rightfully be called communication only if the person who acts has the intention of making something public. Furthermore, she or he has to make use of a socially shared signal system or code in order to make this possible. In case these conditions are not met, bodily conduct should be considered as 'symptomatic' of a certain bodily state rather than being viewed as communication. Shivering, for example is 'symptomatic' of the fact that somebody is cold, but should not be considered as communication about feeling cold.

Anorexia nervosa is often viewed as symptomatic. Feminist explanations especially view the body of the anorectic as part of a social symptomatology. The body is a site of interest for investigators who want to understand subordination and power. The anorectic body refers to experiences of domination and submissiveness and therefore the body becomes symptomatic of particular social situations. It is a signalling system about what these women suffer from, one that is much more ornate than mere words, but a signalling system nevertheless. Anorexia is a sign that the sufferers are entrapped in certain demands that are made upon their bodies. The presence of strong cultural ideals, for example, causes the anorectic women to exaggerate the control over their bodies in order to live up to those standards. A body presentation is created that gives away the anorectic's lack of ego strength and betrays the submission to cultural demands (Chernin, 1986; Lawrence, 1984). In most literature this lack of ego strength is related to certain family dynamics in which the mother plays a crucial role (Bruch, 1978; Chernin, 1986; Lawrence, 1984; Selvini-Palazzoli, 1974). Moreover, it is stressed that the social and cultural system as a whole and not just the family itself is responsible for the way parental behaviour is entrapped in demands that are counterproductive with respect to the anorectic's ego.

By contrasting the symptomatic with communication proper, Wiener and others have drawn a line between communication and signalling a certain state of affairs. Communication is restricted to sending a message. Radley (1991, p. 85) showed that Wiener et al. opened up the possibility for asking questions about those forms of bodily conduct which are in their terms not communicative but symptomatic, although their main objective lies in the reconceptualization of communication. According to Radley, Wiener et al. seem not to have taken advantage of that possibility. He claimed that it is as important to try to discover the social underpinnings of those symptomatic aspects as it is for communication proper. In that sense the borderline between the two cannot be drawn as strictly as Wiener et al. suggested. What is defined as 'symptomatic' has its social underpinnings as well; or, at the very best, we cannot exclude this as a possibility. Studies into the history of manners and bodily practices, for example, show that seemingly symptomatic bodily processes, such as sneezing, spitting and belching, are in fact socially regulated (Elias, 1978). Radley asserted that a study of the body in social life should include the investigation of bodily styles and practices. Mauss already stated in his 1935 essay on 'the techniques of the body' that there exists an 'education of movements' which inscribes itself into expressive style of all bodily performances (Mauss, 1935/1973). It is this project of the culturally inscripted body that we want to pursue.

From the perspective of the anorectic, the body is involved in all kinds of social arrangements. These do not provide a passive background, but rather form the active context in which the so-called 'symptoms' are a form of bodily meaning production that should not be ignored, even if an outside observer (receiver) fails to catch this meaning. Therefore, we would like to broaden Wiener et al.'s restrictive view on communication in such a way that it includes all bodily conduct which contributes to the production of meaning and which is somehow socially regulated. This broadening implies a redefinition of communication. The redefinition we would like to suggest is one in terms of 'co-regulation'.

Communication as Co-regulation

Wiener et al. rightly pose a question about the criteria of communication, but ultimately persist in what could be called the linguistic bias. They narrow their view to those modes of communication which rely on the use of a code or a socially shared signal system. It is obvious that this restriction excludes not only communicative behaviour as it is studied by ethologists, but also those forms of human expressivity which are non-discursive and non-propositional. In her classical study on symbolism, Susan Langer (1951) had already demonstrated that discursive or linguistic symbolism is one way among others of communicating meaning. Others include the non-linguistic modes of symbolization Langer calls rituals. Ritual is a form of *presentational* instead of representational symbolism. While language involves the sequential combination of smaller structural units into larger ones, *presentational* symbolism cannot easily be split up into meaningful units. Presentational forms derive their meaning from the simultaneous coordination of the whole. The meaning of a presentational form like dance, for example, resides not in the combination of smaller behavioural units, but in the expressive quality of the movement as a whole.

In contrast to discursive meanings, presentational forms lack an explicit structure of the either/or kind. They can be considered forms with strong semantics and weak syntax. Therefore they cannot easily be translated into well-articulated statements of a discursive repertoire. Presentational forms can be found in artistic expression, dance and rituals, but also in everyday emotional expression.

That brings us to another reason why communication should be broadened to include those non-linguistic, presentational forms. By claiming that the encoder instead of the decoder of a message provides the final criterion of communication, Wiener et al. persist in the common metaphor of communication as something which is produced somewhere, subsequently transmitted through a communication channel, and finally delivered to a receiver. Fogel (1993) demonstrates that terms like 'sender', 'receiver' and 'signal' belong to the description of 'discrete state communication systems', in which the actors can only be in one of several clear-cut discretely different states (p. 27). In such systems, the actors alternately have to adopt the role of sender and receiver. Although this description may seem adequate in the case of the exchange of written messages like letters or formal oral communications such as debates, it falls short as a description of 'continuous process communications systems'. In a continuous process system it is impossible to determine who is the sender and who is the receiver. Instead the communication dynamically unfolds as a ceaseless flow of mutually induced action and adaptation. Fogel refers to this communicative process as 'co-regulation', 'the dynamic balancing act by which a

smooth social performance is created out of the continuous mutual adjustment of action between partners' (p. 19). So the criterion to decide that a
given interaction is communicative resides in the organization of the system
as a whole and not in one of the participating actors. This point was already
emphasized by Birdwhistell, who was indicted by Wiener et al. for not
distinguishing between communications and signs. By restricting themselves
to the communicative qualities of discrete informational units, Wiener et al.
pass over in silence the actual flow of co-regulated action that specifies the
communicative process.

A comparable point was put forward by Maturana and Varela (1984).
They showed that the metaphor of communication as the transfer of
information through discrete communication channels, appealing as it may
seem in an age of mass media and flows of coded information, is both
biologically and epistemologically inadequate. This view of communication
presupposes that the behaviour produced by the sender is instructive with
regard to what goes on at the receiver's end. Furthermore, the message is
supposed to hold an informational content independent from the interpretation of the receiver or sender. However, it is quite obvious that the
meaning of what is communicated is neither determined by the intentions of
the sender, nor can it be found in the fixed relation between a sign and its
conventional referent. Instead, it is dynamically produced in the communication process itself. Carrying on the phenomenological body project initi-
ated by Merleau-Ponty, Maturana and Varela emphasize the embodied
structure of meaning in the widest possible sense (Maturana & Varela, 1984;
Varela, Thompson, & Rosch, 1991). Its essentially dialogical character,
which points at a very vital *co-construction* of meaning, should not be
overlooked (Hermans & Kempen, 1993; Hermans, Kempen, & Loon, 1992).
To not account for this dialogical character of meaning in which both sides
are emphasized reduces co-constructed meaning to information and co-
regulated action to mere instruction. All that is left is a message.

An important conclusion can be drawn from this co-regulative view of
communication. It implies that a strong emphasis should be placed on what
could be called 'co-regulative skills'. This type of skill should not be
confused with the social skills or competence on which the social skill
approach of mental health generally focuses. This approach relates mental
disorders, like anorexia nervosa, to social inadequacy and a lack of social
competence, especially the competence to deploy the body in social intercourse (Trower, Bryant, & Argyle, 1978). It has mainly been developed as a
social skills training programme for the treatment of mental disorders.
Radley (1991) demonstrates that this approach overemphasizes the body as a
means of control that conforms to the norms of society. Trower et al., (1978)
for example, regard a person as socially inadequate 'if he is unable to affect
the behaviour and feelings of others in the way that he intends and society
accepts' (p. 2). According to Radley, this 'technolized' view of the body

tends to overlook the body as a means of expression. Such a perspective on bodily skills is a very limited one, based as it is on the rather objectifying image of body techniques as something to be judged against an independent social standard and adjusted in accordance with those judgements. This approach to bodily skills is based on an instruction paradigm of communication rather then on a dialogical or co-regulative paradigm. However, as experiences in the field of sports, artistic expression and martial arts teach us, bodily skills are not learned by imposing a prescribed, so-called 'right' form upon individuals. They are learned by a process that involves the progressive development and refinement of bodily sensitivity. This sensitivity does not concern some private world of inner feelings, but on the contrary involves someone's bodily informed knowledge of the life-world. This means that bodily movements have to be felt from the inside as it were, so that they gradually become a part of one's own expressive register. It is not a matter of just imitating a prescribed form. Although the right forms or techniques have to be thoroughly trained, mastery is acquired only when those techniques become part of a personal style in which the expressive and the functional aspects of bodily movements fuse, as in dance, for example.

Co-regulative Skills and the Regulation of Bodily Styles

We have now moved quite far away from Harré's corporeal semantics. Harré borrows ideas from the structural semiotics of Roland Barthes (1985). It is striking, however, that Barthes's notions can be interpreted differently, more in accordance with the co-regulative skills paradigm we are proposing here. While Harré refers to Barthes in order to ground his theory of the body as a sign system, Douglas (1973) extensively quotes Barthes in order to elucidate her conception of style. Style, according to Barthes (1953/1968), springs from the body of the writer, from 'the depths of the author's personal and secret mythology' (p. 16). It is something which enfolds in a spontaneous way beyond his or her control, enacting in a non-representational way the 'erotic body' of the author (Barthes, 1973; Bernink, 1989). So Barthes acknowledges the body in its experiential and expressive qualities, but as was the case with Wiener et al., he also places this type of body outside the realm of the social, and equates it mistakenly with the idiosyncratic, 'secret mythology' of the writer. In addition Barthes places the social constitution and regulation of bodily style and the contribution of style to the production of meaning outside the reach of scientific examination. It is Douglas's merit to have put the notion of style back in the centre of her anthropological research of the body.

According to Douglas, the style of any message will coordinate all channels along which this message is given. Like Langer, she views the body not primarily as the producer of discrete signs. Instead, the signs and gestures of the body acquire their meaning by the expressive use of the body as a whole. Central in Douglas's anthropology of the body is her claim that a social system imposes pressure upon individuals to achieve consonance in all levels of experience, thereby producing concordance among the different means of expression. People are pressed to bring their physical experience into accordance with their social experience. Therefore the social order should be considered an *embodied* order, of which bodily practices and patterns of embodied experience and understanding are an integral part. So, while on the one hand society ritualizes its vital domains by both restricting and refining the possibilities for expression, on the other hand, people have to develop an expressive register or repertory which is sufficiently differ-entiated and geared to the social worlds in which they find themselves.

One way of applying Douglas's conception of bodily style to the field of social psychology is to connect it with our broadened theory of communi-cation and interpersonal relationships. In fact, this involves a return to the features of non-verbal communication presented by Bateson some time ago (1972). He distinguished four features of this non-verbal mode of com-munication: it lacks unambiguous negations, tense and any identification of linguistic mood, and furthermore is metaphoric, which means that it com-municates relations rather than statements about objects or things (p. 139). Like Langer, Bateson stressed the very specific ordering principles of this 'analogic' mode of communication. The lacking of negations, for example, brings about a specific range of problems. Two dogs which bump into one another cannot easily communicate they are *not* going to fight. Instead they have to perform a sham fight by the showing of fangs, engaging in a brawl and discovering that neither wants to kill the other (p. 141). This means that the regulation of non-verbal behaviour involves a clear-cut ritualization of expressive forms, consisting of multiple layers of 'signification'. Moreover, the example of the dogs demonstrates that a regulation of behaviour is possible without the need for a supra-individual moral order and without the explicit need for the discursive or linguistic negotiation of power differ-ences. Instead, ordered forms of behaviour can emerge from the immediate co-regulation of expressive bodily activity.

Anorexia Revisited

Once the body is conceived of as a natural juncture of co-regulative skills, some conclusions with respect to the nature, diagnosis and research of anorexia nervosa can be drawn. Introducing the 'subjectified' or 'selfing' body into an explanation of anorexia places an emphasis on the competence of the subject to claim and sustain an identity. This competence is produced or constituted within a historical process but is nevertheless 'real' in the sense that it is objectified in durable bodily dispositions (Bourdieu, 1990). Viewed this way, anorexia nervosa is not a statement about, or a symbolic reference to, the social position of women, but the embodied expression of a culturally constituted subject. This has some implications for the diagnosis of anorexia.

The diagnostic criteria of anorexia nervosa which are currently used clearly demonstrate the significance of the body in this eating disorder. Both medical and psychological criteria play a part in this diagnosis, which relies on the four criteria of the DSM-IV (American Psychiatric Association, 1994).

First, there must be a persistent refusal to gain weight in spite of being about 15 percent below normal weight. A second criterion is amenorrhea, that is, a prolonged absence of the menstrual cycle. Third, the anorectic must experience an intense fear of gaining weight or becoming fat, and must claim to feel fat even when already underweight. The fourth criterion is the one which occasioned the most influential line of research into the psycho-logical aspects of the body, the so-called 'distorted body image'. This research was inspired by an article of Bruch's (1962), in which she observed that anorexia nervosa involves a disorder of both the perception and experience of the body. Part of the discussion that followed her observations concerned the question of whether perceptual or cognitive factors are most important for an explanation of this distorted body image. Slade and Russell (1973), for example, maintained that the disorder is best understood as a disturbance of the way the body is perceived. However, most researchers emphasize the process of judgement—a cognitive process—in the realiz-ation of the body image (Garner & Garfinkel, 1981; Huon & Brown, 1986).

The way research on body-image distortion is carried out clearly demon-strates its departure from an objectified view of the body. The method applied in the greater part of this research consists of asking women to estimate as adequately as possible the width of their own body, using either simply drawn silhouettes or complex video distortion equipment. By com-paring those estimates to their 'real' body size, it is determined whether the participant has a distorted representation of her own body. In our view, however, this type of research, even though it is related to the real or objective body size as part of a diagnostic criterion, obscures the true nature of the distorted relation anorectics have to their own body. When viewed from the co-regulative skill paradigm, body distortion looks different. According to this paradigm, a non-distorted relation to our bodies does not imply any reference to our objective body size. When walking through a small doorway, for example, we calculate neither the width of the doorway nor that of our bodies. Instead we are capable of acting quite adequately by using an unmediated, tacit knowledge of the environment and of our bodies (Gibson, 1966; Polanyi, 1967). This means that the perception of our bodies is to be understood not as a picture, constructed by ourselves as outside observers, but as an experience that is thoroughly intertwined with our experience of the 'life-world' (Merleau-Ponty, 1945/1962). This perspective raises some serious objections against an understanding of anorexia nervosa in terms of a distorted body image. It is not the image of the anorectic's body that seems to be distorted, but rather the relation to her social world; the selfing capabilities of her body are an integral part of this relationship. Therefore, we need to return to the expressive, communicative body as it was depicted in the preceding paragraphs, in order to examine whether this can provide any insights into the embodied nature of anorexia.

In the distorted image research, the body is not only objectified in the eye of the researcher. What this research does is to ask women to objectify their own body by judging it, as it were, from the outside. Yet, it is exactly this extreme objectification of their own body which constitutes the core of the anorectics' problem. The anorectic does not experience her body as something she is, but as something she has, as some sort of 'non-self'. It seems quite likely that the objectification of her own body keeps her from getting involved bodily in the social world in which she lives. Instead of being a vital constituent of a meaningful relation to her life-world, the body becomes an object of rigid control.

As we have tried to argue earlier, some feminists and social constructionists try to capture the bodily aspect of anorexia nervosa by reducing it to a cluster of discursively constructed meanings. However, as demonstrated above, those meanings pass over in silence the experiential and expressive body of the anorectic herself. By recognizing the central role of the body in the communicative, co-regulative interaction of the self and its social environment, we are able to view anorexia as a distortion of this selfing process. We avoid the static notion of self or self-concept, because what gets distorted is the process of becoming a self—the selfing process, as we call it. This is in accordance with our earlier emphasis on the bodily production of meaning rather than on the ascription of meaning to the body. Instead of asking for the meaning of the excessive slimming of anorectics, we should shift our attention to the competence of deploying their bodies in the social process.

Others as well have shifted the attention from deviant eating behaviour and dismissive judgements about the body to factors related to the self. They focus on social uncertainty and uncertainty about women's own feelings and emotions. By confronting this view with our own, we can make more precise what our view entails.

Anorectics are observed to be especially afraid of spontaneous, informal social relations (Appels, 1983; Bruch, 1977, 1978). Not only their eating behaviour, but their whole bodily style is characterized by restrained expressivity. Restrictive eating behaviour is only one—albeit the most conspicuous—aspect of the anorectic's bodily style. Anorectics are unable to join the vicissitudes of social interactions in an easy, relaxed way. Instead they seem to be constantly aware of themselves, hyper-sensitive to reactions of their social environment. Yet this type of sensitivity is misleading. In competently co-regulated activity there exists a largely automatic and unaware adjustment of one's behaviour to social situations. Anorectics don't seem able to enter into an easy flux of social interactions. They seem constantly preoccupied, watching and monitoring themselves in a rather laborious way. They keep a tight rein on their own doings. This precludes the rather self-evident and easy-going, subtle regulation of their own behaviour. Even though they are hyper-conscious of themselves, anorectics lack a social *souplesse* tailored to the demands of the social situation. In this regard, parents of anorectics often maintain that their daughters were obedient, conforming, non-assertive girls in their pre-anorectic period, which seems to be in sharp contrast with the stubborn and persistent behaviour they display later on in life (Bruch, 1978; Leon & Finn, 1984).

This contrast has brought ego-psychological-oriented theorists, especially, to the conclusion that the anorectic develops a 'false self' or 'pseudo self', an enforced identity, based on the rigid control of her own body. This body control serves to conceal her feelings of worthlessness and lack of auto-nomy. Although the body thus becomes part of a some kind of identity project, we are faced again with the body as something which does not independently contribute to the production of meaning. The notion of a true and a false self easily overlooks the body's resilient contribution to the selfing process. Bateson (1972, pp. 309–337) already made clear that the idea of self-control is based on a mistaken and pathogenic epistemology in which the self is split up into a part that is controlled and a part by which the control is executed. We want to stress that the rigid body control of anorectics involves a practical dualism due to a lack of social *souplesse*. Anorectics experience the body as something they carry with them, some-thing non-self. The mind, then, is imposed upon it as a device which holds firm control over all bodily processes, including expressivity. Bordo (1989) emphasizes the same extreme, dysfunctional dualism. According to her, anorectics are not just obsessed with body weight as such. They fear especially that the weak parts of their body (belly, breasts, buttocks, thighs) will escape their control. Bordo states that the fear of bulging body parts is in fact the 'anxiety about internal processes out of control—unrestrained desire, unrestrained hunger, uncontrolled impulse' (p. 89). By rigidly keeping a check on all of their bodily functions and processes, those women try to cover up their feelings of uncertainty and lack of social competence.

Final Conclusions and Implications

We can now draw some final conclusions about anorexia nervosa and what this disorder has to say about psychology's treatment of the body. Rendering the body of the anorectic as a mannequin that shows the effects of domination and submission, or as a battleground for feminist arguments, dilemmas and discourse, keeps hidden the anorectic's bodily production of meaning. Psychology's rather traditional occupation with discursive meaning holds sway over psychological thinking about the body. Yet anorexia nervosa is not just there to be interpreted as a message or a symptom which results in a judgement from the outside of what these women 'really' seem to convey. The view on communication as co-regulation, espoused in the preceding paragraphs, tries to shift the emphasis away from discursive meaning and messages to the production of meaning within the selfing process. This selfing process implies a social performance which is created out of the continual adjustment of the participants to one another. The minutiae of that process involve kinds of stylized bodily skills that testify to one's ability to take part in the life-world. The body thus becomes a natural juncture of co-regulative skills.

The anorectic's disturbance of bodily practice can now be described more adequately. This description will contain a message for psychology in the sense that psychology's focus should be more on what the body automatically brings about or fails to bring about. Psychology should be more concerned with the bodily production of meaning within the selfing process, instead of restricting itself to socially constructed judgements about the body. The failure of anorectics, if one may put it that way without morally judging those women, is a matter not so much of a distortion of their body image as of a lack of co-regulative skills that serve the selfing process. These skills are not developed adequately. In consequence, the women who suffer from anorexia are much more vulnerable to the pitfalls of an extreme dualistic relation to their own bodies, resulting in bodily dissatisfaction and need for mental control. Research which has been supportive of the view that this dualistic process is often involved frequently limits itself to the assessment of discourse about the body and fails to come to grips with the subtle details of co-regulation. Such theory and research fails to locate the disturbance in the domain of social skills and practices.

Although the emphasis on social skills and co-regulation suggests that the treatment of anorexia nervosa should focus on training and the corroboration of such skills from resources in the direct environment of the anorectic patient, the authors are not sufficiently clinically competent to draw the implications for therapeutic practice. They leave that to the experienced reader, who is invited to develop this view of the body in a full-scale psychological practice.

References

American Psychiatric Association. (1994). *Diagnostic and statistical manual of mental disorders: DSM-IV*. Washington, DC: Author.

Appels, A. (1983). Cultuur en ziekte [Culture and illness]. *De Psycholoog, 18,* 109–132.

Armon-Jones, C. (1986). The thesis of constructionism. In R. Harré (Ed.), *The social construction of emotions*. Oxford: Blackwell.

Averill, J.R. (1980). A constructivist view on emotion. In R. Plutchik & H. Kellerman (Eds.), *Emotion: Theory, research and experience: Vol 1. Theories of emotion*. New York: Academic Press.

Barthes, R. (1968). *Writing degree zero* (A. Lavers & C. Smith, Trans.). New York: Hill & Wang. (Original work published 1953.)

Barthes, R. (1973). *Le plaisir du texte*. Paris: Éditions du Seuil.

Barthes, R. (1985). *The responsibility of form: Critical essays on music, art, and representations* (R. Howard, Trans.). New York: Hill & Wang.

Bateson, G. (1972). *Steps to an ecology of mind*. New York: Chandler.

Berger, P., & Luckmann, T. (1966). *The social construction of reality: A treatise on the sociology of knowledge* Harmondsworth: Penguin.

Bernink, M. (1989). *Inter(ventions) of the body: Preliminary study of the question of the body and sexual difference in Nietzsche, Barthes, Cixous and Irigaray*. Doctoral thesis, University of Utrecht.

Billig, M. (1987). *Arguing and thinking: A rhetorical approach to social psychology*. Cambridge: Cambridge University Press.

Billig, M. (1988). *Ideological dilemmas: A social psychology of everyday thinking*. London: Sage.

Birdwhistell, R. (1952). *Introduction to kinesics*. Louisville, KY: University of Louisville Press.

Bordo, S.R. (1989). Reading the slender body. In M. Jacobus, E. Fox Keller, & S. Shuttleworth (Eds.), *Women, science and the body politic: Discourses and representations*. New York: Methuen.

Boskind-Lodahl, M. (1976). Cinderella's stepsister: A feminist perspective on anorexia nervosa and bulimia. *SIGNS: Journal of Women in Culture and Society, 2,* 342–356.

Bourdieu, P. (1990). *The logic of practice*. Cambridge: Polity.

Bruch, H. (1962). Perceptual and conceptual disturbances in anorexia nervosa. *Psychosomatic Medicine, 14,* 187–195.

Bruch, H. (1973). *Eating disorders: Obesity, anorexia nervosa and the person within*. New York: Basic Books.

Bruch, H. (1978). *The golden cage: The enigma of anorexia nervosa*. Cambridge, MA: Harvard University Press.

Brumberg, J.J. (1988). *Fasting girls: The emergence of anorexia nervosa as a modern disease*. Cambridge, MA: Harvard University Press.

Butler, J. (1990). *Gender trouble: Feminism and the subversion of identity*. New York: Routledge.

Butler, J. (1993). *Bodies that matter: On the discursive limits of 'sex'*. New York: Routledge.

Chernin, K. (1986). *The hungry self: Women, eating and identity*. New York: Harper & Row.

Douglas, M. (1973). *Natural symbols: Explorations in cosmology*. Harmondsworth: Penguin.

Dunbar, M. (1986). *Catherine: The story of a girl who died of anorexia*. Harmonds-worth: Penguin.

Edwards, D. (1991). Categories for talking: On the cognitive and discursive bases of categorization. *Theory & Society, 1*, 515–542.

Elias, N. (1978). *The civilizing process*. Oxford: Blackwell.

Fogel, A. (1993). *Developing through relationships: Origins of communication, self and culture*. New York: Harvester Wheatsheaf.

Garfinkel, P.E., & Garner, D.M. (1982). *Anorexia nervosa: A multidimensional perspective*. New York: Bruner.

Garner, D.M., & Garfinkel, P.E. (1981). Body image in anorexia nervosa: Measure-ment, theory and clinical implications. *International Journal of Psychiatry in Medicine, 38*, 327–336.

Garner, D.M., Garfinkel, P.E., Schwartz, D., & Thompson, M. (1980). Cultural expectations of thinness in women. *Psychological Reports, 47*, 483–491.

Gergen, K.J., & Gergen, M.M. (1983). Narratives of the self. In T.R. Sarbin & K.E. Scheibe (Eds.), *Studies in social identity*. New York: Praeger.

Gergen, K.J., & Gergen, M.M. (1984). Social construction of narrative accounts. In K. Gergen & M. Gergen (Eds.), *Historical social psychology*. Hillsdale, NJ: Erlbaum.

Gergen, K.J., & Gergen, M.M. (1988). Narrative and the self as relationship. *Advances in Experimental Social Psychology, 21*, 17–56.

Gibson, J.J. (1966). *The senses considered as perceptual systems*. Boston, MA: Houghton Mifflin.

Harré, R. (1986). The social contructionist viewpoint. In R. Harré (Ed.), *The social construction of emotions*. Oxford: Blackwell.

Harré, R. (1991). *Physical being: A theory for a corporeal psychology*. Oxford: Blackwell.

Harré, R., & Gillet, G. (1994). *The discursive mind*. London: Sage.

Heelas, P. (1981). Emotion talk across cultures. In P. Heelas & A. Lock (Eds.), *Indigenous psychologies: The anthropology of the self*. London: Academic Press.

Hermans, H.J.M., & Kempen, H.J.G. (1993). *The dialogical self: Meaning as movement*. San Diego CA: Academic Press.

Hermans, H.J.M., Kempen, H.J.G., & Loon, R.J.P. van (1992). The dialogical self: beyond individualism and rationalism. *American Psychologist, 47*, 23–33

Hochschild, A.R. (1983). *The managed heart: Commercialization of human feeling*. Berkeley: University of California Press.

Huon, G.F., & Brown, L.B. (1986). Body images in anorexia nervosa and bulimia nervosa. *International Journal of Eating Disorders, 5*, 421–439.

Jaggar, A.M. (1983). *Feminist politics and human nature*. Totowa, NJ: Rowman & Allenhed.

Jaggar, A.M., & Bordo, S.R. (1992). *Gender/body/knowledge: Feminist reconstruc-tions of being and knowing*. New Brunswick, NJ: Rutgers University Press.

Kitzinger, C. (1987). *The social construction of lesbianism*. London: Sage.

Kitzinger, C. (1992). Theorizing heterosexuality. *Feminism & Psychology*, 2, 293–324.

Kristeva, J. (1978). Gesture: Practice or communication? (J. Benthall, Trans.). In T. Polhemus (Ed.), *The body reader: Social aspects of the human body.* New York: Pantheon. (Reprinted from *Languages*, 1968, *10*, 48–64.)

Langer, S.K. (1951). *Philosophy in a new key: A study in the symbolism of reason, rite and art.* London: Oxford University Press.

Lawrence, M. (1984). *The anorectic experience.* London: Women's Press.

Leon, G.R., & Finn, S. (1984). Sex-role stereotypes and the development of eating disorders. In C. Spatz Widom (Ed.), *Sex roles and psychopathology.* New York: Plenum.

Lenning, A. van (1990). Anorexie: Ben kritisch commentaar op de cultuur? [Anorexia: A critical comment on culture?]. *Tijdschrift voor Vrouwenstudies*, *42*, 128–142.

Lutz, C. (1986). The domain of emotion words in Ifaluk. In R. Harré (Ed.), *The social construction of emotions.* Oxford: Blackwell.

Lutz, C. (1988). *Unnatural emotions.* Chicago: University of Chicago Press.

Macleod, S. (1982). *The art of starvation: One girl's journey through adolescence and anorexia: A story of survival.* London: Virago.

Maturana, H.R., & Varela, F.J. (1984). *The tree of knowledge: The biological roots of human understanding.* Boston, MA: Shambala.

Mauss, M. (1973). The techniques of the body (B. Brewster, Trans.). *Economy and Society*, *2*, 70–88. (Reprinted from *Journal de Psychologie Normale et Pathologique*, 1935, *32*.)

Merleau-Ponty, M. (1962). *Phenomenology of perception* (C. Smith, Trans.). London: Routledge & Kegan Paul. (Original work published 1945.)

Merwe, W.L. van der, & Voestermans, P.P. (1995). Wittgenstein's legacy and the challenge to psychology. *Theory & Psychology*, *5*, 27–48.

Minuchin, S., Rosman, B.L., & Baker, L. (1978). *Psychosomatic families: Anorexia nervosa in context.* Cambridge, MA: Harvard University Press.

Orbach, S. (1985). *Hunger strike: The anorectic's struggle as a metaphor for our age.* New York: Plenum.

Polanyi, M. (1967). *The tacit dimension.* London: Routledge.

Potter, J., & Wetherell, M. (1987). *Discourse and social psychology.* Newbury Park, CA: Sage.

Radley, A. (1991). *The body in social psychology.* New York: Springer.

Ratner. C. (1989). A social constructionist critique of the naturalistic theory of emotion. *The Journal of Mind and Behavior*, *10*, 211–230.

Sampson, E.E. (1993). Identity politics: Challenges to psychology's understanding. *American Psychologist*, *48*, 1219–1230.

Sarbin, T.R. (Ed.). (1986a). *Narrative psychology: The storied nature of human conduct.* New York: Praeger.

Sarbin, T.R. (1986b). Emotion and act: Roles and rhetoric. In R. Harré (Ed.), *The social construction of emotions.* Oxford: Blackwell.

Scheflen, A.E. (1972). *Body language and social order: Communication as behavioral control.* Englewood Cliffs, NJ: Prentice Hall.

Selvini-Palazzoli, M. (1974). *Self starvation: From the intrapsychic to the transpersonal approach to anorexia nervosa.* London: Chaucer.

Shotter, J. (1993). *Conversational realities: Constructing life through language*. London: Sage.

Shotter, J. (1995). In conversation: Joint action, shared intentionality and ethics. *Theory & Psychology*, *5*, 49–73.

Shotter, J., & Gergen, K. (1989). *Texts of identity*. London: Sage.

Slade, P.D., & Russell, G.F.M. (1973). Awareness of body dimensions in anorexia nervosa: Cross-sectional and longitudinal studies. *Psychological Medicine*, *3*, 188–199.

Terwee, S. (1995). Deconstructing social constructionism. In I. Lubek, R. van Hezewijk, G. Pheterson, & C. Tolman (Eds.), *Trends and issues in theoretical psychology*. New York: Springer.

Thomä, H. (1967). *Anorexia nervosa*. New York: International University Press.

Trower, P., Bryant, B., & Argyle, M. (1978). *Social skills and mental health*. London: Methuen.

Unger, R.K. (1989). *Representations: Social constructions of gender*. Amityville, NY: Baywood.

Unger, R.K. (1992). *Women and gender: A feminist psychology*. Philadelphia, PA: Temple University Press.

Varela, F.J., Thompson, F., & Rosch, E. (1991). *The embodied mind: Cognitive science and human experience*. Cambridge, MA: MIT Press.

Vroman, L. (1957). Mens [Human being]. In *Uit slaapwandelen*. Amsterdam: Querido.

Waller, J.V., Kaufman, M.R., & Deutsch, F. (1940). Anorexia nervosa: A psycho-somatic entity. *Psychosomatic Medicine*, *2*, 2–13.

Wiener, M., Devoe, S., Rubinow, S., & Geller, J. (1972). Nonverbal behavior and nonverbal communication. *Psychological Review*, *79*, 185–214.

Wiseman, C.V., Gray, J.J., Mosimann, J.E., & Aherens, A.H. (1992). Cultural expectations of thinness in women: An update. *International Journal of Eating Disorders*, *11*, 85–89.

10

The Psychology and Management of Pain

Gate Control as Theory and Symbol

Robert Kugelmann

ABSTRACT. The theory and treatment of pain have undergone major changes since 1950. Significant has been the gate control theory of pain, first described in 1965. This theory symbolizes a new epistemology and praxis of pain by redefining pain as a process. The redefinition legitimated new treatment possibilities for pain, making all of a patient's existence fair game for professional management. Social uses of the new psychology of pain are examined, in the context of a critique of the object of medical knowledge and power, the patient as a 'person'. In the name of overcoming Cartesian dualism (which today carries a negative value), the new theory and treatment possibilities (which are holistic, therefore 'better') promote a greater technical management of human suffering.

With the development of behavioral medicine and health psychology, psychology and medicine have become increasingly integrated in recent decades. Since 1950, medicine has been moving away from a biomedical model of disease to embrace a biopsychosocial model (see Engel, 1977). The biomedical model 'maintains that all illness can be explained on the basis of aberrant somatic processes' (Taylor, 1995, p. 12), and the biopsychosocial model 'maintains that biological, psychological, and social factors are all-important determinants of health and illness' (Taylor, 1995, p. 13). Taylor indicates that the former emphasizes disease processes, ignores psychosocial factors and even health. The latter addresses both illness and health and reckons health as an achievement rather than as simply the absence of disease. An essential implication of the new model, according to Arney and Bergen (1984), is that when medicine adopted this approach, it 'invented the patient who was also a person, for the first time in its history' (p. 60). This new object of medical treatment, the patient as 'person', means that the totality of the patient's existence, rather than the disease, is in principle comprehended by medical expertise. Along the same lines, Armstrong (1983) argues that by the late 1940s in Britain 'the medical gaze began to fix with more tenacity on the patient's personality' (p. 108) and on the social sphere surrounding the patient. These two analyses, influenced by Foucault's (1973, 1979, 1980) reading of the history of modern subjectivity, show that the 'personhood' of the patient is as much a construct of medical knowledge and power as had been the passive and silent patient of the biomedical model.

This change in the object of medical treatment—from disease to existence—is not a liberation from dehumanizing objectification. It signifies an alteration in the meaning of being a patient.[1] The extension of health care, under the slogan of treating the person not the disease, is no advance if one assumes, as I do, that professional expertise ought to have limits. Its proponents argue that the new model has arisen to deal with chronic diseases, which have become more prominent as infectious diseases have been conquered and as life expectancy has increased (Gatchel, Baum, & Krantz, 1989). Insofar as patients suffer chronic conditions, treatment aims not to cure but to manage. The latter involves 'physician and patient . . . in a search for an optimal life strategy which respects a distant, somewhat vague idea of the social order that is part of the normative structure of life' (Arney & Bergen, 1984, p. 92).

What is problematic in the biopsychosocial model is its claim to comprehend all existence and to provide professional management for disease and health. This comprehension of existence, its 'totalization', to use Lévinas's (1961/1969) term, is problematic not because it ignores individual uniqueness, but because it masks ethical imperatives in the guise of scientific findings about the nature of health. This paper describes this masking as it occurs in the treatment of chronic pain. By disguising moral imperatives as scientific theory, professionals can claim authority over ever-increasing areas of existence (see McKnight, 1978, for an analysis of care as the 'mask of love').

Taking off the mask over the hidden morality does not resolve the difficulty. Biopsychosocial medicine favors the technological management of existence. The way it describes existence biases intervention toward technical, professionalized treatment of existence. The biopsychosocial model is a powerful, deceptive metaphor that converts non-scientific, non-technological treatments of disease into techniques that can be owned by modern professions. The biopsychosocial metaphor converts vernacular healing practices into turf claimed by modern professions (see Zola, 1978, for a good general discussion of medicalization). In other words, the new model reconstructs not only the patient but also the treatments.

Chronic pain is worth studying in relation to the changed medical models. Chronic pain is widespread, apparently increasing over time, to the point where it has been called an epidemic (Nachemson, 1994; Osterweis, Kleinman, & Mechanic, 1987). Many pain patients, when they decide that there is no quick fix for their pain, or when an insurance company recommends it, turn to a pain clinic for treatment. Pain clinics to varying degrees espouse a biopsychosocial approach to pain. The development of this approach and its legitimation are my concerns. In particular, I focus on changes since 1950 in the theory and treatment of chronic pain. The gate control theory, introduced in 1965, serves as a focal point in this analysis. The gate control theory symbolizes the new 'world' of biopsychosocial medicine, and I consider its symbolic character in two ways: by examining the symbol itself and by indicating the social uses of the theory as it has affected practice. In this new world there is emphasis on the subjective nature of pain. The new model legitimates greater psychotherapeutic treatment of pain, which is no longer spatially located in the body defined anatomically; pain is now a process. Finally, the new theory serves as a lever to reconstruct, to legitimate and hence to expropriate heretofore marginalized treatments. The locus of all these changes is the pain clinic, an institution unique to the second half of the 20th century, a growth industry, and the place for the professional exploitation of chronic pain.

Pain in the Biomedical Model

'Pain involves perception of noxious impulses and a reaction thereto' (Bonica, 1952, p. 1582). In 1950, pain was viewed medically as a sensation, along the lines of vision and touch. This sensation theory, which had developed late in the 19th century, was the received view but not the only theory of pain available when pain clinics began. It states that pain, like other sensations, is mediated by specific nerves. In opposition to this theory was the summation theory: 'Pain is mediated by the tactile nerves and . . . it results from the summation of their excitations in the gray substance of the spinal cord' (Dallenbach, 1939, p. 343). While neither the sensation theory nor any version of the summation theory could adequately account for all pain phenomena, in medical textbooks the sensation theory dominated (Bonica, 1990, p. 8; Schiller, 1990).

The Cartesian Space of Pain

The sensation theory can be approached as a symbol of a 'world' of pain, the world of professional treatment before 1950. The symbol represents what we can call the existential possibilities for professional treatment in the period. To represent the sensation theory world of pain, consider an illustration from Descartes's 1644 treatise *Of Man* (Figure 1). Melzack and Wall (1965), who helped end this world and establish a new one, point to this very picture and state: 'To call a receptor a "pain receptor" . . . is a psychological assumption; it implies a direct connection from the receptor to a brain center where pain is felt' (p. 971). The Cartesian image implies a direct relationship between an interiority and an exteriority. In fact, there are two types of interiority: that of the body and that of the soul. Outside lies the observer, who, as the

FIGURE 1. Symbol of pain in the bio-medical model, showing Cartesian space. (From 'Traité de l'Homme', by R. Descartes, 1644/1974, in C. Adam and P. Tannery (Eds.), *Oeuvres de Descartes* (Vol 11. Figure 7), Paris: Vrin)

image suggests, can see into the interior of the body. Finally, the figure in the illustration is a solitary figure, an autonomous individual.

This Cartesian space of pain, which was in fact that of the first half of the 20th century and not the 17th century, was a divisible space (Figure 2). Since pain existed in that space as a signal, it could be interrupted: the foot could move, a surgeon could cut the nerve, the soul could distract itself. Above all else, pain *signalled*: it represented danger in the external world or damage to the body. Each region of this divisible space had its professional caretakers. Physicians anatomized the body, psychiatrists the soul, and physicists the fire.

The solitary figure with his camp fire is independent and self-reliant. He can manage by himself. The viewer observes this person from a distance. Beyond the figure and the fire, there is a rudimentary background. A message of the picture seems to be: This person has a degree of autonomy. Despite the fact that we, the viewers, can peer into his innards, despite the fact that the body facing us is dissectable, he does not need us. He is an object in Cartesian space, but over there, at a distance from us.

The Cartesian symbol of pain is an image of the autonomous individual, who can potentially control pain through specific interventions, chiefly by interrupting the nerve pathways. This symbol, especially of the pain pathway, reveals that the sensation theory spatialized pain. Pain had not been spatialized previously. The dominant understanding of pain prior to the sensation theory had been the ancient one, which dates back to the Greeks, which held pain to be a passion of the soul. Passions of the soul, especially in their Aristotelian formulation, are not spatial. Spatialization makes possible visualization, which in turn facilitates mechanistic possibilities for professional, technological intervention.

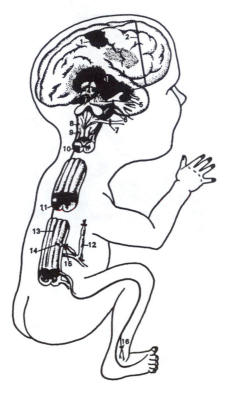

FIGURE 2. Pain in the biomedical model, showing the divisibility of the space of pain. (From 'Neurosurgical Procedures for the Control of Pain', by C.S. MacCarty and R.L. Drake, 1956, *Proceedings of the Staff Meetings of the Mayo Clinic, 31*, p. 208. Schematic diagram illustrating various surgical procedures designed to alleviate pain, published with permission from the Mayo Foundation for Medical Education and Research.)

Psychogenic Pain

In the Cartesian symbol, pain disappears from view when it enters the soul. This vanishing act proved the undoing of the sensation theory, which had thus to be elaborated to account for psychological factors in the experience of pain. 'Pain can be separated into two components: the perception of pain [resulting from the stimulation of pain receptors] and the reaction to pain [resulting from the central or psychological elaboration of the pain sensation]' (Bonica, 1990, p. 9). This psychosomatic addendum sought to square the sensation theory with the common experience that pain expression and feeling do not correspond easily to tissue damage. J.J. Bonica (1990), the anesthesiologist who spearheaded the development of modern pain clinics, later criticized this attempted reconciliation because it 'assumes a one-to-one relationship between the intensity of the stimulus and pain perception and relegates the reaction to pain as a secondary response consequent to the sensation in a straight-through push-button or alarm system fashion' (p. 9). The argument went: If there be pain, it must be a sensation, and it must normally signal tissue damage. What the subject does with this sensation, what of memory and anticipation is added to it, turns pain the sensation into pain the perception.

But sometimes pain exists without any physiological indications. The patient might be deriving pleasure or some other benefit from the pain. Even if originally associated with trauma, the flesh had long ago healed, but the pain persisted. Such anomalies were gathered under the heading of psychogenic pain. Psychogenic pain is said to exist when there is no demonstrable organic cause for pain, yet the patient complains of it. This type of pain could not be treated, strictly speaking, by the anesthesiologist in a pain clinic. The diagnosis seems to have been a dumping ground for types of pain not easily assimilated to the sensation theory. Critics of the latter condemned the tendency to call unknown pain psychogenic. William K. Livingston, a surgeon at the University of Oregon Hospital in the 1940s and 1950s, whose book, *Pain Mechanisms* (1943/1976), did much to change the received view of pain, criticized this practice, especially in cases of phantom limb pain, because 'to classify certain types of pain as "psychic" pain is purely arbitrary, because all pain is a psychic perception' (p. 70). Bonica (1953) complained of 'the rather widespread tendency to diagnose a pain as "psychic in origin," because no organic etiology is obvious during a brief and not too careful examination made in the busy practitioner's office' (p. 134). The diagnosis had the onus of the imaginary, since only the organic is 'really real'. The temptation to dismiss puzzling cases must have been great, for Bonica quotes the French surgeon René Leriche (1939), who pleaded with practitioners in the 1930s to take patients' complaints of pain seriously (a complaint still heard; see Melzack, 1992).

For critics of the sensation theory, psychogenic pain was real, because 'clinical pain must be considered as fundamentally a psychobiological phenomenon which is not easily classified as either a sensation or emotion' (Bonica, 1953, p. 135). Often the sensory component of pain is less important than the emotional, which is conditioned by upbringing, culture and personality. For Bonica (1953), who claimed that the sensation theory accounted for many pain phenomena, psychogenic pain properly speaking arises 'from the projection of psychic conflicts to some organ without any abnormal activity or tension in the organ to which the pain is referred' (p. 137). The controversy over psychogenic pain shows the uncertainty in the understanding of pain in the minds of the clinicians dealing with pain patients. The status of pain and of pain clinics was fluid in the late 1940s and subsequent years.

The Management of Chronic Pain

The career of a patient with intractable pain changed between 1950 and the present. General practitioners provided most of the medical treatment for pain in 1950. If the pain proved resistant to treatment, then the patient could be referred to a specialist, such as an anesthesiologist or psychiatrist. Some patients were further referred to one of the few clinics specializing in the treatment of intractable pain. The assumption at the time was that pain was symptomatic of an underlying disease; pain itself was not considered a disease.

Pain clinics began to appear in the 1930s, although they were rare until after World War II, as places where medical specialists, especially anesthesiologists, managed intractable pain. The treatment of choice was the nerve block, 'the injection of a solution of a local anesthetic agent, or some other drug with a special affinity for nerve tissue, into a painful part, or into the immediate vicinity of afferent nerves carrying pain impulses' (Alexander, 1954, p. 585). Treatments also included nerve section, neurosurgery (e.g. prefrontal lobotomy) and the administration of narcotic and analgesic drugs. J. Rubin, an anesthesiologist, described the pain clinic which began in 1948 at the Philadelphia General Hospital. Rubin's clinic handled pain arising from a variety of diseases, including cancer, arthritis and back pain. Indicative of the limits of the treatment, Rubin (1951) noted: 'Many patients have been sent to the Pain Clinic for whom nerve block therapy was not indicated. Complete study often revealed that more definitive therapy was available for such patients in other branches of medicine' (p. 602). Pain clinics at the time had limited scope and their procedures were biomedical.

Anesthesiologists at the time saw in pain clinics a natural extension of their practice. The field was relatively low in status and pay (see Starr, 1982). R.A. Gordon (1949) found that with the development of regional anesthesia, 'the activities of the anaesthetist have ceased to be confined to the operating theater, and that he has gradually come to the position of a collaborator with, and at times a consultant to members of the medical profession working in other fields' (p. 251; see also Schiller, 1990, p. 40). In an editorial in 1950, Howard Dittrick called pain clinics 'an opportunity for expansion' (p. 60). The editorial clearly presents the pain clinic as a novelty:

> Recently I visited a hospital where the anesthesia department has established a service to the profession for the diagnosis and treatment of pain. The group calls this activity a Pain Clinic. The plan has been submitted to the local medical society and no objection to it has been raised. The facilities of the Clinic are available to any physician and the diagnostic survey is made upon payment of a moderate fee. The Clinic is open one day a week, but provision is made for emergency appointments. Patients are accepted only when referred by a private physician. Each patient is examined by an anesthesiologist and a neurosurgeon, but when necessary other specialists are consulted. If indicated, one diagnostic block with recommendations are sent to the referring physician. Usually no subsequent treatment is carried out by the Clinic. (p. 60)

Dittrick argued that 'the meaning of the term anesthesia (without feeling) would indicate that when treatment is required to obliterate pain, such treatment should be in the hands of an anesthesiologist' (p. 60).

Despite the opportunities for expansion of the practice of anesthesiology, the biomedical model kept the scope narrow. Beyond the call for collaboration among specialists, the time-honored place of the general practitioner was secure. Even in the early work of Bonica, the emphasis was on what any physician could do to treat pain. In introducing the idea of the pain clinic, Bonica (1953) stressed:

> I am *not* suggesting or advocating that these procedures are the sole responsibility of, nor that they should be performed exclusively by, the anesthesiologist. On the contrary, the primary purpose of this book is to acquaint physicians in all fields of medical endeavour with this form of diagnosis and therapy in the hope that it will be employed more widely. (p. 181)

In fact, Bonica stated that the pain clinic should not infringe on the private physician's turf, for the patient remains in the care of the referring physician; the pain clinic 'acts mostly in a consulting capacity' (Bonica, 1953, p. 181). Nevertheless, Bonica hoped that pain clinics would be formed 'in every locality' (p. 182). In these early pain clinics, treatment possibilities were limited. The relationship between the private general practitioner and the patient was the ideal context for handling pain medically. Beyond this narrowly defined professional domain was the rest of the patient's life, largely uncharted and no immediate responsibility of any physician.

In the writings of the physicians who held the early pain clinics, there was a discrepancy between clinical and theoretical understandings of pain. Reading what physicians of the 1940s and 1950s said about pain management leads to the conclusion that the clinical understanding of pain did not square with theory. Physicians dealing with chronic pain lamented the inadequacy of the physiological understanding of pain and the failure of procedures that ought to work according to the received view of pain. Yet these physicians were committed to medical science, which meant that arguments from clinical experience were necessary but insufficient grounds for reformulating theory. Experimental results alone could reframe theory and so legitimate alternative forms of treatment.

Pain Viewed Clinically

From the clinical perspective, pain was a complex perceptual and emotional experience. Alexander (1954), an anesthesiologist who began a pain clinic in 1947, stated the fact plainly: 'Pain is a highly personal affair. It is entirely subjective in nature' (p. 580). For him, this fact was decisive for understanding the effect of any treatment. In discussing nerve blocks, Alexander commented that since pain is subjective. 'the interpretation of the results must be made largely on the basis of the patient's report as to the effect of the procedure upon *his* pain' (p. 586). Then, in this article devoted to the procedure of administering nerve blocks, Alexander wrote:

> In the complicated cases—*e.g.*, the long-standing causalgic cases, carcinomatosis, etc., even the most discerning patient may have difficulty in determining to what extent or in what way his pain has been modified. When we consider the multitude of correlative, extraneous factors which may modify his reaction to the change, it is understandable that he is unable to give an explicit estimation of relief.
>
> *In spite of all this, more than sixty per cent of all patients who are blocked for pain have some appreciable degree of relief.* This is true independently of the skill or experience of the operator in a significant series of cases. It necessitates only that the operator be sincere in his attempt to give the patient relief. (p. 586)

While Alexander underscored the success rate, the independence of success from the skill or experience of the operator bears notice. Sincerity is a crucial element in the treatment. Not that he doubted the physiological action of the blocking procedure; rather he understood that the block was as much a psychological treatment as a somatic one. Moreover, sincerity is not a technical or professional trait, because anyone can be sincere. Alexander even played down technical acumen in this regard. There was a non-professional, non-technical component to the management of pain in the biomedical model.

Swerdlow (1972), an anesthesiologist who began a pain clinic in England in 1962, similarly drew attention to the non-professional aspect of pain management: 'The cooperation and understanding of the patient's relatives is also necessary; they can assist by keeping the patient interested and active so that he does not sit around and brood too much about the remnant of pain' (p. 406). Like Alexander, Swerdlow presents a limited role for the pain clinic in the totality of the treatment of the patient. The consultant deals only with the biomedical component of pain.

What Alexander and Swerdlow expressed was an awareness of an interpersonal dimension that transcends professionalism. The phenomenological philosopher Lévinas (1961/1969) describes this transcendent dimension: it is the ethical relation with an other who is incomprehensible because he or she is not an object to be known, but an other who faces and converses with me, who calls my activity into question. What I am arguing is that the Cartesian space of pain implicitly respected the transcendence of the other, the patient, through the recognition of limits of professional intervention. What the recent history of pain indicates is that these boundaries have been erased, in the name of an expanded sense of professional responsibility.

In practice, physicians viewed pain as a complex phenomenon that medicine could only partially treat. Non-medical aspects of the pain had to be respected, but they were not handled medically. Or they could not be handled medically. Livingston described how frustrating it was to try to eliminate pain surgically. Despite all efforts, all too often pain returned: 'I have been increasingly impressed with the *dynamic* characteristics of pain, its urgency and its remarkable ability to find a new route when the customary channels have been blocked' (Livingston, 1943/1976, p. 26). Pain slipped through the surgeon's hands as it skirted the anesthesiologist's needle.

Pain in the Biopsychosocial Model

In the three decades after 1950, there has been, to use an overworked phrase, a paradigm shift in the understanding and treatment of pain. The causes for this shift are legion, and neither a 'top-down' nor a 'bottom-up' understanding suffices. From the top, a new theory of pain, the gate control theory, appeared in the 1960s, unifying the explanatory virtues of the earlier sensory and summation theories. The new theory legitimated new clinical practices. Equally, persistent pain provided a powerful critique of medical practice, leading patients to demand new forms of treatment. Providing a rich setting for both theory change and patient critique were social and economic factors that instigated change in clinical practice.

While elements of a revised physiological theory of pain were available for several decades, only in the 1960s did a new synthesis take place (Schiller, 1990). The real break with earlier understandings occurred in 1965, with Melzack and Wall's gate control theory. The gate control theory of pain incorporated elements of both the sensation theory and the pattern theory, and stated that pain occurs only as a result of complex interaction of afferent and efferent signals in the nervous system, all converging on the gate control mechanisms in the spinal cord. Melzack and Wall (1965) in their seminal paper wrote: 'The model suggests that psychological factors such as past experience, attention, and emotion influence pain response and perception by acting on the gate control system' (p. 978). Or as Melzack had stated in 1961, 'pain becomes a function of the whole individual, including his present thoughts and fears as well as his hopes for the future' (p. 49).

Melzack had been a postdoctoral fellow with Livingston between 1954 and 1957. He recalled that Livingston advocated attempts

> ... to restore normal inputs. . . . Do everything to break the vicious circle of pain; use physiotherapy; help the patients psychologically—in short, try every possible way to modulate activity in the internuncial pools to block its abnormal reverberatory activity. . . . Cutting nerves, he pointed out, only deprives the physician of avenues to modulate the input. (Melzack, 1976b, p. ix)

The gate control theory attempted to depict schematically the pathways open to such modulation.

The gate control theory integrated physiological and psychological aspects of pain. I cannot judge the adequacy of its account of neural functioning; my interests lie in the social uses made of the theory rather than its value as physiology.[2] The gate control theory altered the discourse of pain, thereby helping to establish a different set of possibilities for the professional treatment of pain. Melzack (1976a) was aware that the gate control theory had symbolic significance: 'It is clear that the theory rode in on a "Zeitgeist," and both men [i.e. Melzack and Wall] were astonished by its wide acceptance' (p. 136).

The New World of Pain: From Cartesian Spatiality to Gate Control Temporality

In contrast to the divisible space of the Cartesian image, the domain of the gate control theory is comprehensive, interconnected, dynamic. The schematic diagram which produces this domain (Figure 3) depicts the different contributions of the central nervous system to the physiological mechanisms of pain. On the left, marked 'input', are nerves from the periphery into the spinal cord. The 'gate control system', inside the spinal cord, is the site where these inputs are modulated, both by themselves and by efferents from the brain. This flowchart puts together components that existed in different regions of Cartesian space. All differences now have the same status. Pain is less a signal than a *process*. The process occurs as the various components contribute in an excitatory or inhibitory fashion to the self-regulating

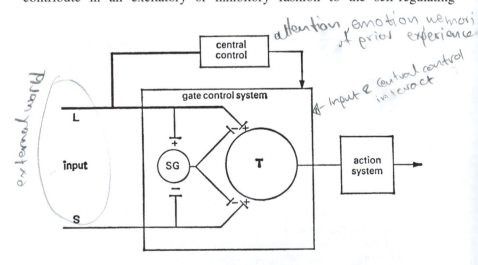

FIGURE 3. Symbol of pain in the biopsychosocial model: the gate control theory. (Reprinted with permission from 'Pain Mechanisms: A New Theory', by R. Melzack and P. Wall, 1965, *Science, 150*, p. 975. Copyright 1965 American Association for the Advancement of Science.)

circuits. In the region labelled 'input' the formerly external world makes its contribution. The 'central control' involves inputs from 'central nervous system activities subserving attention, emotion, and memories of prior experiences' (Melzack & Wall, 1965, p. 976). The 'gate control system' is the decisive region, where input and central control interact in a single site of information transfers. However, pain does not result when the 'action system' is activated, although that is essential to pain. 'Pain . . . does not consist of a single ring of the appropriate central bell, but is an ongoing process' (Melzack & Wall, 1965, p. 976).

The diagram depicts time, not space. Since it is not really a spatial image, but a 'narrative' or depiction of 'flow', differences between inside and outside, self and other, mind and body are not charted. Or to say it from the position of the diagram itself, they do not exist: they are false problems, mistakes of perspective. Outside and inside are not metaphors that have meaning in this flowchart; all experience can be put into the process. With the sleight of hand of calling the psychosocial and cultural world 'central input', the mystery of soul and body is effectively eliminated.

As Cartesian space opened up possibilities for division, this flowchart promises unlimited potentials for connection. The gate control theory did not cause the increased emphasis on non-surgical manipulations—which the flowchart does not preclude—but rather this theory is an emblem of possibilities for treatment. In this new world of pain, surgical, psychological, social and spiritual modulations all serve the same purpose, the influencing of the gate control mechanism and its central connections. While literally a schematic drawing of an area of the spinal cord, in fact it contains the whole of human experience made manageable.

The 'holistic approach' so widely acclaimed these days is manifest in the flowchart of the gate control theory. The chart represents the new terrain for professional intervention into pain. Like a satellite photo revealing new prospects for mining enterprises, the schema of gate control shows the 'necessity' for greater involvement in pain for an ever-enlarging variety of professionals—psychologists, physical therapists, social workers, biofeedback technicians and spiritual guides of all kinds. The central difference between pain before 1950 and pain after 1950 is that now all domains of existence fall within one discourse, one set of techniques of intervention, one reimbursement scheme.

To say it in other words, the gate control theory provided a new metaphor for pain. The metaphor asserts: pain is a process that can be depicted in a flowchart. The force of the metaphor is to make pain into an essentially technical process, a programmable process. In accentuating process as technique, it invites a response that is equally technique-oriented. Pain becomes a puzzle, a challenge (see Melzack 1973, 1982). This puzzle, challenge or process can be handled in a variety of ways. All are referred to this flowchart and its implicit promise of technical management.

194 SICK AND HEALING BODIES

Pain Redefined

At the same time that the gate control theory was being formulated, a new definition of pain was proposed, which was accepted by the International Association for the Study of Pain in 1979. Merskey and Spear cited 'conflict between physiology and psychology' over pain, especially regarding psychogenic pain. Drawing on the observation that there is no one-to-one correspondence between pain and tissue damage, they proposed rejecting the division of pain into a sensory aspect and a reaction aspect—the ad hoc hypothesis of the 1940s designed to save the sensation theory of pain. This distinction confused a physiological event (nerve impulse) with a psychological one (pain), leading to two problematic situations: (1) denying that pain exists when a person says it does, simply because there is no physiological evidence for it (phantom limb pain was the primary example); (2) attributing pain to a wounded person who denies feeling it. Thus 'to call pain which is primarily related to physical disturbances "organic" and other pain "psychogenic" can thus be inconvenient and even illogical' (Merskey & Spear, 1967, pp. 61–62). They define pain as 'an unpleasant experience which we primarily associate with tissue damage or describe in terms of tissue damage or both' (p. 65). This definition calls pain not a sensation, not a reaction to a sensation, but a perception or an experience, an emotionally charged experience. Merskey's definition converged with the gate control theory. The coincidence of these two appearances at the same time suggests that pain already had entered into a new existential order that made such reunderstandings evident.

The definition, revised by the International Association for the Study of Pain (Merskey was a member of the subcommittee that drew up the definitions), reads as follows:

> An unpleasant sensory and emotional experience associated with actual or potential tissue damage, or described in terms of such damage.
> — Note: Pain is always subjective. Each individual learns the application of the word through experiences related to injury in early life. . . . Many people report pain in the absence of tissue damage or any likely pathophysiological cause; usually this happens for psychological reasons. There is usually no way to distinguish their experience from that due to tissue damage if we take the subjective report. If they regard their experience as pain and if they report it in the same ways as pain caused by tissue damage, it should be accepted as pain. This definition avoids tying pain to the stimulus. (International Association for the Study of Pain, 1979, p. S217)

The patient's report of pain is now fundamental to the definition of pain. Pain, to be pain, must be described. Here we see the formulation of the new medical object, the patient-as-person. No longer can the physician, within the 'clinical gaze' (Foucault, 1973), point to the spot in the body where the pain sensation originated. Pain occurs now within an existence understood as a process, as much as in the body defined as visible object.

The new definition of pain amplifies one aspect implicit in the gate control metaphor: Central to the process is the patient's input. Indeed, access to the process charted in the metaphor of the gate control is only through the patient's description of pain. The life of the patient needs to be mapped onto the flowchart in order to be understood. The social site for this mapping is a new entity, the pain clinic.

The New Pain Clinic

Bonica began a pain clinic at Tacoma General Hospital in 1946, which brought together a multidisciplinary team for the treatment of chronic pain; Bonica's clinic has been acclaimed the world's first (Procacci, 1974, p. 295), despite the existence of earlier pain clinics. What made Bonica's clinic different was the multidisciplinary approach. For Bonica (1974a), 'the basic concept of the multidisciplinary approach is essential to the great success in this field' (p. 282). While only a few pain clinics existed in the early 1960s, by 1987, there were 1,500 in the United States alone (US Department of Health and Human Services, 1987).

What accounts for the dramatic growth of these centers? 'An increasing recognition that chronic pain is a distinct burden for the health care and disability systems' (Csordas & Clark, 1992, p. 383) led to increased funding, beginning in the mid-1970s, by the Social Security Administration and private insurance companies. The social and economic pressures to expand treatment for chronic pain are complex, and they include demands by patients not only for more treatment, but also for certain types of treatment. Nixon's 'opening of China' led to an interest in acupuncture, which became part of what Kotarba (1983) calls the 'chronic pain subculture' (p. 74). There was a similar rise in interest in methods such as biofeedback and hypnosis. While individual methods have had uneven fates over the past two decades, the trend toward multidisciplinary treatment of pain has continued. Finally, in the 1970s there was a surge in the medical research on pain. Bonica (1990) argues that medical research was hampered by an inadequate understanding of pain:

> The predominant concern with anatomical and physiological research on pain, consequent to the widespread assumption that pain was a purely sensory experience, caused emotional and psychologic factors to be relegated to secondary roles or to be considered byproducts of the sensation. . . . Consequently, the crucial roles of psychologic and environmental factors in causing chronic pain behavior in a significant number of patients were not studied and defined until recently. (p. 12)

Bonica implies that the new theoretical understanding of pain played a critical role in legitimizing pain research and treatment.

Revolution in the Psychotherapy of Pain

In the pain clinics, armed with a new theoretical explanation for pain, psychology redefined its place in the medical treatment of pain. The gate control theory helped to alter understanding and treatment of pain. As Schwartz and Parris note, until the gate control mechanisms were proposed, there had been no 'unifying theory' for the pain clinics. 'In particular, the theory's emphasis on both ascending and descending modulating systems laid down a framework into which multiple disciplines, such as medicine, psychology, and physical therapy, could fit their contributions' (Schwartz & Parris, 1991, p. 5).

For an understanding of pain to alter the view of the medical and psychological communities, the evidence and arguments had to be physiological.[3] Melzack and Wall provided a new theoretical basis of pain, and one that was congruent with the developing biopsychosocial model. Melzack and Casey (1968) argued early on that the gate control theory would change medical practice:

> Pain can be treated not only by trying to cut down the sensory inputs by anesthetic block, surgical interventions and the like, but also by influencing the motivational-affective and cognitive factors as well. Relaxants, tranquilizers, sedatives, suggestion, placebos, and hypnosis are known to influence pain, but the historical emphasis on sensory mechanisms has made these forms of therapy suspect, even fraudulent, almost a sideshow in the mainstream of pain treatment. Yet ... these methods deserve more attention that they have received. (p. 435)

The theory did not *create* new forms of treatment; it made them *legitimate*. Moreover, it made prevailing forms of treatment, the heavy emphasis on surgery and medication, suspect.

Initially the role of psychologists at pain clinics had been assessment and traditional psychotherapy, but by the late 1960s, the situation had changed. That was when the gate control approach to pain met another significant development in postwar psychology: behavior therapy. Since pain is no longer defined as only a sensation, pain is as pain does. 'The gate control theory of pain suggests that psychology has much to offer in both understanding and treating pain' (Turk, Meichenbaum, & Genest, 1983, p. 82). As the theory was multidimensional, so was the treatment. For Wilbert Fordyce, a psychologist at the University of Washington and innovator of the behavioral treatment of pain, the significance of the gate control theory was that it undermined the mind–body dualism that had dominated psychological thinking about pain. No longer was it necessary to distinguish between organic and psychogenic pain. Now, he states, 'pain was conceptualized as behavior. As such, pain could be seen as subject to the same laws or influences as any other form of behavior' (Fordyce, 1985, p. xi). The work of Fordyce represents the new psychological approach to pain in the pain clinics. Fordyce began working in Bonica's clinic in 1969, 'applying principles of operant conditioning to the management of patients with chronic pain' (Bonica & Fordyce, 1974, p. 299). If the gate control theory offered an explanation of pain that redefined it as a process rather than a sensation, the work of Fordyce and others provided a 'behavioral technology' (Fordyce, 1976, p. 4) for altering that process. However, according to Gamsa (1994, p. 9), behavior therapy of pain is basically warmed over sensation theory. In sensation theory, there was 'real' or sensed pain, with overlays of psychological factors. Behavioral therapy for pain seeks to eliminate the latter, in a belief that some 'pain behavior' is in response not to real pain, but to social reinforcement. This may be a clear example of the social use of the theory: Fordyce did not need the gate control theory to legitimate behavior therapy for pain, but the gate control theory, with its aura of 'overcoming Cartesianism', provided a scientific justification for behaviorist manipulation.

The differences between Fordyce's and other behavioral approaches to pain pale before their radical departure from pre-gate control therapies of pain. His goals include the reduction in 'pain behaviors' and the increase in 'well behaviors' (Bonica & Fordyce, 1974, p. 301). In the related cognitive– behavioral approach, 'self-management techniques, in which the patient is taught to directly alter behavior' (Keefe, 1982, p. 903), are emphasized as a way of aiding the patient reframe the pain experience. These techniques occupy a place within the larger multidisciplinary approach of pain clinics. Gamsa (1994, p. 9) observes that 'cognitive approaches to the treatment of pain were inspired in large part' by the gate control theory, but that unlike the 'pure' behavioral treatment of Fordyce, they take into consideration and try to modify the experienced meaning of pain. The behavioral and cognitive–behavioral treatments of pain actualize the vision symbolized by the gate control flowchart. Whereas in Cartesian space, pain was over there in the body or mind of the figure by the fire, in the flowchart pain has no particular location. Ironically, because pain is defined as essentially subjective, it is more rigorously objectified. The flowchart expands the field of objectification by elimination of the dichotomies inside/outside, mind/body. In principle, nothing is invisible in the flowchart. The behavior therapist observes pain behaviors (grimacing, restriction of movement, verbalized complaints). By manipulating the responses of others to expressions of pain, the therapy attempts to silence those expressions and replace them with 'well behaviors', that is, functional behaviors. Alternatively, in its cognitive mode, behavior therapy attempts to alter the meaning of pain so it does not interfere with a productive life. Pain is, by implication, either meaningless or correctly meaningful only when it is not socially disruptive. The therapist is part of the flowchart, trying to make these modifications in the central input. Pain is a kind of raw material that patient and treatment team together fashion into an acceptable product.

The New Morality of Biopsychosocial Treatment

In praising 'breakthroughs' and 'advances' in pain management in recent years, Taylor (1995) correctly identifies a major change in the 'technology of pain control': 'the responsibility for pain control has shifted from the practitioner to co-management between patient and practitioner. This is an important psychological shift in that it gives patients a sense of participation in and control over their situation' (p. 594). Patients must be responsible if the new technologies are to work, since behavior therapy, biofeedback, relaxation, guided imagery and other psychosocial techniques require the consent and active participation of patients. The call for patients to become 'responsible' is widespread in pain management and in biopsychosocial medicine generally (Matarazzo, 1980). More clearly than in the necessity for active patient participation in biofeedback, cognitive–behavioral therapy, and the like, the insistence on personal responsibility shows the implicit morality of the new medicine. Access to the flowchart of the patient's existence only occurs with the patient's assumption of responsibility. So what does the call for responsibility imply?

Over and above following medical directives (which compliant patients had been expected to do in the biomedical model), the call to personal responsibility is above all else a call to openness. One can be angry or depressed, so long as one is open about it. Openness means that inputs are still occurring in the flowchart of existence. And if the patient is inputting, then the patient is participating in the process of management. Significantly, most often placed in opposition to responsibility is not irresponsibility, but learned helplessness or passivity. Helplessness or passivity has no place in the gate control flowchart. This form of biopsychosocial irresponsibility amounts to the admission of tragic limits, which the chart cannot admit.

The openness of the flowchart of existence excludes, beyond a tragic sense of limits, genuine conflict and the incomprehensible character of another person, an Other. Conflict is excluded to the extent that the flowchart provides a structured way to handle all 'inputs'. It imposes what Arney and Bergen (1984) call 'the tyranny of harmony' (p. 172, citing Sisk, 1977). Pain as a measure of an inhumane society has no place in this totalizing world. But dissent is important and necessary because the Other is beyond the grasp of any epistemology. Relations with others transcend comprehension of them (Lévinas, 1961/1969). Pain management in particular, and biopsychosocial medicine in general, by imposing a morality of responsibility, are deeply exploitative.

The Expropriation of Healing Techniques

The further consequence of the new model for pain is the progressive expropriation (a term I borrow from Illich, 1976) of healing techniques. By healing techniques I mean those practices, mostly culture-bound, with which people have responded to pain over the centuries. They are practiced by people who are not modern professionals (Zola, 1978), and who learn the technique through some kind of apprenticeship. The flowchart of pain enables the appropriation of these techniques by discovering that they really work and providing an explanation for them. Because the explanation is scientific, it paves the way for them to be owned by a professional group, which can then seek to exclude lay practitioners from the practice. To chart this process would carry us too far afield, so I restrict my comments simply to examples of theoretical expropriation. The nature of this expropriation is that in place of the indigenous discourse which accounted for the efficacy of the practice is substituted a scientific explanation that then can be appropriated by a scientifically trained professional group.

Bonica visited China in the early 1970s as Chairman of the Ad Hoc Committee on Acupuncture of the National Institutes of Health and the American Society of Anesthesiologists (Bonica, 1974b). He reported witnessing the extensive use of acupuncture in Chinese medical settings. While he did not doubt the efficacy of acupuncture in a variety of treatments, he cautioned that 'acupuncture should be considered an experimental method to be used in laboratory studies, controlled clinical trials, and clinical settings' (p. 1551). Prudent advice, given the context of scientific medicine. Moreover, he concluded: 'by permitting the continued use of acupuncture by qualified practitioners working under uniform and supervised conditions, it should constitute a pragmatic solution to the real problem of public clamor for acupuncture therapy' (p. 1551). Acupuncture needs to be incorporated into the scientific epistemology to be accredited.

Melzack (1977) studied the analgesic effects of acupuncture treatment and concluded it does control pain. His reframing of acupuncture shows how Bonica's conclusion could be realized: 'Even the effects of acupuncture on some kinds of chronic pain are put into focus within the framework of the gate theory. They are no longer seen as mysterious, but simply as an example of the modulation of pain by sensory input' (p. 90). The use of the term 'mysterious' denigrates non-scientific knowledge and 'simply' appropriates this traditional practice for scientific medicine. Lost in 'simply' would be the image of the body as a microcosm, central to Chinese medicine. Now acupuncture becomes a way of modifying the input in the pain process.

As a second example, I cite Melzack's (1989) essay on 'Folk Medicine and the Sensory Modulation of Pain'. Reviewing such practices as cupping, moxibustion and other forms of counter-irritation, he observes that such stimulation controls pain because it activates 'brain stem mechanisms that exert a descending inhibitory control over transmission through the dorsal horns as well as at higher levels in the somatic projection area' (p. 902). He is referring, of course, to the flowchart. Can the day be far off when bloodletting and cupping return as forms of medical practice, now that they have been given the imprimatur of scientific legitimacy?

Gate Control as an Emblem of Discipline

In the book that popularized the gate control theory, Melzack (1973) stated: 'Perhaps, then, we should not aim at totally abolishing pain but, rather, at reducing it to bearable levels' (p. 200). Pain clinics take this advice to heart. Many of the people who partake in their programs have reached 'the end of the line' (Csordas & Clark, 1992, p. 391). Pain patients are all told that they must learn to live with their pain, that no one can 'fix' it.[4] They are told that they must modify their thoughts and actions in order to make pain manageable. The idea is to avoid what appeared to be excesses of the pre-gate control era:

> Many of these patients are exposed to a high risk of iatrogenic complications from improper therapy, including narcotic addiction, or are subjected to multiple, often useless, and at times mutilating operations; a significant number give up medical care and consult quacks. (Bonica, 1974a, p. 275)

In place of emphasizing these external forms of treatment, the new approach stresses the responsibility to be open. Surgery and medication are not precluded, of course, given the multidimensional meaning of pain. But for many patients with chronic pain, the route taken is one of increased discipline with the mandate that they assume personal responsibility for their pain and its treatment. They learn to discipline their activity, since pain is a behavior, by avoiding pain-enhancing behaviors and learning 'well behaviors' (Turk et al., 1983, p. 317). They learn to think different thoughts, to improve coping skills, to visualize, and to visualize in a productive way. They learn to be open, to 'process' what is going on with them. Above all, they learn not to expect the practitioners to do all the work, that they as patients are partners in healing. They should not expect, however, that the professionals should relinquish their salaries or expertise.

The significance of these changes is that now a person in intractable pain becomes more existentially engaged in medical treatment. Since pain is a multifaceted, essentially subjective experience, the patient-as-person is required to participate 'as a person' in the health care system that seeks to comprehend and help him or her. The new conception of pain serves to construct the pain patient and pain treatment. The gate control theory helped to put an array of professionals at the gates to subjectivity, to colonize and reform it.

What are no longer recognized in the biopsychosocial chart of existence are limits. There are no limits to intervention into the patient's life. Limits are eliminated theoretically and symbolically in the chart, and in practice, by the mandate for the patient to be a responsible and open team-member. This situation is not unique to the problem of pain; it is endemic in psychology and medicine generally (Stam, 1988). The absence of limits has two major consequences. First, it eliminates the possibility of shame. Shame is above all a sensibility of exposure. According to Erikson (1963), 'shame supposes that one is completely exposed and conscious of being looked at. . . . One is visible and not ready to be visible' (p. 252). The gate control understanding of pain is shameless. All is potentially visible, if not through the X-ray, then through the patient's openness and cooperation. Second, pain clinics, armed with psychosocial technologies of pain, silence pain as social protest. If pain is truly epidemic today, then something is terribly wrong, not only with patients, or 'inadequate' pain technologies, but with the social matrix that produces suffering. To tempt people in pain to be co-managers in such a social world only deepens our true helplessness.

Notes

1. For purposes of clarity, let me make some provisional definitions. When someone says that he or she does not feel well, that person is ill or sick. If that person submits to medical ministrations, he or she becomes a 'patient', occupying a position toward which medical knowledge and treatment can be directed. In the biomedical and the biopsychosocial paradigms (to use Engel's, 1977, terms), these positions differ. In the former, the patient occupied a position of a detached and passive observer; one abdicated one's body and let it become an anatomical object. The new position is that of an engaged co-manager of a complex of biological, psychological, social, spiritual systems.

2. I restrict discussion to the gate control theory, although there are other theories of pain today in competition with it (Crue, Kenton, Carregal, & Pinsky, 1980). Also I am not discussing the role of endorphins in pain. These other theories of pain share with the gate control theory a biopsychosocial approach, and that is the main point.

3. See McCloskey (1984) for a presentation on the rhetoric of inquiry in the social sciences. Although he primarily discusses economics, the arguments about 'modernism' apply equally to psychology and medicine. Essential to modernism is a belief in methodology: 'It is the business of methodology to demarcate scientific reasoning from non-scientific, positive from normative' (p. 484). As applied to the study of pain, one could state the issue baldly: Given the numerous perspectives on pain as a passion, as an experience, etc., there was no need for the gate control theory for the alteration of practice. What the gate control theory did was provide an account compatible with the biopsychosocial model and modernism. It helped preserve expert dominance of the field even as that field incorporated hitherto marginal practices.

4. In the new biopsychosocial medicine which manages lives, rather than cures diseases, 'fix' has become a four letter word. As Schwartz and Parris (1991) write: 'One major liability of the [sensation theory] approach is still present in modern times; this is the notion that pain can be "fixed" by a surgical procedure, drug, or other procedure' (p. 4).

References

Alexander, F.A.D. (1954). The control of pain. In D.E. Hale (Ed.), *Anesthesiology* (pp. 579–611). Philadelphia, PA: F.A. Davis.

Armstrong, D. (1983). *Political anatomy of the body: Medical knowledge in Britain in the twentieth century* Cambridge: Cambridge University Press.

Arney W.R., & Bergen, B.J. (1984). *Medicine and the management of living.* Chicago, IL: University of Chicago Press.

Bonica, J.J. (1952). Management of intractable pain with analgesic blocks. *Journal of the American Medical Association, 150,* 1581–1586.

Bonica, J.J. (1953). *The management of pain.* Philadelphia, PA: Lea & Febiger.

Bonica, J.J. (1974a). General clinical considerations (including organization and function of a pain clinic). In J.J. Bonica, P. Procacci, & C.A. Pagni (Eds.), *Recent advances on pain* (pp. 274–298). Springfield, IL: Charles C. Thomas.

Bonica, J.J. (1974b). Therapeutic acupuncture in the People's Republic of China. *Journal of the American Medical Association, 228,* 1544–1551.

Bonica, J.J. (1990). History of pain concepts and therapies. In J. Bonica (Ed.), *The management of pain* (2nd ed.; Vol. 1, pp. 2–17). Philadelphia, PA: Lea & Febiger.

Bonica, J.J., & Fordyce, W.E. (1974). Operant conditioning for chronic pain. In J.J. Bonica, P. Procacci, & C.A. Pagni (Eds.), *Recent advances on pain* (pp. 299–312). Springfield, IL: Charles C. Thomas.

Crue, B.L, Kenton, B., Carregal, E.J.A., & Pinsky, J.J. (1980). The continuing crisis in pain research. In W.L. Smith, H. Meskey, & S.C. Gross (Eds.), *Pain: Meaning and management* (pp. 1–20). New York: SP Medical & Scientific Books.

Csordas, T.J., & Clark, J.A. (1992). Ends of the line: Diversity among chronic pain centers. *Social Science and Medicine, 34,* 383–393.

Dallenbach, K. (1939). Pain: History and present status. *American Journal of Psychology, 52,* 331–347.

Dittrick, H. (1950). The pain clinic. *Current Research in Anesthesiology and Analgesics, 29,* 60.

Engel, G. (1959). Psychogenic pain and the pain-prone patient. *American Journal of Medicine, 26,* 899–918.

Engel, G. (1977). The need for a new medical model: A challenge for biomedicine. *Science, 196,* 129–136.

Erikson, E.H. (1963). *Childhood and society* (2nd ed.). New York: Norton.

Fordyce, W. (1976). *Behavioral methods for chronic pain and illness.* St Louis, MO: C.V. Mosby.

Fordyce, W.E. (1985). Foreword. In G.M. Aronoff (Ed.), *Evaluation and treatment of chronic pain* (2nd ed., pp. xi–xii). Baltimore, MD: Williams & Wilkins.

Foucault, M. (1973). *The birth of the clinic: An archeology of medical perception* (A.M. Sheridan Smith, Trans.). New York: Vintage.

Foucault, M. (1979). *Discipline and punish: The birth of the prison* (A. Sheridan, Trans.). New York: Vintage.

Foucault, M. (1980). *The history of sexuality: Vol. l. An introduction* (R. Hurley, Trans.). New York: Vintage.

Gamsa, A. (1994). The role of psychological factors in chronic pain: I. A half century of study. *Pain, 57,* 5–15.

Gatchel, R., Baum, A., & Krantz, D. (1989). *An introduction to health psychology* (2nd ed.). New York: McGraw-Hill.

Gordon, R. (1949). Application of nerve block in diagnosis and treatment. *Canadian Medical Association Journal, 60*, 251.

Illich, I. (1976). *Medical nemesis: The expropriation of health.* New York: Pantheon.

International Association for the Study of Pain, Subcommittee on Taxonomy. (1979). Pain terms: A list with definitions and notes for usage. *Pain, 6*, 249–252.

Keefe, F.J. (1982). Behavioral assessment and treatment of chronic pain: Current status and future directions. *Journal of Consulting and Clinical Psychology, 50*, 896–911.

Kotarba, J. (1983). *Chronic pain: Its social dimensions.* Beverly Hills, CA: Sage.

Leriche, R. (1939). *The surgery of pain.* London: Bailliere, Tindall & Cox.

Lévinas, E. (1969). *Totality and infinity: An essay on exteriority* (A. Lingis, Trans.). Pittsburgh, PA: Duquesne University Press. (Original work published 1961.)

Livingston, W.K. (1976). *Pain mechanisms: A physiological interpretation of causalgia and its related states.* New York: Plenum. (Original work published 1943.)

Matarazzo, J.D. (1980). Behavioral health and behavioral medicine: Frontiers for a new health psychology. *American Psychologist, 35*, 807–817.

McCloskey, D.N. (1984). The rhetoric of economics. *Journal of Economic Literature, 21*, 481–517.

McKnight, J. (1978). Professionalized service and disabling help. In *Disabling professions* (pp. 69–92). Boston, MA: Marion Boyars.

Melzack, R. (1961). The perception of pain. *Scientific American, 204*, 41–49.

Melzack, R. (1973). *The puzzle of pain.* New York: Basic Books.

Melzack, R. (1976a). Pain: Past, present, and future. In M. Weisenberg & B. Tursky (Eds.), *Pain: New perspectives in therapy and research* (pp. 135–145). New York: Plenum.

Melzack, R. (1976b). Foreword. In W.K. Livingston (Ed.), *Pain mechanisms. A physiological interpretation of causalgia and its related states* (pp. v–xi). New York: Plenum.

Melzack, R. (1977). The gate theory revisited. In P. LeRoy (Ed.), *Current concepts in the management of chronic pain* (pp. 79–92). New York: Symposia Specialists Medical Books.

Melzack, R. (1982). *The challenge of pain.* New York: Basic Books.

Melzack, R. (1989). Folk medicine and the sensory modulation of pain. In P. Wall & R. Melzack (Eds.), *Textbook of pain* (2nd ed., pp. 897–905). Edinburgh: Churchill Livingstone.

Melzack, R. (1992). Humans versus pain: The dilemma of morphine. In F. Sicuteri (Ed.), *Pain versus man: Advances in pain research and therapy* (Vol. 20, pp. 149–159). New York: Raven Press.

Melzack, R., & Casey, K.L. (1968). Sensory, motivational, and central control determinants of pain: A new conceptual model. In D. Kenshalo (Ed.), *The skin senses* (pp. 423–443). Springfield, IL: Charles C. Thomas.

Melzack, R., & Wall, P. (1965). Pain mechanisms: A new theory. *Science, 150*, 971–979.

Merskey, H., & Spear, F.G. (1967). The concept of pain. *Journal of Psychosomatic Research, 11*, 59–67.

Nachemson, A. (1994). Chronic pain—the end of the welfare state? *Quality of Life Research, 3*(1), S11–S17.

Osterweis, M., Kleinman, A., & Mechanic, D. (1987). *Pain and disability*. Washington, DC: National Academy Press.

Procacci, P. (1974). Discussion of Bonica, J.J. In J.J. Bonica, P. Procacci, & C.A. Pagni (Eds.), *Recent advances on pain* (pp. 294–298). Springfield, IL: Charles C. Thomas.

Rubin, J. (1951). Experience with a pain clinic. *Anesthesiology, 12*, 601–603.

Schiller, F. (1990). The history of algology, algotherapy, and the role of inhibition. *Pubblicazioni della Stazione Zoologica di Napoli*, Section II: *History and Philosophy of the Life Sciences, 12*, 27–50.

Schwartz, D.P., & Parris, W.C.V. (1991). Historical perspectives on pain management. In W.C.V. Parris (Ed.), *Contemporary issues in chronic pain management* (pp. 1–8). Boston, MA: Kluwer Academic.

Sisk, J.P. (1977). The tyranny of harmony. *The American Scholar, 46*, 193–205.

Stam, H.J. (1988). The practice of health psychology and behavioral medicine: Whither theory? In W.J. Baker, L.P. Mos, H.V. Rappard, & H.J. Stam (Eds.), *Recent trends in theoretical psychology* (pp. 313–325). New York: Springer.

Starr, P. (1982). *The social transformation of American medicine*. New York: Basic Books.

Swerdlow, M. (1972). The pain clinic. *British Journal of Clinical Practice, 26*, 403–407.

Taylor, S. (1995). *Health psychology* (3rd ed.). New York: McGraw-Hill.

Turk, D.C., Meichenbaum, D., & Genest, M. (1983). *Pain and behavioral medicine: A cognitive–behavioral perspective*. New York: Guilford.

US Department of Health and Human Services. (1987). *Report of the commission for the evaluation of pain*. Washington, DC: US Government Printing Office.

Zola, I. (1978). Healthism and disabling medicalization. In *Disabling professions* (pp. 41–68). Boston, MA: Marion Boyars.

11

From Dysappearance to Hyperappearance:

Sliding Boundaries of Illness and Bodies

Arthur W. Frank

A review of:

José Luis Bermúdez, Anthony Marcel and Naomi Eilan (Eds.), *The Body and the Self*. Cambridge, MA: MIT Press, 1995. 376 pp. ISBN 0–262–02386–5.

Kathy Davis, *Reshaping the Female Body: The Dilemma of Cosmetic Surgery*. New York & London: Routledge, 1995. 211 pp. ISBN 0–415–90632–6.

Arthur Kroker and Michael A. Weinstein, *Data Trash: The Theory of the Virtual Class*. Montreal: New World Perspectives [in USA, St Martin's Press], 1994. 165 pp. ISBN 0–920393–23–3.

Drew Leder (Ed.), *The Body in Medical Thought and Practice*. Dordrecht: Kluwer Academic, 1992. 258 pp. ISBN 0–7923–1657–6.

Deborah Lupton, *The Imperative of Health: Public Health and the Regulated Body*. London: Sage, 1995. 181 pp. ISBN 0–8039–7936–3.

Emily Martin, *Flexible Bodies: Tracking Immunity in American Culture—From the Days of Polio to the Age of AIDS*. Boston, MA: Beacon, 1994. xxiii + 320 pp. ISBN 0–8070–4627–2.

S. Kay Toombs, *The Meaning of Illness: A Phenomenological Account of the Different Perspectives of Physician and Patient*. Dordrecht: Kluwer Academic, 1993. xvi + 161 pp. ISBN 0–7923–2443–9.

S. Kay Toombs, David Barnard and Ronald A. Carson, *Chronic Illness: From Experience to Policy*. Bloomington: Indiana University Press, 1995. xiv + 221 pp. ISBN 0–253–36011–0.

Mary G. Winkler and Letha B. Cole (Eds.), *The Good Body: Asceticism in Contemporary Culture*. New Haven, CT: Yale University Press, 1994. 247 pp. ISBN 0–300–05628–1.

IRIS MARION YOUNG, *Throwing Like a Girl and Other Essays in Feminist Philosophy and Social Theory*. Bloomington: Indiana University Press, 1990. 213 pp. ISBN 0–253–36857–X.

ABSTRACT. Ten recent empirical studies of the body are reviewed with particular reference to illness. Discussion is organized around the relations of body to world, body to self, social mediations of embodiment and physical reshapings of the body. Particular attention is given to recent work of Kathy Davis on elective cosmetic surgery, Emily Martin on the immune system, Kay Toombs on the phenomenology of chronic illness, and Iris Marion Young on women's embodiment.

Eight years ago, when I was reading in preparation for my first omnibus review of social-scientific studies of the body, I could sustain a pretense of addressing the scope of the literature. 'Bodies are in', I wrote, 'in academia as well as in popular culture' (Frank, 1990, p. 131). I could hardly have predicted, however, the ubiquity of bodies today, both as the subject of scholarly writing and as a focus of popular culture. Because bodies are everywhere, no pretense can be made of surveying the recent literature. Thus I sought to reduce my scope to the more modest topic of ill bodies.[1]

The 'ill body' has an apparent self-evidence as a point of departure, but depart is what the student of illness, and of bodies, quickly does. Several years ago Arthur and Marilouise Kroker (1987, pp. 29–30) wrote that health is *outside* the body.[2] The recent literature is catching up with this prescient observation; this literature suggests a body that seems to move progressively *outside itself*. One task of this review is to make that strange-sounding phrase—the body outside itself—sensible. The body moving outside itself is unstable both as an analytic category and as a social phenomenon. It is no easy thing to say what the body is, and the books discussed here all struggle with that instability.

A useful introduction may be to consider a book that stands out as different from the others, *The Body and the Self* (Bermúdez, Marcel, & Eilan, 1995), and seek to specify this difference. To orient their readers to the concerns of this volume, Eilan, Marcel and Bermúdez (1995) suggest three subareas of body study: (a) the concept of self-consciousness, which has been largely the preserve of philosophers; (b) how people 'represent and use our bodies' (p. 2), which, although they do not say so, has been the focus of anthropology, history, sociology and more recently of gender studies and cultural studies; and (c) studies of 'sensory physiology, neurology, and motor control' (p. 2). The papers blend philosophical and psychological arguments to consider questions of body image and self-consciousness.

The common theme of the collected papers is intentionality, but the traditional phenomenological usage of this term is given greater specificity by demonstrating self-consciousness and physiology to be interdependent at the level of proprioception. The considerable contribution of the papers is to deconstruct the boundary between self-consciousness and physiology. The papers deserve to be called *deconstructive* in this basic sense: two categories that once seemed separable are shown to be not oppositional but mutually dependent, and in that mutual dependence, neither can be privileged over the other.

Thus in Bermúdez et al. intentionality is no longer an exclusive capacity of consciousness, but is now the interaction of psyche and soma. Yet in another sense the papers impose a new restriction on intentionality. Because they tend to equate self-consciousness with body image, the papers direct the body's intentionality onto itself. Intentionality is not turned outward onto the world; the bodies in these papers are generally decontextualized, having no distinct social milieu. The social implications of the phenomenology of Husserl and Merleau-Ponty are absent in this collection.

In contrast to Bermúdez et al., the other books being reviewed adopt, with variation in practice but consensus in principle, the perspective that Drew Leder calls the 'lived body'. Leder draws on the German distinction between *Leib*, living bodies, and *Körper*, 'used to designate inanimate or dead bodies'. He places phenomenological investigations on the side of *Leib* and mainstream medical thought on the side of *Körper* (Leder, 1992, p. 25). The papers in Bermúdez et al. are certainly about animate bodies, and they make reference to the same phenomenological philosophers that Leder draws on: Husserl and Merleau-Ponty. Why, then, are these papers not about the 'lived body'? The difference, I propose, has to do with narrative.

While many of the writers in Bermúdez et al. could claim, with justification, that they *are* writing about the lived body as 'an "intending" entity' (Leder, 1992, p. 25), the best way of expressing what is not 'living' about their bodies may be to say that these bodies *have no story*. When the authors do place the body within a 'case history' (e.g. Cole & Paillard, 1995), this story is virtually devoid of meaning for those living it: the body remains an object-body for investigation by an other who claims to speak for that body on the basis of his or her expertise. In contrast to this approach, the living subject-body of the other books is very much a story-telling body. Different authors take varying perspectives on the body's ability to know itself through its stories of itself, but they all take these stories seriously. For the other authors, to make sense of the body is to struggle with the narratives in which embodied self-consciousness expresses itself. To claim to study the lived body, the investigator must interpret the body's stories of itself, as these stories struggle to interpret the body to itself.

The narrative construction of the lived body is exemplified by Kay Toombs, whose work appears in three of the books under review. Toombs is among those authors whose writing merges their own experiences of embodiment with their studies of bodies, refusing to differentiate 'lived experience and scientific conceptualization' (1993, p. 26). What seems to separate Toombs's lived experience from the phenomenology found in

Bermúdez et al. is her *narrative* intentionality. Her intentionality begins with issues of proprioception—how the physical situation of her body in a wheelchair affects her view, and thus her consciousness, of the world and others in it—but moves to a territory never considered by Bermúdez et al.— intentionality as self-consciously living out a story that is told in relation to other stories. Whether this is called narrative intentionality or dialogical intentionality, what is involved is a layer of self-reflection—a hermeneutics—that is lacking in the phenomenology of Bermúdez et al. In Toombs's *The Meaning of Illness*, as in the other works under review, an embodied author tells about bodies creating themselves as they tell their stories.

This shift to the narrative intentionality of the lived body both reflects and perpetuates the ongoing dissolution of the disciplinary boundaries that have organized traditional academic study. Academic disciplines can no longer be clear-cut because the categories in which people once organized their lives no longer work as neat compartments for experience. Emily Martin (1994) marks this dissolution:

> My fieldwork has made clear to me that the categories of social analysis that we once found so useful to describe our lives—gender, race, class, work, home, family, community, state and nation, science and religion—are no longer sufficient to describe, let alone analyze, the phenomena of the contemporary metropolis. (p. xvi)

The categories of what Martin calls 'social analysis' are no longer useful because, as she finds, they no longer describe the realities of people's lives: 'the very borders are often in flux' (p. xvi).

What sets this flux in motion is the instability of the body. Martin's analysis of this instability begins with how the immune system, as physiology and as trope, dominates lay and scientific understandings of bodies. Lay and scientific conceptions of the body as an immune system create a sense of flux as to what is body and non-body, what is inside and out, and what is believed to affect or not to affect the body.

Scholars like Toombs and Martin have abandoned the cool certainty of the papers in Bermúdez et al. as to what 'the body' *is*. The body clearly is not a stable *point* of departure for the organization of either academic study or one's own life. What is found repeatedly throughout the recent literature is the flux, permeability and deconstruction of body boundaries.

What, then, *is* the body? One significant response is provided by Arthur and Joan Kleinman (1994), asserting the need for their field, medical anthropology, 'to examine how culture infolds into the body and, reciprocally, how bodily processes outfold into social space' (p. 710–711; parentheses omitted). In a later paper, Arthur Kleinman (1995) specifies this trope of infolding and outfolding: 'the social world enters into cardiovascular, endocrinological, and neurobiological processes so as to pattern responses. In turn, bodily and self processes project into social space, bringing affect and embodied meaning to bear upon social life' (p. 180). I return to the Kleinmans at the end of this paper; for now, let me modify their terms.

I understand the body as *a recursive process of inscription and projection.* Social and cultural processes inscribe the body with meanings, and the body, which is always more than these meanings, projects its realities onto social spaces. The process is recursive: the body organizes the culture and society that inscribe this same body with meaning. Both movements of this recursive process take place in narratives. Narratives are both inscribed on bodies—as, for example, in cultural standards of beauty—and projected from the body onto society: for example, the body's pain constructs the stories a person tells, and Glass (1995) argues that a society's pain constructs its larger political narratives.[3] These various narratives both complement and contest each other.

With respect to the scholarly literature, the Kleinmans (1994) contend that 'the study of the processes that mediate and transform the bodily forms of social experience has yet to commence' (p. 711). Since they completed their paper, the study of how bodily forms are mediated and transformed has certainly begun in Kay Toombs's studies of embodiment in chronic illness, in Emily Martin's report on how understandings of the immune system are changing our sense not only of the ill body but also of the working body, and in Kathy Davis's interviews with women who quite consciously choose the risks of body-altering surgery. In all three studies, culture inscribes the body, the body projects itself into social space, and the boundary of these reciprocal movements is in flux.

Flux, however, does not organize a review, so as topic headings I suggest five very general propositions. Each of these may be something of a truism in body studies, yet the contribution of the literature under review is to advance our understanding of how each proposition is true, for whom, with what consequences. The propositions are as follows:

1. The experience of *illness* calls attention to the body, making body awareness a significant issue for consciousness.
2. We know the *world* through our bodies.
3. The sense of *self* is constructed and experienced through the body.
4. Body experience, as how we know both world and self, is mediated.
5. In postmodern times, the body is increasingly experienced as *reshapable*; physiology has become a question, not a given.

As a final introductory note, let me emphasize the comment made by one of Martin's interviewees: 'So the body does have a natural life of its own . . . . and there are ways which we can affect [this natural history] and ways we can't' (quoted in Martin, 1994, p. 124). In the current distrust of 'essentialisms', many studies suspect the idea that the body has 'a natural life of its own' and resist the implication that this life cannot, in some respects, be affected. The books under review seek to recognize how this 'natural life' is real, but rarely is the body's solitary 'own'. We learn from these books how bodies share their natural life more than common sense often realizes.[4]

1. Dysappearing Bodies: Illness as Awareness

Martin (1994) writes at the beginning of *Flexible Bodies* that her 'concern is how our taken-for-grantedness about the body is generated' (p. xiii). One way to study the body's taken-for-grantedness is to consider where it ends; thus Toombs (1995) writes: 'I must—as a matter of course—constantly take my body into account' (p. 12). Her body's unreliability, caused by progressive multiple sclerosis, requires careful inquiry and planning regarding building entrances, special accommodations and seating. Her body involves her with others, who can offer necessary help or unwanted intrusion (pp. 16–17).

Drew Leder (1990; reviewed in Frank, 1993) coins the term 'dysappearing' to refer to the body's loss of taken-for-grantedness during illness. The body's appearance to consciousness results from the dysfunction caused by illness; thus the body *dysappears*. One of Martin's interviewees expresses this dysappearance:

> You think about the body as being, if you think about it, and you don't do it that often, unless it's acting up, and you really don't think about it, you just take for granted that all these things are working, the heart is pumping and the blood's flowing. You take it for granted, till something goes wrong. (quoted in Martin, 1994, p. 177)

When 'something goes wrong', the taken-for-granted body can become what Toombs (1992) calls 'inescapable embodiment' (p. 134). The inescapability is also an alienation: 'I still have difficulty recognizing my increasingly peculiar gait as my own', Toombs writes (p. 135).

Serious illness, in causing the body to 'dysappear', also changes the sense of self. Lonny Kliever (1995), seeking to understand the behavior of the burn victim Dax Cowart, writes:

> . . . experiences of severe and unrelenting pain often reorder the patient's familiar relationships between 'self' and 'body.' Experiences of great pain are shocking reminders that the self depends on the body, that selves are radically contingent. For persons who are chronically ill, severely handicapped, or grossly disfigured, the body moves from the background to the foreground of their experienced world. (p. 60)

Kliever describes the paradox that just when the body becomes the totality of the ill person's world, the body loses its 'familiarity and unity' (p. 60). To the observer this mix of totality and loss may be a paradox; to the ill person it can be Toombs's 'inescapable embodiment'.

The ill body is experienced as an 'oppositional force' with an 'opposing will of its own' (Toombs, 1992, p. 129). But here the firm boundary between healthy and ill bodies deconstructs. Iris Marion Young (1990), in one of her remarkable essays on the experience of female embodiment, suggests that the female body is perpetually dysappearing:

> We [women] often experience our bodies as a fragile encumbrance, rather than the media for the enactment of our aims. We feel as though we must have our attention directed upon our bodies to make sure they are doing what we wish them to do, rather than paying attention to what we want to do *through* our bodies. (p. 174)

Certainly Young's example of slowing down her male hiking companions because of her feminine bodily reticence crossing a stream is hardly the 'inescapable embodiment' of Toombs's restriction to her wheelchair. But as significant as the difference of degree is, the similarity remains: both experience a dysappearing body.

Martin's analysis of popular conceptions of the immune system further deconstructs the boundary of health and illness. Martin demonstrates that people throughout society orient to the immune system as a primary aspect of bodies; in their concern over the state of their immune systems, their bodies are constantly dysappearing. Foregrounding the immune system as a primary fact of one's own embodiment produces a self whose condition in the world is an anxiousness of 'empowered powerlessness', described as 'feeling responsible for everything and powerless at the same time' (Martin, 1994, p. 122). Everything in one's life can affect the immune system, but only some of these effects can be controlled. In an age of immune consciousness, the body is perpetually dysappearing as 'the enormity of the "management" tasks, of controlling one's body and health, becomes overwhelming' (Martin, 1994, p. 123). Selves exist in a continuing dilemma of 'universal agency and helplessness' (Martin, 1994, p. 135).

Again, no claim is intended that these anxieties over the state of the immune system, real as they are, are equivalent to being told that one is, right now, seriously ill. My point is the *persistence of dysappearance* as a defining condition of what I prefer to call 'postmodern times' (Frank, 1995a). Dysappearing bodies are no longer exclusively ill or traumatized bodies. The body's taken-for-grantedness may be less taken-for-granted than it used to be.

Finally, dysappearance is not only appearance as dysfunction; it also denotes *loss*. Toombs's difficulty experiencing her 'increasingly peculiar gait' as her own body is a loss. Those who have lost the familiarity of their bodies, Kliever (1995) observes, experience the concomitant 'loss of their "voice"' (p. 60). Having a 'voice' is rarely defined, but seems to imply the capacity to be a subject who speaks of him- or herself. The basis of this speech is familiarity with one's own body. Loss of this familiarity both impairs the capacity to be a subject—to assert oneself as the linguistic 'I'—and involves loss of the coherence of self-image necessary to be an object in one's own speech.[5]

Throughout the body literature, self, body and voice appear as inter-dependent. In an age in which the body/self relation is characterized by Martin (1994) as 'empowered powerlessness', finding and sustaining a 'voice' is frequently expressed both as a goal and as a problem. Each of the books being reviewed is in its own way concerned with restoring some measure of voice to bodies that have dysappeared.

2. The Body's World

Studies emphasizing the body as capacity for proprioception tend to begin with how the world becomes known through the body. A relation of difference between body and world is presupposed. Recent work decon-structs the body/world boundary: where one ends and the other begins blurs. Thus Young (1990) glosses Merleau-Ponty: 'The body's movement and orientation organizes the surrounding space as a continuous extension of its own being. Within the same act in which the body synthesizes its surrounds, moreover, it synthesizes itself' (p. 149).

To be a *subject* in the world is to create that world in a 'meaning-giving act' (Young, 1990, p. 147); Young's essays combine phenomenology, autobiography and politics to elucidate this act. In a series of theses (for want of a better term) about the particularity of women's embodiment, Young specifies the dynamics of the body/world interdependence claimed by Northoff, Schwartz and Wiggins (1992) in their oxymoronic statement that the boundaries of world and body are 'distinct but intersecting' (p. 146). I want to give Young's argument a greater generality by suggesting that what she writes about women's bodies is an equally valid description of ill people's bodies.

First, with respect to what Young (1990) calls the body's 'openness to the world', she distinguishes the cultural ideal of the subject's capacity to *transcend* the body, to be more than the flesh seems to allow, against the female body's *immanence*: its fundamental weight; in Toombs's term, its inescapability. Women's capacity for transcendence, Young argues, is at most '*ambiguous*', remaining 'laden with immanence'. Women's embodi-ment is not natural but social, resulting from their bodies being 'touched as well as touching ... grasped as well as grasping' (p. 148). Young's description applies to ill persons of both genders. Hospital patients are subject to being grasped by a variety of strangers, often with minimal explanation and no apology. Immanence is enforced over transcendence not only by the sensations imposed by the disease, but also by the social treatment of the diseased body.

Second, Young characterizes female embodiment as 'an *inhibited intentionality*, which simultaneously reaches toward a projected end with an "I can" and withholds its full bodily commitment to that end in a self-imposed "I cannot"' (p. 148). Toombs (1993) describes her illness condition in precisely the same terms: 'In illness bodily intentionality is frustrated. . . . The "I can" is rendered circumspect' (p. 63). 'For the person with gait disturbance', Toombs (1992) writes, 'stairs which were formerly simply there "to be climbed" now represent obstructions "to be circumvented" or avoided' (p. 130). Space *constricts*, both for women as described by Young (1990, p. 151) and for the ill as described by Toombs (1992, p. 130); thus the body's intentionality within its space becomes inhibited. When Young (1990) writes of the inhibiting disjunction between the projected possibility of 'someone' who could perform some action, and the subject's sense of what are 'truly *her* possibilities' (p. 149), she describes Toombs's everyday reality.[6]

Third, Young (1990) understands the female body as standing 'in *discontinuous unity* with both itself and its surrounds' (p. 149). In Young's description we meet, once again, the quality of constant dysappearance: 'Feminine bodily existence is frequently not a pure presence to the world because it is referred onto *itself* as well as onto possibilities in the world' (p. 150). If Martin is right, as I believe she is, and we do live in a time of generalized 'empowered powerlessness', then there is no 'pure presence' for anyone. Young clearly evokes 'pure presence' as an idealization. Her point is that a woman can never be *as* pure a presence as a man; a disabled woman like Toombs is then at a multiple disadvantage. In her wheelchair, Toombs is a nexus of vulnerabilities, fixed there to be '*looked at and acted upon*', in Young's phrase (1990, p. 150; cf. Toombs, 1992, pp. 132; 1995, pp. 16–17).

Eventually Young (1990) herself invokes illness as metaphor, writing that: 'Women in sexist society are physically handicapped' (p. 153). When this statement is read in the context of her essay, which does not otherwise refer to illness experience, physical disability is a metaphor for sexist handicap. When Young is read alongside of Toombs, being 'physically handicapped' is a literal expression of the restrictions that, to *very* different degrees, attend most 'normal' embodiment. Many people exist in body/world relations of ambiguous transcendence, inhibited intentionality and discontinuous unity.

Reading Young and Toombs fills in how the boundaries of world and body are, in the phrase of Northoff et al. (1992), 'distinct but intersecting'. The further question is how most people orient to this intersection as they negotiate their bodies' ways through the world. Here we can turn to Martin, who alone among these books has an extensive interview sample and a range of fieldwork experiences. Martin's hypothesis is that people relate bodies to the world through the mediation of a particular scientific/cultural view

(1994, p. 37; discussed in section 4, below). This view, however, is by no means univocal: if the notion of body as immune system is dominant for all, people still have multiple understandings of their bodies' relation to their world.

At one extreme are many who believe that 'the boundary between the body ("self") and the external world ("non-self") is rigid and absolute' (Martin, 1994, p. 53). Martin associates this understanding with the dominant model of contagion in popular images of disease during the 1950s, although many immunologists still maintain a rigid self/non-self dichotomy. The immune system is thus understood, in both lay and scientific terms (though with differing specificity), as being able to differentiate the self from the foreign. This understanding is expressed in the metaphor of the body as police state: 'Every body cell is equipped with "proof of identity"—a special arrangement of protein molecules on the exterior' (Martin, 1994, p. 54).

Other immunologists critique the self/non-self dichotomy as 'mechanical' and instead understand the immune system as a 'network of communicating cells that can learn from and adapt to experience' (Martin, 1994, p. 109). The popular adaptation of this view is found among those who 'see themselves as persons or bodies in a system with no clear, stable borders within it and no place outside it on which to stand' (Martin, 1994, p. 121). This latter understanding has a greater affinity to what Martin presents as the emerging cultural ideal, the 'flexible body'. The flexible body expresses more than a body's relation to its world; it is also the body's relation to what is differentiated as a self.

3. Body and Self

The body is no longer conceptualized as a mere vehicle for the self, but neither have body and self entirely collapsed into each other. Toombs's disabled body may be inescapable, but it does not render her a disabled self. As a self contingently within a disabled body, Toombs frequently has to contest being treated as insensible by others who identify too closely her body with her self. Young's essays on women's embodied 'handicap' could not be written if her non-handicapped self could not reflexively engage this body. This reflexive engagement is complex: Young's political project seeks to affect women's embodiment via their reading her writing, but this reading may depend less on 'intellectual' understanding than on embodied recognition of what women's bodies share. Because selves *can* recognize what bodies do share, I consider Young's writing to be just as 'generalizable' as Martin's, even if she has no interview sample to document her arguments.

The mutual dependence of body and self is nicely illustrated by Northoff et al.'s presentation of a case of eczema. The disease is both cause and outcome of the patient's compulsive scratching. The patient says, 'I scratch much more than I itch. Scratching has become an obsession. I bring on itching by scratching. . . . Bob told me: when you are scratching, nothing important exists for you' (quoted in Northoff et al., 1992, p. 148). Northoff et al. comment that for this woman the skin is no longer a boundary between self and world, but 'becomes a wall without doors where neither access nor exit is possible' (p. 149). Scratching is both a means of treating her body like an other-object (she stops 'only when I draw blood' [quoted on p. 148]), but she also scratches 'in order to experience her body as a lived body' (p. 150). Thus they conclude that 'it is impossible to separate the physiological and psychological' (p. 151).

In contrast to this assessment, Toombs, as the self in the disabled body, has to separate the physiological from the psychological, lest she become for herself the diminished object that others often treat her as being. Toombs (1995, p. 16) describes how the self is 'diminished' by the body's loss of upright posture: 'Verticality is directly related to autonomy' (1992, p. 132). She writes of the 'bodily detachment' (1992, p. 133) that disability brings. As she loses her 'sense of position and movement', she recognizes that these are 'integral to the experience of the body as one's own' (1992, p. 132). With the loss of bladder and bowel control, detachment turns to 'alienation of body from self'. 'Not only does it fail me, but it is capable of causing me deep humiliation and shame,' Toombs writes (1992, p. 133). Here the body is unquestionably the 'it' about which a separable if not separate self writes.

Northoff et al. (1992, p. 142) 'intertwine' the physiological and the psychological, and Toombs experiences the detachment and alienation of her body from her self. A third and more complex stance, reflecting yet another experience of the body, is presented by Young in her self-analysis of 'pregnant embodiment'. For Young (1990), 'Reflection on the experience of pregnancy reveals a body subjectivity that is decentered, myself in the mode of not being myself' (p. 162).

Young's pregnant body is no longer the exclusive space of her self alone:

> Pregnancy challenges the integration of my body experience by rendering fluid the boundary between what is within, myself, and what is outside, separate. I experience my insides as the space of another, yet my own body. . . .
>
> The first movements of the fetus produce this sense of the splitting subject; the fetus's movements are wholly mine, completely within me, conditioning my experience and space. Only I have access to these movements from their origin . . . which I can tell someone but which cannot be an object for both of us in the same way. (p. 163)

Young writes that the 'integrity' of her body is 'undermined' by pregnancy; she no longer can place firm boundaries between self and other, body and world.

Young's experience of pregnancy can be understood as a different mode of Leder's bodily dysappearance. Instead of appearing in its dysfunction, the body makes itself apparent in a new mode of wholly embodied creativity: 'The pregnant woman experiences herself as a source and a participant in a creative process. . . . she *is* this process, this change' (Young, 1990, p. 167). Thus if the pregnant woman is a 'split subject' in some respects, she also discovers a new, synthetic unity in her embodied creativity.

Young (1990) turns her analysis of the pregnant body into a generalized critique of the young male bias in the normative construction of 'health':

> Only a minority of persons, however, namely adult men who are not yet old, experience their health as a state in which there is no regular or noticeable change in body condition. For [these men] a noticeable change in their bodily state usually does signal a disruption of dysfunction [Leder's dysappearance]. Regular, noticeable, sometimes extreme change in bodily condition, on the other hand, is an aspect of the normal bodily functioning of adult women. Change is also a central aspect of the bodily existence of healthy children and healthy old people, as well as some of the so-called disabled. (p. 169)

This line of argument leads Young (following Sally Gadow) to formulate an awareness in which the body is neither the 'transparent mediator of our projects' (the ideal of transcendence) nor 'alienated resistance or pain' (immanence) (pp. 164–165). Beyond these dichotomous alternatives, she argues the possibility of experiencing the body 'in an aesthetic mode'. 'That is, we can become aware of ourselves as body and take an interest in its sensations and limitations for their own sake, experiencing them as a fullness rather than a lack' (p. 165).

My own bodily experience in athletics draws me to this notion of an aesthetic mode of awareness; an athlete can take an 'interested' attitude towards pain, for example. But my experiences of illness remind me that for many the body's sensations and limitations are a lack. Toombs (1993) writes of the 'sense of chill or dread' that derives from being 'irrevocably bound to suffer whatever this particular body suffers' (p. 60). In Toombs's darkest evocations of her embodiment, there is little question of an 'aesthetic' interest in the body. The physiological and the psychological must be clearly separated:

> . . . the body is experienced as a '*hidden presence*' in that, as biological organism, it includes events, processes, and structures over which I have no control and of which I have no awareness. In a sense my body seems to 'carry on' without me and to have no need of me. (Toombs, 1993, p. 61)

Lest this last phrase appear hyperbolic, consider a pregnancy story rather different from the account given by Young. The ethicist Peter Singer (1994, pp. 9–11) relates a case where the pregnant mother had 'died', but the court ordered her kept alive on life support until the baby could be delivered by caesarian section. Here the body literally does 'carry on' without the self that it has no need of.

None of these views—Northoff et al. Toombs, Young—excludes any of the others; rather they circumscribe a spectrum of experiences of bodies and selves. What now must be brought into the equation are the social forces that mediate the relations of bodies, selves and worlds. In the case Singer presents, mediations multiply: a court orders a hospital to employ a technology to maintain the woman's body in a certain state. The following section shows that this complex interplay of mediations is by no means unusual in postmodern times.

4. Mediated Bodies

Our bodies' experiences of knowing our worlds and ourselves are, common-sensically, internal; studies show, however, that experience is increasingly mediated by external forces. The books under review suggest two axes of this mediation. One axis involves body alienation and enhancement, a relation that is not a continuum because enhancement can be alienating, at least in some circumstances and on some interpretations. The circumstances bodies are placed in, and interpretations of those circumstances, are mediated by the other axis, local worlds and cosmopolitan worlds.

The social mediation of the body is most easily recognized as *alienation*. Feminist critiques of medicine are obvious examples; thus Young (1990) glosses a common criticism of obstetrical practices: 'A subject's experience or action is alienated when it is defined or controlled by a subject who does not share one's assumptions or goals' (p. 168). Toombs's (1995, pp. 49, 74) parallel account of the medical treatment of the disabled make it clear that more than obstetrical practices are involved. As Toombs (1993) shows in brilliant detail in *The Meaning of Illness*, physician and patient inhabit different life-worlds:

> The patient takes for granted that the physician recognizes the illness as primarily and essentially a threat to his or her personal being. The physician assumes that the patient understands the disease (albeit incompletely) in terms of the 'objective' clinical data. (p. 23)

Since the 'interchangeability of standpoints' is necessary for communication to occur, the breakdown of this interchangeability is a precursor to mutual alienation.

In Young's descriptions of medicalized childbirth, the woman and her physicians each know the body in the different ways described by Toombs. The woman experiences childbirth as a lived body; the physicians seek to reduce the lived body to machine-readable output. Thus 'medical instruments objectify internal processes in such a way that they devalue a woman's experience of those processes . . . the woman's reports are no longer necessary for charting the progress of her labor' (Young, 1990, pp. 168, 170).

In contrast to these alienating mediations of the body, Allison Moore (1994) describes feminist therapy as bodily *enhancement*. Her own work tries 'to help battered women begin to modify the cultural and interpersonal conditioning that keeps them trapped in abusive relationships' (p. 43). The woman's relationship to her body is still being mediated, but in this instance the objective is to enhance the woman's own capacity for experiencing, and then choosing, how she wants her body and her self to be treated. In both Young's and Moore's examples, however, what is alienating and what is enhancing can be contested. Some women might experience medical instrumentation as enhancement, and others might find therapy to be objectifying and alienating. Significantly, both examples involve health.

We gain further perspective on the contestable nature of bodily experiences in health care when we consider Martin's inquiry into how new emphases on the immune system are redefining health. She asks, 'Are we seeing the development of a "health currency" in terms of which exceedingly diverse and widely ranging forces and causes affecting health can be measured in the same coin?' (Martin, 1994, p. 192). In this question we can hear the contest of alienating and enhancing aspects of 'health'. We can also hear a shift from health being defined in local terms to more cosmopolitan definitions necessary to health as common currency.

The pre-eminent accounts of how *local worlds* mediate understandings of bodies, health, fertility and death are found in anthropological accounts (Balshem, 1993; Cátedra, 1992; Devisch, 1993; Zito & Barlow, 1994) which I have either reviewed elsewhere (Frank, 1995b) or which exceed the limits of this review. Although local worlds can be either alienating or enhancing, the emphasis in the literature is on their potential for enhancement. Thus Kleinman (1995) links local worlds to possibilities of embodied resistance to oppression. How local resistance functions to enhance the subject's own embodied experience, and embodied resistance, can be seen in Anthony Weston's depiction of the 'self-care' movement.

Weston (1992) describes self-care as attempting to 'reclaim the body from medicine's control'. In self-care, 'ordinary people' attempt 'to learn and use medical techniques for themselves' (p. 69). Self-care is one aspect of a reaction against medicine's assertion of its 'rights over the body' (p. 72). Self-care seeks to de-mystify bodily processes that medical expertise has mystified. The complementary form of this reaction is holistic medicine, which Weston defines as attempts to 're-mystify' or 're-enchant' the body that medical systems, as bureaucracies legitimated by science, has disenchanted (p. 69).

The most vocal of the local worlds of self-care practice have been feminist groups. Weston quotes *Our Bodies, Ourselves*, a publication of the Boston Women's Health Book Collective: 'in an age of professionals, we are the experts on our selves' (quoted in Weston, 1992, p. 71), and their selves *are* their bodies. With the massive international success of *Our Bodies, Ourselves*, however, the discourse of a local world becomes cosmopolitan; thus the local/cosmopolitan axis is no more linear than the axis of alienation and enhancement.

If *cosmopolitan* worlds can enhance body experience, the literature contains only the briefest hints of how; the emphasis is clearly on the alienating effects of cosmopolitan discourses and practices. The universalistic claims of medicine are easy targets. Thus Mary Brown Parlee criticizes the medicalized discourse of premenstrual syndrome, writing that science and biomedicine are neither disinterested nor exclusively about the treatment of physical disease. Both are also

> ... human activities socially organized in particular ways to produce, among other things, authoritative discourses about illnesses and how they are to be treated. One effect of these discourses is to medicalize (and thereby contain and control) deviant or potentially subversive experiences and actions. (Parlee, 1994, p. 101)

Parlee represents the postmodern argument that the claim of cosmopolitan discourses to be 'authoritative' across the contingencies of local worlds is a kind of colonization. As cosmopolitan discourses reformulate and evaluate the experiences of local worlds in their own universalistic terms, these discourses 'contain and control' what might be 'potentially subversive' in local actions.

Parlee (1994) emphasizes how drug companies, among other *institutional* interests, create premenstrual syndrome as 'a physically based illness' (p. 103). This critique of how the body's health is not simply mediated but dictated from above by discourses that cut across institutional and professional boundaries is given more extensive documentation in Deborah Lupton's study *The Imperative of Health: Public Health and the Regulated Body*, a title which expresses the book's political perspective. 'Health' is no longer the experience of a lived body but has become an 'imperative' enforced by various regulations imposed on the body.

Lupton combines, without significant qualifications as to local origins, materials on public health practices from Australia (where she writes), North America and western Europe. The implication of her method is that the cosmopolitan discourse of public health has effaced the particularities of local worlds: readers in the United States will presumably find Australian public health practices relevant to their own situation, just as Australian readers will find British practices relevant. With respect to Martin's suggestion, quoted above, of an emerging 'health currency', Lupton's politics might lead her to be critical of this currency, yet her own method trades in the common coin that Martin argues is emerging. I do not mean to suggest, however, that Lupton herself is any more ambivalent than the situation she studies: Martin's common currency is emerging, but it is not yet here, and its emergence is a mixture of benefits and losses. I only wish Lupton were more reflectively ambivalent.

Lupton's theoretical framework is dominated by Foucault's late conceptualization of 'governmentality'.[7] Institutional discourses, particularly 'helping' institutions, formulate the self as requiring both self-discipline and external surveillance. Thus:

> Health promotion relies on the model of the rational, unified self, consciously making decisions about one's conduct in everyday life in the quest for self-improvement and social success and integration. . . . Sickness has become a marker of the body 'taking over' reason, revealing the essential nature of the body as fragile and mortal. (Lupton, 1995, pp. 8–9)

Perhaps because Lupton's work relies more on her extensive review of the health literature than on her own fieldwork, which figures only marginally in the text, her work tends to privilege discourses and institutions over individual voices and agency: the body is more an object for institutional regulation than a means of individual resistance.[8]

In her conclusion Lupton recognizes that greater attention to individual agency might have given her study a somewhat different direction. Her concept of agency remains, however, highly conditioned by social position:

> . . . the interaction of discourse, practices of the self, and subjectivity in the context of health promotional and other governmental imperatives is not stable. The ways in which discourses are taken up and integrated into self-identity are at least partially contingent on the flux of individual's positions in the workforce, in the lifecycle and the interaction of institutions such as the economy, the family, the school. (Lupton, 1995, p. 149)

The most subtle and provocative conceptualization of this 'flux' is undoubtedly in Emily Martin's *Flexible Bodies*, which is, on my reading, the work that ought to set the agenda for the next 'generation' of studies (the space of a generation in the field being about five years). More than any other writer reviewed here, Martin captures the inscription *and* projection of the body, the fine line between alienation and enhancement of bodies, and the subtle interaction of regulation and agency.

Martin (1994) begins with Pierre Bourdieu's influential concept of *habitus*, which she defines as 'dispositions laid down in early childhood, patterns that make it possible for people to live in a world filled with taken-for-granted meanings' (p. 15). In contrast to analyses based on *habitus*, Martin proposes the essential importance of '*practicums*', which 'foreground *training* and *education*' (p. 15). '"Practicums" involve learning about new concepts of the ideal and fit person . . . learning that is embedded in some sort of complex physical–mental experience' (p. 15). Practicum learning is more self-conscious than habitus dispositions, it is often institutionally related, though it also takes place in non-institutional settings. Most distinctive to Martin's conception of the body, agency and society is her view that 'the complex combination of physical and psychological experiences evoked [in practicum learning] often means that the "teachers" are not exactly in control of the outcome' (p. 15). Thus indeterminacy is given a larger place than it seems to have in Bourdieu's social world.

Practicum learning seeks to develop the 'flexible body', and the key to flexible bodies is assumed to lie in the functioning of the immune system. Thus Martin effectively links physiology itself, body practices that affect physiology, scientific and popular discourses of physiology, and institutional structures. The flexible body is simultaneously a personal achievement, a scientific topic (as immunity), a 'powerful commodity', and a basis on which institutions can discriminate among persons (p. xvii).

The centre of Martin's analysis is public knowledge of, and orientation to, the immune system. She shows how the popularization of science leads not only to reconceptualizing bodies, but to creating different experiences of embodiment, and even different bodies. Public knowledge of the immune system has reached what Martin calls *saturation*:

> ... the general public comes to know that the body is made up of an immune system ... awareness of and regard for the body's health as defined by the functioning of the immune system have come to be so general in society that one cannot avoid it, wherever one turns. (p. 184)

Martin and her graduate student colleagues interviewed 225 people representing a variety of educational and occupational backgrounds; remarkably, only a few had not heard of the immune system. One of these was legally blind, leading Martin to conclude that '[b]eing isolated from public culture—for whatever reason—may be the only way to escape acquiring, relating to, and worrying about an immune system' (p. 72). Uniform awareness of the immune system does not mean, however, compatible accounts of what it is, and part of the fascination of Martin's data is the diversity of descriptions people give.

'Flexible bodies' are defined, in their *interior* aspect, in terms of the 'strength' of their immune systems. The immune system is strongest when it is able to meet the threat of new antigens; what is most remarkable about the immune system is its capacity to neutralize (the verb here would be contested among different theories of immune functioning) an unthinkably large variety of external threats. Thus 'strength' is defined as flexibility of response. 'Flexibility' then becomes a generalized metaphor for the optimal body. At the institutional level of analysis, Martin shows how organizations sustain an ideal of 'flexible specialization' (p. 245), which requires employees who are flexible bodies. The capacity of the body to fit into a variety of institutional slots is the *exterior* aspect of flexibility.

As I read Martin I recalled sitting on my university's curriculum commit-tee when the Dean of Education requested that students being trained as high school teachers be allowed to take three one-semester courses in several different disciplines rather than the larger number of courses that had previously been required in one discipline for a minor to an education degree. His reasoning was that the school board wanted to hire teachers who were flexible—who could be fitted into the broadest variety of classrooms—rather than limited by their subject specializations. Students who took conventional academic majors were suspect because their assumed special-ization rendered them inflexible for administrative purposes. This is the flexibility Martin claims organizations of all sorts now seek, but my example falls short of her analysis because it does not involve the body.

Flexible Bodies contains one of the most unusual photographs I've seen in a social science monograph: Emily Martin herself hangs suspended in a harness, some distance above the ground, 'after jumping off the "pamper pole" during a course in experiential training for a corporation' (p. 215). In the contemporary corporation, being a flexible body means being physically flexible, and Martin presents data on how much corporations are spending on physically challenging 'experiential training' to develop and screen their employees. This training is intense: the 'pamper pole' is so-called because so many trainees soil their pants while perched at the top of it. Thus the flexible body is no longer metaphoric for flexible skills, as it was in my education example. Flexible bodies now mean *bodies* that are flexible.

Martin argues the linkage between the cultural conceptions of a flexibly strong immune system as central to the body and corporate emphasis on flexible employee bodies. Two points seem particularly important. First is Martin's awareness of the politics—the potential for new forms of discrimination—inherent in this linkage. On this point Martin provides a complementary analysis to Lupton's politics of public health. Scientific and popular emphasis on the interior body can be an ideological ruse, perpetrated to 'divert attention to interior entities [immune systems] and processes [and] divert attention from social problems' (p. 186; cf. pp. 180–181).

> At stake is what kinds of bodies we imagine will be able to survive the next eruption of Ebola or the development of a more virulent flu or crowd disease. At stake is what kind of mechanism we imagine will enable some of us—and not others—to evolve into successful, healthy workers, surviv-ing in higher-order organizations. (pp. 244–245)

At stake is whether flexible bodies will become the new form of racism, or whether society can 'relish both the flexible, lean, and agile, and the stable, ample, and still' (p. 248). But Martin is far more sensitive than Lupton to the reality of bodies as more than discourses. Her fieldwork among persons dying of AIDS leaves little doubt that immunity, whatever its metaphorical and ideological uses, is also an absolute condition of embodiment.

Second, although Martin does not make the point in this way, emphasis on the immune system deconstructs the difference between external mediation of the body and the body's internal processes. Thus one of her interviewees exemplifies an understanding of the body—oddly parallel to Young's description of pregnancy—in which the boundary between external and internal is no longer relevant:

> I mean, you become a substance upon which many things can grow, can grow and flourish. . . . You become this incredibly rich ground upon which to multiply. (quoted on p. 126)

But can any of us entirely choose what will 'grow and flourish' on the 'rich ground' of our bodies? As Martin says about practicum learning, we are not exactly in control of the outcome. Nor are our bodies any longer 'ours' in an individualist sense.

Martin's multi-faceted analysis justifies her statement, which is both a hypothesis and a conclusion, that 'what goes to make up a person in these times is being reconfigured' (p. xvi). Clearly some form of power is being exercised in this reconfiguration, but 'no one can tell whether he is dealing with a new source of power', Martin writes (p. 16). The latter qualification is not evasion on her part, nor does it represent an incompleteness in her research. Rather it is the nature of our times to observe the effects of power while being uncertain as to the sources or novelty of this power.

The books under review show that the mediation of bodies is both enhancement and alienation; power can be power *over* or power *for*, and which power is operating in which practice is often not clear in postmodern times. The ambiguities of power are nicely developed in Margaret Miles's (1994) paper on eating disorders, a well-worn topic that continues to yield fresh analysis in Mary Winkler and Letha Cole's anthology *The Good Body*. Miles's argument is that eating disorders are certainly 'dangerously self-destructive' (p. 51), but are also pleasurable for the woman herself:

> I will contest both the understanding of eating disorders as an attempt by the powerless to control *something*, and the suggestion that young women starve themselves in order to look like the models they see in the media. (p. 51)

Instead, eating disorders are 'a female strategy for imagining and achieving pleasure' (p. 51).

Miles's analysis rests on placing eating disorders in the tradition of female asceticism.[9] Asceticism is a way that women can 'resist socialization' and develop 'an alternative to the pleasure of assuming the roles and capabilities established by one's society' (p. 51). Asceticism is the 'pleasure of no pleasure' that forges 'a permeable and vivid connection between the living body and the psyche' (p. 54). Miles then provides a provocative restatement of Leder's 'dysappearing body', suggesting yet another mode of this dysappearance:

> Perhaps the ultimate question is, 'What sets the body thinking?' In health
> and ordinary circumstances, psyche and body seem to maintain a tenuous
> connection at best; one's body comes to be noticed only when it 'acts up'.
> Ascetic practices, however, alter the body world and make the mind notice
> that it feels, not more-of-the-same, but different and *differently*. (p. 54)

This question leads Miles to question the 'myth of individual autonomy,
self-directedness, a chosen self that is cultivated, exercised, trained and has
articulated and examined values' (p. 52). Individual autonomy is an issue in
all these books. Miles's proclamation that autonomy is a myth recalls
Martin's observation, quoted above, that in the body's practicums, the
teacher may not be 'exactly in control of the outcome'. For all the body is
trained, the trainer cannot know what the body will become in that training.
When the body's own determination is recognized, the autonomy of self
begins to slip, with profound implications for our understandings of social
practices and our expectations of other people.

Miles takes us to the threshold of the next section on the physical
reshaping of bodies when she writes: 'Desire can then [in asceticism] be
worked with, pointed toward an object of choice, *designed*' (p. 55). In eating
disorders this work with desire leads to a redesigning of the body through
self-imposed fasting. As Miles shows, this reshaping of the body has a long
tradition. In the next section we move to newer technologies of reshaping the
body, and the problems of this section—mediation as enhancement and as
alienation, and the status of the person as agent of her own reshaping—
become more immediate and complicated.

5. Hyperappearing Bodies

The established role of medicine with respect to eating disorders is to deny,
to pathologize, this form of desire (if Miles is correct and such it is); here
medicine stands *against* reshaping the body. Kathy Davis's (1995) study of
why women seek cosmetic surgery, *Reshaping the Female Body*, casts
medicine in the opposite role of *enabling* the desire to design the body.
Davis finds that women do not exactly ally themselves with surgeons; on the
contrary, her research affirms Toombs's argument that physicians and their
patients inhabit two different life-worlds. Davis writes that even when
surgeons talk about appearance, they 'seemed to speak a different language
than their patients' (p. 130). Davis portrays women as at least believing they
are *using* medicine for their own purposes and this use stands in contrast to
Young's descriptions of how obstetrical medicine uses women. As often
throughout the literature, these accounts reflect not only different occasions,
but also different conceptions of agency and embodiment.

Davis's research began with her curiosity that discussions of elective
cosmetic surgery rarely included the perspectives of the women undergoing

these treatments. Her project was to treat these women not as 'cultural dopes' but as 'knowledgeable and active' subjects (pp. 57, 106). She found that the typical trajectory of choosing surgery begins with a woman's sense of being 'a prisoner of her body . . . never able to escape its constraints' and 'doomed to a life of misery' so long as that body remains unchanged (p. 100). After various attempts to forget her bodily defect and live a normal life, women discover and elect surgery.

Women describe the experience of surgery as empowering: 'It also gave me a kick,' a woman tells Davis, 'like, I'll be damned, but *I really did it*. You know? I got it together. I dared to do it. And I still feel that way' (quoted on p. 102). From this quotation we can begin to appreciate Davis's claim that elective cosmetic surgery is less about cultural norms of beauty and more about 'becoming an embodied subject rather than an objectified body' (p. 114). The male gaze may still be implicated, but far more indirectly than other accounts suggest.

Perhaps most interesting are women's reactions to failed surgery, and Davis is clear that about half of elective cosmetic surgeries do fail in some significant sense, many requiring further surgeries to fix the original. Women's descriptions of these failures are still dominated by a sense of agency; having *done* the operation seems to be more important than its success. Davis concludes:

> The difference seems to be less a matter of how her body looks than of agency. Whereas she previously presents herself as a hapless victim of fate, she now portrays herself as an agent in interaction with her circumstances. ('you have to keep going', 'You just can't stop and forget about it.') (p. 143; cf. p. 146)

I was first interested in Davis's study because elective cosmetic surgery seems to represent a leading edge of what I call 'proactive medicine', that is, medical practice devoted not to its traditional business of restitution and repair but instead to taking a body that is neither diseased nor injured and attempting to make it better than it 'naturally' is.[10] But the women Davis interviews do *not* see themselves being enhanced by surgery; they understand their surgery in fairly traditional medical terms, as repairing what previously was not normal (p. 101). Medicine, in the personae of cosmetic surgeons, is not being proactive here. Davis shows that women are using medicine proactively.

If a watershed is to be found, it seems to be less in medical practice than in how actors accomplish the reshaping of their bodies. In anorexia, the body is reshaped by refusing to take in what is external; the most decisive body boundary is maintained to a point when life literally does depend on it. In cosmetic surgery, what was external to the body merges fluidly into the body. The woman quoted above ('I dared to do it') has been caused gruesome pain by her breast implants, but she does not define the implants as the cause of suffering. She does not even seem to define surgery as suffering; thus the continuity of cosmetic surgery with earlier ascetic practices is questionable. Despite the pain they have caused, the woman feels the implants 'belong' to her; she does not notice they are there. The woman continues:

> ... but I'm not always thinking—what I used to worry about—'These things are in there, they don't belong to me.' I *could* have felt that way, but luckily I didn't. My immediate reaction was: 'This is me.' At least, for sure, my left breast, but it's even the way I feel about the other one now, too. It's just *me*. (quoted on p. 143)

Davis shows that women do *elect* surgery, and they make decisions with full knowledge of the risks. Women may even have to overcome medical resistance to performing surgery.[11] But it will remain unresolvable whether women's 'agency' in electing surgery only reflects the false consciousness instilled by a patriarchal culture, since some version of 'internalized oppression' cannot be refuted by any number of interviewed women declaring in the most certain terms that they alone decided and they knew what they were doing. The interest of Davis's research seems to lie elsewhere. What these women indisputably do is to deconstruct an individualist sense of their 'own' bodies: their accounts break down any stable opposition of me and not-me, inside and outside.

Other studies show this interior/exterior boundary being unstable, but Davis goes well beyond Northoff et al.'s case presentation of eczema or Young's meditations on pregnancy. In the quotation above, the woman proclaims that what is patently *not* 'her' *is* her; and recall that this woman has experienced surgical failure requiring intensely painful and still incomplete reconstruction.

Miles's argument that women with eating disorders are not 'ill' in any medical sense but are engaged in a form of ascetic pleasure leads her to suggest that more than illness can be involved in the body's dysappearance. Similarly women achieving cosmetic surgery are clearly not ill; they are active *subjects* of medical intervention. These women's bodies may initially dysappear—in Leder's sense—with their presurgical awareness of being prisoners to some imperfection. But after surgery, even failed surgery, the body *hyperappears* as the realized form of what it never has been. This enhanced body is nonetheless claimed as normal and the woman's own. The importance I attribute to Davis's research is that it most clearly depicts— though hints are also found in Martin—the hyperappearing body.

The woman who claims her breast implants as *hers* poses the question of how complete this deconstruction of one's body's boundaries can be; this question is clearly at the core of postmodernity. One answer is suggested by Arthur Kroker and Michael Weinstein (1994) in their meditation on the next stages of the information age, *Data Trash*. For Kroker and Weinstein, today's silicone gel implants are the crude precursors of eventual chip implants, with which the flesh and the machine will achieve their final 'interface'.

The cultural belief that the body not only can but *should* be surgically augmented is one facet of what Kroker and Weinstein call the age of 'recline', which is dominated by a 'wish to be replaced by technology' (p. 161). The following passage suggests their argument:

> The will to virtuality is infected by the nostalgic belief, even as the behavioral organism seeks to become a prop, that technology is meant to serve the flesh. That belief is held cynically because it is obvious that the terms of the relationship were reversed long ago. The question must be raised as to why there should be any flesh at all. . . . It makes perfect sense to conclude that if there are going to be total environments, there should also be specially produced nervous systems to sense them. The deep wish of reclining (humanity?), after all, is the wish to be replaced. The fin-de-millennium is the half-way house, the hospice, of a reclining species. Virtuality is what you do for/with/to (inferior) human nervous systems in a period during which custom-made nervous systems are being prepared and tested in human organisms. (p. 47)

Unfortunately readers do not learn much about where these tests are being conducted and what they consist of.

We do read about the French police offering a choice to drivers caught without their seat belts fastened: either a $50 fine

> . . . or taking a ride in a torture machine that simulates what it feels like when your car rolls over. It looks like an amusement park ride but it's meant to scare you straight. For your own good. Is it any wonder that France produced Foucault? Virtual disciplinization. (p. 86)

As provocative a story as this is, it establishes the recline thesis less effectively than Davis's research does. Davis's version of women's agency, read according to Kroker and Weinstein, reappears as the wish to be replaced and to call that replacement one's own self. Custom-made nervous systems may not yet be ready for installation, but the *willingness* to incorporate non-self and call it self is already apparent. The body is becoming whatever can be made of it, using whatever technology is available for remaking.

The credibility of Kroker and Weinstein is also enhanced by reading Martin. The next stage of the flexible body may well be the computer-wired body, with which the flesh becomes 'a functioning interfaced body'. The ultimate flexibility is what Kroker and Weinstein call 'the wireless body' (p. 17).

Finally, I take Kroker and Weinstein more seriously as I read Bill Gates quoted in my morning paper, forecasting 'computers so small you won't actually notice the computer itself' and saying about virtual reality: 'The ability to pretend you're somewhere is something I'm very excited about' ('Computers', 1995). Gates seems to take for granted that 'somewhere' is somewhere *else*. The ultimate effect of virtual reality may be to instill a sense that even when I am conscious of being where my body is, I feel as if I'm pretending to be there. The hyperflexible body is the virtual body. In the age of recline the body aspires to become a pretend body, a wired body with no inside or outside, no boundary of me or not-me. Hyperappearance is beyond pretend and real. In the virtual world it no longer makes sense to ask if Davis's interviewees make decisions based on a false consciousness, because there is no 'real' situation as a referent against which consciousness can be 'false'.

To attribute a dystopian conclusion to the literature would, however, miss much of what else is said. Kroker and Weinstein calls themselves 'critics IN the Net, not OF it' (p. 156); resistance to recline still seems possible. Despite Martin's (1994) reservations about the exclusionary realities of corporations making flexible bodies their preferred form, she perceives a positive side to what is happening:

> . . . many (myself included) may feel delight at some of the changes being brought about in the new flexible corporations: the elimination of some old hierarchies between management and labor, the effort to include women and minorities, the integration of mental and manual skills on the job, the wish to treat workers as whole people. (p. 248)

Toombs (1995, p. 21) not only proclaims her need to 'reclaim my life', she performs this reclaiming in her writing, which displays a self that has outwritten the limitations of her body. Various technologies play a considerable part in her reclaiming.

Reclaiming is also evident in Weston's descriptions of both self-care and holistic care. Weston (1992) describes what may be the singular recognition of the holistic shift in medicine:

> . . . the body really *is* a sort of mystery: not to be mystified, to be sure, but certainly to be respected in a new kind of way. The aim, again, is to speak of the body as something *more* than it is presently made to seem—but something not so easily, and not so appropriately, pinned down. (p. 78)

Holistic medicine is only one of many insistences 'on the *indeterminacy of the body*', and modern medicine is but one 'face of the all-too-determinate body' (Weston, 1992, p. 80).

How postmodern body indeterminacy need not indicate 'recline' is clearly stated in Tu Wei Ming's essay on the Confucian ideal of the body. Here also there is no inside or outside, but eliminating this boundary now effects a profound social responsibility:

> Indeed, we do not have our bodies as given realities; we *become* our bodies as we relate to, communicate with, and appropriate from the social and natural world in which we are a part.
>
> Our bodies are, therefore, the human form of the vital energy of the great transformation that we assume at birth. More appropriately, our bodies are the gifts entrusted to us by our parents and by Heaven so that we can fully embody our humanity.
>
> . . . we do not own our bodies; we are our bodies ontologically and we become our bodies existentially. (Ming, 1992, pp. 91–92)

Is the body headed toward virtuality in an age of recline, or will people understand their bodies as gifts, given so that we can 'fully embody our humanity'? Certainly at this moment, both visions are equally possible, and the only sensible conclusion is that each in its own way will occur. The literature under review is, however, anything but morally neutral about the future.

Epilogue: Bodies Who Theorize

The final boundary effaced by the literature under review is that between the subjects who write research reports and the bodies that are the objects of those reports. My favorite images from these readings are of Kay Toombs in her wheelchair, confronting airline officials who look right over her, at her husband, and ask him if 'SHE' can walk at all, to which he replies, 'No, but SHE *can* talk' (1995, p. 17). And Emily Martin, volunteering as a care-giver to persons with AIDS, feeling her rubber gloves fill with the water that has washed one man's soiled body and wondering what risk she is exposing herself to, as those bodily fluids pass into the 'deep cracks I get in my hands in the winter' (1994, pp. 136–137). And Iris Marion Young describing her own pregnancy in order to call into question the descriptions of earlier phenomenologists. And Kathy Davis, being asked by one of her interviewees why *she* would be interested in studying their cosmetic surgery (1995, p. 109).

What *do* the Kleinmans mean by culture 'infolding' into the body and bodily processes 'outfolding' into social space? Cosmetic surgery is the infolding of cultural norms into the bodies of women (and men), and flexible specialization is the outfolding of the body, not just as metaphor, into corporate space. The research project infolds into the body as the soiled, infected water fills Martin's gloves, and bodies outfold into theory as Toombs's disability and Young's pregnancy become their respective insights. The best work does not simply do research on the body; it is embodied research. I read the point of that embodiment as ethical. To write about the body is not to theorize abstractly; it is to join fates with other bodies. This work is not only 'research'. It is the construction of a common autobiography of shared humanity, and the assertion of a responsibility for the future of that autobiography.

Notes

1. My choice of ill bodies, as opposed to sporting bodies, gendered bodies, media-represented bodies or many other possibilities, represents both my own research interests (Frank 1991a, 1995a) and what is probably the largest 'substantive area' in the body literature (Featherstone & Turner, 1995).
2. The Krokers wrote this as a gloss on the sociology of Talcott Parsons (see Frank, 1991b, p. 207).
3. On the body as the basis of political narratives, see Feldman (1991).
4. Although the term 'social construction' has become a popular tag used to emphasize matters of context and interrelationship, I resist it because it de-emphasizes bodies' 'natural history'. Social construction carries the implication that the body's history is not 'natural', and thus anything can be affected. See note 6.
5. Thus Michael Ignatieff (1994), in his autobiographical novel *Scar Tissue*, describes his understanding of his mother's Alzheimer's disease: 'My mistake had been to suppose that a memory image could subsist apart from an image of the self, that memories could persist apart from the action of speaking or thinking about them from a given standpoint. . . . She was wondering who the "I" was in her own sentences' (p. 53).
6. Although Toombs (1995) writes that she has begun 'to reclaim my life' (p. 21) in ways that are 'enriching' (p. 20), she is equally uncompromising in her statement that: 'Harsh though the reality may be, there is nothing intrinsically good about chronic, progressive multiple sclerosis. Nothing' (p. 20). Here we see clearly the body having a 'natural life of its own' (Martin's interviewee, quoted earlier) and the limits of how this life can be affected.
7. Among the books being reviewed, a useful presentation of Foucault is found in Spitzack (1992).
8. For a complementary view of public health, driven predominantly by the author's own work in the field as well as fieldwork, see Balshem (1993). Balshem is able to depict practices of resistance that Lupton cannot find in the secondary literature, and she is able to recognize the basic truth of public health: bodies do get sick, and sickness is caused by a complex interplay of personal choices and environmentally imposed risks. Lupton, however, does recognize her own bias; see p. 131.
9. This territory continues to be explored in a recent work by Caroline Walker Bynum (1995). In this work, however, Bynum seems wary of presentist implications of her research; those implications are still most fully developed in her earlier book (1991).
10. Examples of proactive medicine include the medicalization of infertility, which involves the paradox of a 'natural' physical condition being defined as a disease in order to justify body-enhancement as medical cure. An eye clinic that I pass on my way to work advertises its new laser surgeries in large letters printed on its wall: 'Freedom from glasses', which is quite different from the traditional medical promise of freedom from partial vision. The leading edge of proactive medicine, however, is clearly genetic manipulation. In all these practices we see the technological reshaping of the body.
11. Davis's research was in the Netherlands, which, at the time of the research, had a higher per capita rate of elective cosmetic surgery than the United States, and which covered much of this surgery under government medical insurance. To qualify for government coverage, women had to persuade skeptical, cost-conscious medical authorities that they needed surgery. Thus the argument that surgery is instigated by money-hungry physicians is not relevant to her findings.

References

Balshem, M. (1993). *Cancer in the community: Class and medical authority*. Washington, DC: Smithsonian Institution Press.

Bynum, C.W. (1991). *Fragmentation and redemption: Essays on gender and the human body in medieval religion*. New York: Zone.

Bynum, C.W. (1995). *The resurrection of the body in western Christianity, 200–1336*. New York: Columbia University Press.

Cátedra, M. (1992). *This world, other worlds: Sickness, suicide, death and the afterlife among the vaqueros de Alzada of Spain*. Chicago, IL: University of Chicago Press.

Cole, J.L., & Paillard, J. (1995). Living without touch and peripheral information about body position and movement: Studies with deafferented subjects. In J.L. Bermúdez, A. Marcel, & N. Eilan (Eds.), *The body and the self* (pp. 245–266). Cambridge, MA: MIT Press.

Computers on way to invisibility: Gates. (1995, 4 December). *Calgary Herald* (Reuters), p. A6.

Devisch, R. (1993). *Weaving the thread of life: The Khita gyn-eco-logical healing cult among the Yaka*. Chicago, IL: University of Chicago Press.

Eilan, N., Marcel, A., & Bermúdez, J.L. (1995). Self-consciousness and the body: An interdisciplinary introduction. In J.L. Bermúdez, A. Marcel, & N. Eilan (Eds.), *The body and the self* (pp. 1–28). Cambridge, MA: MIT Press.

Featherstone, M., & Turner, B.S. (1995). Body & society: An introduction. *Body & Society, 1*(1), 1–12.

Feldman, A. (1991). *Formations of violence: The narratives of the body and political terror in Northern Ireland*. Chicago, IL: University of Chicago Press.

Frank, A.W. (1990). Bringing bodies back in: A decade review. *Theory, Culture & Society, 7*(1), 131–162.

Frank, A.W. (1991a). *At the will of the body: Reflections on illness*. Boston, MA: Houghton Mifflin.

Frank, A.W. (1991b). From sick role to health role: Deconstructing Parsons. In R. Robertson & B.S. Turner (Eds.), *Talcott Parsons: Theorist of modernity* (pp. 205–216). London: Sage.

Frank, A.W. (1993). When bodies are other: An applied phenomenology [Review of D. Leder, *The Absent Body*]. *Bulletin of the Canadian Society for Hermeneutics and Postmodern Thought. 8*(1), 13–17.

Frank, A.W. (1995a). *The wounded storyteller: Body, illness, and ethics*. Chicago, IL: University of Chicago Press.

Frank, A.W. (1995b). An agenda for professional reflection: Place, power, and the other of medicine [Review of M. Balshem, *Cancer in the Community*, D. Hilfiker, *Not All of Us Are Saints*, and A. Verghese, *My Own Country*]. *Second Opinion, 21*(1), 53–59.

Glass, J. (1995). *Psychosis and power*. Ithaca, NY: Cornell University Press.

Ignatieff, M. (1994). *Scar tissue*. Toronto: Penguin.

Kleinman, A. (1995). The social course of chronic illness: Delegitimation, resistance, and transformation in North American and Chinese Societies. In S.K. Toombs, D. Barnard, & R.A. Carson (Eds.), *Chronic illness: From experience to policy* (pp. 176–188). Bloomington: Indiana University Press.

Kleinman, A., & Kleinman, J. (1994). How bodies remember: Social memory and bodily experience of criticism, resistance, and delegitimation following China's Cultural Revolution. *New Literary History, 25*(3), 707–723.

Kliever, L.D. (1995). Rage and grief: Another look at Dax's case. In S.K. Toombs, D. Barnard, & R.A. Carson (Eds.), *Chronic illness: From experience to policy* (pp. 58–76). Bloomington: Indiana University Press.

Kroker, A., & Kroker, M. (1987). *Body invaders: Panic sex in America*. Montreal: New World Perspectives.

Leder, D. (1990). *The absent body.* Chicago, IL: University of Chicago Press.

Leder, D. (1992). A tale of two bodies: The Cartesian corpse and the lived body. In D. Leder (Ed.), *The body in medical thought and practice* (pp. 17–35). Dordrecht: Kluwer Academic.

Miles, M.R. (1994). Textual harassment: Desire and the female body. In M.G. Winkler & L.B. Cole (Eds.), *The good body: Asceticism in contemporary culture* (pp. 49–63). New Haven, CT: Yale University Press.

Ming, Tu Wei (1992). A Confucian perspective on embodiment. In D. Leder (Ed.), *The body in medical thought and practice* (pp. 87–100). Dordrecht: Kluwer Academic.

Moore, A.M. (1994). The good woman: Asceticism and responsibility from the perspectives of battered women. In M.G. Winkler & L.B. Cole (Eds.), *The good body: Asceticism in contemporary culture* (pp. 36–48). New Haven, CT: Yale University Press.

Northoff, G., Schwartz, M.A., & Wiggins, O.P. (1992). Psychosomatics, the lived body, and anthropological medicine: Concerning a case of atopic dermatitis. In D. Leder (Ed.), *The body in medical thought and practice* (pp. 139–154). Dordrecht: Kluwer Academic.

Parlee, M.B. (1994). The social construction of premenstrual syndrome: A case study of scientific discourse as cultural contestation. In M.G. Winkler & L.B. Cole (Eds.), *The good body: Asceticism in contemporary culture* (pp. 91–107). New Haven, CT: Yale University Press.

Singer, P. (1994). *Rethinking life & death: The collapse of our traditional ethics.* Melbourne: Text Publishing Company (in North America, St Martin's).

Spitzack, C. (1992). Foucault's political body in medical praxis. In D. Leder (Ed.), *The body in medical thought and practice* (pp. 51–68). Dordrecht: Kluwer Academic.

Toombs, S.K. (1992). The body in multiple sclerosis: A patient's perspective. In D. Leder (Ed.), *The body in medical thought and practice* (pp. 127–137). Dordrecht: Kluwer Academic.

Toombs, S.K. (1995). Sufficient unto the day: A life with multiple sclerosis. In S.K. Toombs, D. Barnard, & R.A. Carson (Eds.), *Chronic illness: From experience to policy* (pp. 3–23). Bloomington: Indiana University Press.

Weston, A. (1992). On the body in medical self-care and holistic medicine. In D. Leder (Ed.), *The body in medical thought and practice* (pp. 69–84). Dordrecht: Kluwer Academic.

Zito, A., & Barlow, T.E. (Eds.). (1994). *Body, subject and power in China.* Chicago, IL: University of Chicago Press.

Index

acupuncture, 195, 199
agency, and communion, 66
AIDS, 222
Alcoff, Linda, 97
Alexander, F. A. D., 189–90
alienation, 217, 218, 220
Allen, Jennifer, 106, 113
American Psychologist, 55
anesthesiologists, 188–9, 191, 199
angelic eye, 32
Angenot, Marc, 146
anorexia nervosa, 10–1, 161–2, 168–9, 171, 173–7, 225; and distorted body image, 174–5; and feminist explanations, 166, 168; and identity politics, 166; and self-regulation, 176–7; and social constructionism, 162; and the body, 161–2, 168–9, 171, 176–7; and the ideal of slenderness, 165; explanations of, 164–6
Aristotle, 32, 97
Armstrong, D., 182
Arney, W. R., and Bergen, B. J., 182, 198
art, 142, 153–4
art establishment, 152
artistic field, 142
Atkinson, R. C., and Shiffrin, R. M., 75, 80–4
Augustine, St., 97

Baerveldt, Cor, 10–11
Bakan, D., 66
Bakhtin, Mikhail, 155
Balinese cockfight, 19, 26
Balshem, M., 230
Barthes, Roland, 172
Bartlett, F. C., 84

Bateson, G., 173, 176
Baumeister, R. F., 54
Bayer, Betty, 8
Becker, Howard, 144
behavior therapy: in the treatment of pain, 196–7, 200
behavioral medicine, 182
Bennington, G., 84
Berger, Harry, 109
Berger, P. L., and Luckmann, T., 57, 163
Bermúdez, J. L., Marcel, A., and Eilan, N., 206–8
bio-power, 121
biology: contesting terms of, 120; definition of sex, 122; human, 57, 63
biology of meaning, 65
biomedical model, 182, 186, 190
biopsychosocial model, 10, 11, 182–4, 191, 196, 198, 200–1
Birdwhistell, R., 167, 171
Blake, W., 50
bodily functions, 14
body: and activism, 121; and anorexia nervosa, 161–2, 168–9, 176–7; and body talk, 105; and Buddhism, 42; and cognition, 77, 86; and communication, 167–8, 172; and culture, 10, 209; and epistemological uncertainty, 98; and experiential realism, 46; and expression, 16, 28; and feminism, 9, 42, 99; and feminist-constructionism, 35–6; and history, culture and community, 48; and ideology, 116; and illness, 10, 206, 209, 213, 216, 230; and influencing machine, 89; and pain,

body, *cont.*
11, 194, 209–10; and Pentecostal religious revival, 43; and phenomenology, 33; and politics, 49; and preconceptual meaning, 46–7; and psychology, 6, 96; and sense of self, 209; and social constructionism, 31, 162–3, 230; and social intercourse, 171–2; and style, 22, 172; and temporality, 114; and universal variables, 58; and 'woman', 114; as a 'selfing' device, 162; as a recursive process of inscription and projection, 209, 220; as elusory, 6; as ground and figure, 27; as mannequin, 167, 177; as property, 109; as signifying medium, 115; as tag-along to feminist discourse, 108; as visual territory, 141; becomes subjectified, 65; designed, 224; disabled, 215; distorted image of, 174–5; dysappears, 210, 212; early Christian views of, 40–1; fashioned in psychology, 103; female, 96, 213; flexible, 214, 221–2, 228; healthy and ill, 211; hostility to, 40; hyperappearing, 224, 226; in sociology, 146; lived, 207; material aspect, 15; mechanized, 2; metaphors of psychology, 1–4; outside itself, 206; physiological, 4; precultural, 36; reclaim, 218; reproductive, 95; research on the, 229; taken-for-granted, 210–1; transcend vs immanence, 212; transgendered, 130; virtual, 228–9; what is, 98; women's, 146, 217–8
Body and the Self, The, 206
body ideal, 105
body image: and self-consciousness, 206; distorted, 174–5; healthy, 113
body politics, 167
body-kinds, 124–5
Bonica, J. J., 186–7, 189, 195, 197, 199
Boole, George, 79, 80

Bordo, Susan, 102, 176
Boskind-Lodahl, M., 166
Boudon, Raymond, 146
Bourdieu, Pierre, 9, 10, 38–9, 49, 142–8, 153, 155–6, 220–1
Bourne, E. J., 54
Boyarin, D., 40–1
Braidotti, Rosi, 153
Broadbent, D. E., 82
Brown, Beverly, and Adams, Parveen, 111
Brubaker, Roger, 146
Bruch, H., 174
Bruner, J., 57, 63–5
Buddhist thought and practices, 42–3
Butler, Judith, 35–7, 42, 96, 112, 121–2, 123, 135, 156–7
Bynum, C. W., 41, 101, 230

capital: artistic, 153; disciplinary, 142, symbolic, 145
Cartesian: dualism, 4, 5, 7, 46, 77, 123, 184, 197; space of pain, 185, 190, 192–3, 197
Casey, K. L., 196
childbirth, 217
Chinese medicine, 199
Chomsky, N., 91
Chow, Rey, 157
Christianity, 41
chromosomal differences, 135
chronic conditions, 183
chronic pain subculture, 195
class, 154
classification, 100
co-construction of meaning, 171
co-regulation, 170–3, 177
cognition, 73; and computation, 74, 81; and différance, 84; and interpretation, 84; and sexual difference, 78–9; and the body, 77–8; and the corporeal, 79, as behaviourist, 76; as masculine, 87; disembodied, 75, 85; distinguished from mind, 90; embodying, 80; is embodied, 86; limits of, 85; not impartial, 90

cognitive psychology, 74, 75; and trace, 82–83; as information processing, 81; feminist interventions in, 88, 90
cognitive science, 74, 85, 91
Cole, Letha, 223
communication, 167–8, 170, 171, 173; non-verbal, 173
comportment, 17
computer metaphor, 73
conception, 100–1
constructionism, 66; blueprint of, 57
constructomania, 37
consumer culture, 23
control, internal-external locus of, 62
corporations, 222
corporeal: powers, 34; semantics, 167, 172
corporeal psychology, 123
corporeality, masculine: and power, 110
corps-sujet, 59, 65
cosmetic surgery, 224–6, 229–30
Cowart, Dax, 210
Cox, Harvey, 43
Craik, Kenneth, 3
critical ethnography, 153
cross-cultural psychology, 54
culture: and self, 67; as co-orienting system, 63
Cushman, P., 55, 58
cybernetics, 4

Danziger, Kurt, 1
Darwin, C., 44
Date Trash, 226
Davis, Kathy, 209, 224–7, 229–30
de Lauretis, Teresa, 157
Delphy, Christine, 122, 135
Dempsey, Shawna, 152
Derrida, J., 75, 83–4
Descartes, R., 32, 45, 59, 77, 97, 184–5
desire, bodily: and the social order, 111
dialogical relations, 67
différance, 83–4, 87
disabled, 217
disciplines, 9–10; traditional, 154
discourse, 37, 143

discursive acts, 37
displays, 13, 15–6, 17–23, 25, 27–8
dispositions, 143
Distinction, 144
Dittrick, Howard, 188–9
Dora: and Freud, 115
doubt, 60
Douglas, M., 172–3
Drawing the Line, 150, 152, 156
DSM-IV, 174
dualism, 5
dualisms, 99
dysappearance, 27
dysappearing body, 210–11, 223

eating disorders, 223
eczema, 214–5
embodied action, 15
embodied discourses, 38
embodiment, 7, 13, 14, 15, 17, 21–3, 27–8, 31, 39, 42, 126, 131; and rhetorical-responsive model, 38; domestication of, 155; female, 123; gendered, 101; male, 123; women's, 102, 212
emotion, 44–5
empirical, 12
Engels, F., 49
enhancement, 218, 220
Enlightenment, 32; science and progress, 97
epistemology, 7
Epstein, Robert, 91
Erikson, E. H., 201
ethnicities, 155
ethnography, 157
evaluative universal, 62, 64
Evans, Martha, 95, 103
exemplar sensible, 24
exemplification, 24–5
experience, 107
experiential realism, 46–7
Eye Body, 141, 154

fact and fiction, 147
Feldman, A., 230
female form: ideal, 104
femininity, 95

feminism, 9, 42, 102, 106–7, 142; and
    the body, 115, 177; in psychology,
    73
feminist: artists, 142; psychologists,
    103; standpoint, 106; theory, 73,
    153
feminists: radical, 112, 125; post, 125
Ferguson, Kathy, 102
field, 145–6
fields: disciplinary, 143; artistic, 143
Flexible Bodies, 210, 220, 222
flirtation, 20–21, 24
Fogel, A., 170
Fordyce, W., 196–7
Foucault, M., 36, 102–3, 121–2, 135,
    183, 220, 230
Frank, Art, 11
Freud, S., 66, 86, 95, 115

Gadow, Sally, 216
Game, Ann, 144–5, 147–8, 153, 155,
    157
Gamsa, A., 197
Gardner, H., 85
Gates, Bill, 227–8
Geertz, C., 19, 55, 57
gender, 133; and constructivist
    perspective, 135; and sex, 8, 9,
    121–2, 124–5, 131, 133–4, 136;
    and 'gendertrash', 130; in
    photography, 153
genderqueer, 130
Gendertrash, 127
Gergen, Kenneth, 134, 164
Gergen, Mary, 134
Gesell, Arnold, 2
Gibson, E., 34–5
Gillett, G., 167
Ginsburg, G., 57
Glass, J., 209
Gleason, M. W., 38–9
Goffman, E., 16–7, 21
Good Body, The, 223
Goodman, N., 24–5
Gordon, R.A., 188
grid: illusory, 130; of identities, 130
Grosz, E., 77, 123

Haacke, Hans, 155

habitus, 9, 11, 39, 143, 145, 147–8,
    153–4, 220
Hall, G. Stanley, 2
handicapped: physically, 213
Haraway, Donna, 134
Hare-Mustin, Rachel, and Marecek,
    Jeanne, 109–10
Harré, R., 56, 122–6, 129–30, 131,
    133–4, 135–6, 164, 167, 172
healing techniques, 198–9; and
    expropriation by professionals, 199
health: currency, 218; promotion, 220;
    public, 219, 222
health psychology, 182
Heelas, P., 57
Heidegger, Martin, 143
history, culture and community:
    absence of, 48
history of science: feminist, 101
Hixon Symposium, 91
Hofstede, G., 58
holistic medicine, 218, 228
Hollingsworth, L. S., 100
Homer, 44
hominid body, 47
Hutchinson, Marcia Germaine, 113
hyperappearance, 224, 226
hysteria, 95

identities, 5, 16; and style, 16
ideological individualism, 48
ill body, 206
illness, 10
imagination, 59
immune system, 211, 214, 221–2;
    strength of, 221
Imperative of Health, The, 219
individual, 6; and autonomy, 224;
    autonomous, 185
individualism, 5, 66; and
    foundationalism, 33, 35
infertility, 230
influencing machine, 87–8
information, 3, 82
intentionality, 206–7; inhibited, 213
Internal Model Principle, 59
International Association for the Study
    of Pain, 194

Irigaray, L., 9, 75, 79, 86–7

James, W. T., 44
James, W., 61
Jay, M., 32
Johnson, M., 46–7
Judeo-Christian tradition, 41
Juhasz, Alexandria, 142

Kant, I., 97
Keller, Helen, 78
Kelly, Mary, 152
Kempen, Harry, 8
Kinsey, Alfred, 2
Kiss & Tell, 150, 152
Kitzinger, Celia, 109, 121–2
Kleinman, Arthur, 208–9, 218, 229
Kleinman, Joan, 208–9, 229
Kliever, Lonny, 210–11
Körper, 207
Koss, Mary, 108
Kotarba, J., 195
Kristeva, J., 167
Kroker, Arthur and Marilouise, 206
Kroker, Arthur, and Weinstein,
        Michael, 226–8, 230
Kugelmann, Robert, 11

Lacan, J., 86, 111
Lacanians, 112, 116
Lacquer, T., 100
Laird, J. D., 45
Lakoff, G., 46–7
Langer, Susan, 170, 172–3
language acquisition, 63–4
Lashley, Karl, 88
Leder, Drew, 7, 10, 27, 207, 210, 216,
        223, 226
Leib, 207
Leriche, René, 187
Levin, D. M., 32, 33, 40
Lévinas, E., 183, 190
life-world, 175
Linneaus, Carl, 100
Livingston, W. K., 187, 191
Lock, Andrew, 56
Loebner Contest, 91
logocentrism, 142

long-term store, 82
Lovers and Warriors, 142, 149–52,
        154–5
Lupton, Deborah, 219–20, 222, 230

MacKinnon, Catherine, 111–2, 113
male imaginary, 86
Malone, Kareen, 8
Mapplethorpe, Robert, 147; affair, 152
Marcus, Sharon, 107–8
Markus, H. R., and Kitayama, S., 65
Martin, Emily, 132, 208–9, 210–14,
        218–24, 226–9
masculine: desire, 79; dispassion, 86;
        morphology, 86
masculinity, 131
Matlin, M. W., 81
Mauss, M., 39, 169
McCloskey, D. N., 201
McCulloch, W. S., and Pitts, W. H., 80
Meaning of Illness, The, 208, 217
medical/scientific discourses, 132, 135
medicine: existential engagement in,
        200; holistic, 218, 228; proactive,
        225
Melzack, R., 184, 191–2, 196, 199–200
memory, 75, 80
Mercer, Kobena, 157
Merleau-Ponty, M., 20, 24, 26, 33, 46,
        86, 171, 212
merry-go-round, 17–8
Merskey, H., and Spear, F. G., 194
Merwe, W. L. van der, 37
metaphor, 46
Miles, Margaret, 223–4, 226
Miller, G. A., and Gazzaniga, M. S., 85
Min-ha, Trinh T., 157
mind: and body, 96; as information
        processing machine, 74;
        computational approach to, 72, 75,
        80; distinguished from cognition,
        90; neurological approach to, 72
Ming, Tu Wei, 228–9
monocultural views, 54, 56
Moore, Allison, 218
Morrow, Raymond, 146
motor-bike gang, 18, 25–6

näive realism, 67

narrative(s), 207, 209; intentionality, 208
narrotomania, 37
natural kinds, 124
nature vs culture, 122
Neel, Alice, 147
Neisser, U., 74
neuro-cognitive sciences, 72
neuron, as logical proposition, 80
Nietszche, F., 33, 46
Northoff, G., Schwartz, M. A., and Wiggins, O. P., 212–5, 217, 226
nudes, 95

object-body, 31–5, 40, 44, 207
objectivism, 36
ocularcentrism, 32–6
oppression and domination, 49–50
Orbach, S., 166
organism, metaphor of, 1–3
Osgood, C. E., 62
Other, the, 98, 131, 198
Our Bodies, Ourselves, 218–9

pain, 11; and cognition, 197; and cosmetic surgery, 226; and experience, 194, 197; and healing techniques, 198–9; and pain clinics, 186–9, 195–6, 200–1; and patient responsibility, 198; as a technical process, 193; as passion of the soul, 185; as social protest, 201; chronic, 183–4, 187, 189, 195; conceptualized as behavior, 196–7, 200; distinguish perception of and reaction to, 186, 194; gate control theory of, 184; gate control theory of, 191–7, 199–201; new definition of, 194; non-medical aspects of, 190–1; phantom limb, 187; psychogenic, 186–7, 194; psychotherapeutic treatment of, 184, 195–7; sensation theory of, 184, 186–7; treatment of, 188, 190, 195–6, 198, 200–1
Parlee, Mary Brown, 9, 219
Parmar, Pratibha, 157
Parsons, Talcott, 230

patriarchy, 113
pedagogy of the oppressed, 7
Pentecostalism, 43
performance art, 141–2; 152
Perkins, Rachel, 109
phallocentrism, 142
Phelan, Peggy, 147–8, 153, 155–6
phenomenological feminism, 105
phenomenological-body, 33–4
phenomenology, 7, 33, 35, 207; and felt-body, 35
photography, 149–51
Pizanias, Caterina, 9
Plato, 32
Plutchik, R., 64
polarities, 66
politics, bodily dimension, 49
pose, pudica, 94
power, 223; and knowledge, 111
practicum(s), 220–1, 223
pregnancy, 215–6
Prince, Richard, 152
prise de position, 145
proactive medicine, 225
psyche, 91
psychoanalysis: feminist, 152–3
psychologists' representations, 121
psychology: and dominant discourses, 30, 44; and the body as subject-matter, 161; cognitive, 8; of the body, 5–6
psychoneuroimmunology, 67
public health, 219

queer: and genderqueer, 130; bashing, 152; community, 152
queer communities, 142
Quinby, Lee, 96

race, 154
Radley, Alan, 6, 7, 10, 167–9, 171
rape, 107–8
religious practices, 7
representational: politics, 9; practices, 129
repression, 109
reproduction, 95, 101
Reshaping the Female Body, 224

Risatti, Howard, 153
Risseeuw, C., 65
ritual, 18, 170
Robbins, Derek, 145
role distance, 17
Romanyshyn, R. D., 33–4
Rotter, J. B., 62
Rubin, J., 188

Said, Edward, 157
Salomon, Nanette, 94–5
Sampson, Edward, 7–8
Scheflen, A. E., 167
Scheper-Hughes, N., 49
Schiebinger, Londa, 99–100
Schneemann, Carolee, 141–2, 154–5
Schwartz, D. P., and Parris, W. C. V., 196
science: idealized picture of, 132; value-free, 67
Scott, Joan, 107
Sedgwick, E. K., 44
self, 8, 55–6, 59–60, 175; and non-self, 214; as constructed, 56; independent vs interdependent, 65
self-conceptions, 55, 65
self-construction, 8
self-options, as biological, 65
self-regulation, 176
self-universals, 55
selfing, 55; process, 162, 175, 177
sensory register, 82
sex: and gender, 8, 9 121–2, 124–5, 131, 133–4, 136; and gender categories, 128; and gender identity, 126; as natural, 36; one-sex models, 100; psychological theories of, 134
sexual difference, 78–9
sexual orientation, 164
sexual pleasure: lesbian, 152
sexuality, 14, 121, 131
sexually taboo practices, 153
shame, 201
Sheets-Johnstone, M., 34–5, 46–8
Sherman, Cindy, 152
Shilling, Chris, 146
short-term store, 82

Shotter, J., 38, 164
Shweder, R. A., 54
signs, 173
Simmel, G., 7, 21–4, 26, 28
Singer, Peter, 216
Skinner, B. F., 2
Slade, P. D., and Russell, G. F. M., 174
Slobin, D. I., 64, 65
social constructionism, 31, 36, 39, 57–8, 124, 230; and conversation, 164; and the body, 162–4, 230; and sex, 133
social life, 14
social order: as embodied order, 173
social, body as, 6
society: patriarchal, 146; racist, 146
sociology: absent body in, 146; deconstructive, 144; of art, 144
souplesse: social, 176
space-orienting task, 62
Spence, J., 55–6, 58, 61, 65–7
Spivak, Gayatri C., 157
Stanley, Liz, and Wise, Sue, 131
Starback, Jana, 152
Stewart, Susan, 9, 142, 149–50, 152–4, 156
Stine, Jean Marie, 126
Stone, Allucquere R., 123
story-telling, 207
style, 172
stylization, 23
subject-body, 207
Swerdlow, M., 190
symbolic order, 112–3, 115
symbolic capital, 145
symbolize, to, 13
Symposium on Information Theory, 91
Synnott, A., 40
system: metaphor of, 3–4

Tacoma General Hospital, 195
tactile-kinesthetic sense, 34
Tao, 66
Tausk, Victor, 75, 88–90
Taylor, C., 39
Taylor, S., 182, 198
teacher training, 222

techniques of the body, 169, 172
Teena, Brandon, 126
Telling Sexual Stories, 157
temporality, 114
Theory & Psychology, 6, 122
theory, embodied, 144
time, experience of, 62
Toombs, Kay, 207–10, 213–7, 228–30
totalization, 183
trace, 82–4, 87
transcendence, 20
Transsexual Menace, 129
Transgender Tapestry, 126, 136
transgender: activists 9, 127–9; and
    psychological theories, 128;
    biomedical conceptualizations of,
    133; community, 129; naming of,
    129–30; movement, 129;
    organizations and publications,
    127; persons, 127, 132; relations
    with other activists, 128
transsexual, 127–9,
transsexualism, 131
Trower, P., 171
True Inversions, 150, 156–7
Turing, A. M., 8, 75–80; test, 75–80,
    91
Turner, Bryan, 146
Turner, T., 5–6

universal child speaker, 64
universal self-aspects, 61, 66; as
    variables, 61, 63
universals, in language, 64

Vancouver, 149, 156; lesbian
    community in, 149
Varela, F. J, and Maturana, H. R., 171
Venus Pudica, 94
Vico, G., 8, 46, 59–60
virtual disciplinization, 227
virtuality, 227, 229
Voestermans, Paul, 10–11, 37
voice, 95; loss of, 211–12
Vroman, Leo, 162

Wacquant, L. J. D., 39, 143–5, 153
Wall, P., 184, 191–2, 196
Wertheim, W. F., 65
Wessels, M., 81
Weston, A., 218, 228
Wiener, M., 167–71
Wilchins, Riki Anne, 129–30
Willis, P.E., 18, 25
Wilson, Elizabeth, 8
Winkler, Mary, 105, 223
Wolff, Janet, 144
women: artists, 143, 147; mystics, 101
women's: discontent, 104;
    emancipation, 99; oppression, 99
Wonham, W., 59, 65
worlds: cosmopolitan, 219; local, 218
Wundt, W., 55

Young, Iris Marion, 211–7, 226, 229

Zajonc, R. B., 45